Exploring Christian Literature

Edited by
Michael J. McHugh

Christian Liberty Press

Exploring Christian Literature
Editor: Michael J. McHugh
Reviewer: Kathleen A. Bristley
Designer: Eric D. Bristley

Christian Liberty Press
is a division of:

Christian Liberty Academy Satellite Schools
502 West Euclid Avenue
Arlington Heights, Illinois 60004
Phone (847) 259-4444

Acknowledgements
For the courtesy extended in permitting use of copyrighted selections, grateful acknowledgment is made to the following publishers or authors:

Michael P. Farris
Teaching Your Child to Work © 1993

The Thomas Y. Crowell Co.
The Story of Martin, the Cobbler © 1937

W. H. Auden
The Unknown Citizen © 1950

Maranatha Publications
How to Become a Dynamic Speaker © 1985
The Power of the Pen © 1985

Ruth E. McDaniel
The Crucible © 1993
The Value of a Dollar © 1993
The Search for the City of Satisfaction © 1993

John J. Floherty
The Sinking of the Titanic © 1947

Doug Rennie
Only If We Have To © 1997

J. Gresham Machen
All Nature Sings! © 1947

❧ Preface

The study of literature is an important part of every young person's educational experience.

In good literature, one can meet and experience life by entering the lives of others for a time. The stories, poems, and biographies in this text will help the student realize that he is not alone in the challenges and wonders of life.

True Christian literature is preoccupied with glorifying Almighty God and strengthening the lives of all those who are sincerely seeking to worship and serve the Lord Jesus Christ. Young people in America today, especially Christian teenagers, desperately need to be exposed to reading material that will help them develop a Christ-centered worldview.

Not all of life is pleasant; not all problems are simple. Therefore, this literature text will present the student not only with delights but also with decisions; life does that too. Christ, the Master Teacher, told stories to help others gain insights and make decisions in a godly manner. Reading stories is still one of the best ways to develop a proper understanding of how to apply Biblical truth to everyday life.

We sincerely hope that this reading material will be used by God to strengthen the Christian home and school.

Michael J. McHugh
Arlington Heights, Illinois
1994

Walking by Faith

If, on a quiet sea,
    Tow'rd heaven we calmly sail,
With grateful hearts, O God, to thee,
    We'll own the fav'ring gale.

But should the surges rise,
    And rest delay to come,
Blest be the sorrow, kind the storm,
    Which drives us nearer home.

Soon shall our doubts and fears
    All yield to thy control:
Thy tender mercies shall illume
    The midnight of the soul.

Teach us, in every state,
    To make thy will our own;
And when the joys of sense depart,
    To live by faith alone.

CONTENTS

🔥 Introduction

Many of the reading selections contained in this text are short stories. A short story is a fictional narrative of prose, usually under 10,000 words, that provides the reader with entertainment and insight.

A good short story will have well-developed characters that are involved with real-life believable situations. To properly understand any story, it is helpful to know the basic elements of structure that make up a well-written story. Well-educated readers will be concerned with what happens in the story—*the main plot*, who makes it happen—*the characters*, and the message that the author intended to impart—*the theme*. In addition, other elements should be routinely considered, such as *setting* (the time, location, and general circumstances) and *the mood* (the particular emotional tempo that the author presents with regard to his subject or audience), as well as the overall *unity* or *flow* of the story. A good work of prose will have each of these literary components working together in a sensible whole.

For the Christian, it is also important to analyze each story in light of Biblical principles to determine whether the "message" contained in the work harmonizes with Holy Scripture. Virtually all writers have a purpose to convey or some principles to impart through their writings. It is the responsibility of each child of God to determine whether the message contained in a particular story has a positive or negative life application. Too many Christian young people, and adults, have been duped into believing that ideas and principles can be neutral. The fact is, every single idea promoted by man has ultimate consequences for good or evil. A person's character is molded by his thoughts and actions: "For as he thinketh in his heart, so is he." (Proverbs 23:7)

It is very important that students learn how to accurately identify the key components of each reading selection. As a starting point, students should routinely attempt to identify any or all of the following components:

a)   *the main plot*

b)   *the key characters*

c)   *the primary theme*

d)   *the setting*

e)   *the mood or emotional style*

f)   *the appropriate life application or moral.*

Students who take the effort to carefully analyze the key parts of each story will be better equipped to comprehend the motives of the writer and, hopefully, use these skills to improve their own writing. Helpful comprehension questions have been provided in the text for selected writings. These questions can and should be used as a starting point for healthy discussion with others. They can also be used to analyze the key points of the story or poem. It should be understood that the questions in the text are not designed to be totally comprehensive and perfectly adequate. They are merely a starting point and basic guide for students to follow.

In addition, a helpful glossary of terms is often included at the end of each lesson that provides students with definitions for the particularly essential or difficult words contained in each reading selection. It is very important for students to utilize this information as they strive to expand their vocabulary skills and comprehension.

Obviously, the above information will need to be modified when students begin to analyze the poetry selections in their text. Nevertheless, students may still use some of the previously mentioned techniques to critique poetry while they also focus on new considerations such as a poem's meter and rhyme.

Finally, readers may also wish to utilize the following questions as they seek to properly analyze their reading selections. Some of these questions will not apply to each and every story in the text.

1. What is the main idea or thrust of the author's writing?

2. Who was the leading character(s) in the story?

3. Who are the secondary characters in the story?

4. Is there a key paragraph in the author's writings?

5. Do you agree with the message of the author?

6. Do you think that the writing style that the author used was effective? Would another style have been better?

7. Was the main message of the author consistent with Biblical Christianity?

8. Describe the mood of the story, as well as your own emotional response to it.

9. What purpose do you think the author was trying to accomplish with his story or poem?

May the Lord grant you wisdom as you study this text and wrestle with the issues of life.

1 *The Miner*

by Chelsea C. Fraser

Search where you will among the occupations of mankind, you will find no calling more humble than that of the miner. Nor will you find a calling more hazardous, more risky to life and limb, than his.

A miner's life is often considered a commodity that is worth risking because his fellow human beings must have coal and iron, copper and lead, silver and gold, garnets and diamonds, and because this is the only way in which he can put bread in the mouths of his dear ones living in that weather-worn little shack over yonder in the valley. Then, too, there are times when his rugged nature is called upon to show a greater test of heroism—those times when, owing to the sudden peril of his comrades, he has a chance to exhibit the supreme degree of self-sacrifice and the acme of true courage.

Rough? Yes, very, very rough is the miner. But underneath that rough manner, the stolid look, the coarse speech, beats the heart of a fighter, and often the tender mercifulness of a woman. Let us try to forget his lack of schooling, his meager "manners," his strong love for spending his hard-earned wage in idle ways. Instead let us admire in him that sterling quality, bravery, which he possesses in such average abundance. As we sit in our easy chair before the fireplace on a cold winter's night and gaze dreamily and cozily into the curling red flames, let us see him laboriously digging out the coal, flat on his back in the slimy, cold water, hacking, hacking away, from morning till night, while ugly calluses from his hard flinty bed spread here and there on his body, and great masses of slate threaten to fall on him, or deadly mine gases to asphyxiate him.

So great is the peril in mining, hardly a month goes by before we read in the newspapers about some dire mine accident which has nearly, or actually, snuffed out the lives of one or more miners. This, too, in spite of the fact that today the United States has a Bureau of Mines which for some years has been doing its utmost to educate miners and mine owners to the perils of their calling and to encourage inventors, scientists, and engineers to produce methods and appliances looking toward the prevention of such dangers and the rescue of the victims themselves before they are robbed of their lives.

In South Africa, near Kimberley, is one of the most famous diamond mines in the world. It is known as the De Beers Mine.

On the afternoon of June 5, 1897, those outside the entrance to this mine shrieked with terror in their native tongue. Behind them, creeping in a thick, slow-moving, irresistible mass, flowed a stream of blue mud from the belly of the tunnel.

The mine filled with blue mud.

No one knows just why, but sometimes diggers and blasters in a diamond mine strike a soft bit of earth, and this causes a great rush of mud. The mud does not burst outward with explosive force, as water might go; but comes silently and stealthily, like a thief in the night, and with such speed that miners are often caught from behind in its relentless talons before they suspect their danger. Then it goes gliding on along the passage, swallowing everything in its path.

Higher and higher it rises, swells and rolls, till the whole tunnel is sometimes filled with the thick, suffocating mass, as molasses might run through the neck of a bottle.

Such was the rush of blue mud in the De Beers Mine on the afternoon named. After the count had been made of those who had escaped from the tunnel, it was found that two Kafir "boys" were missing. As these fellows were working in the thousand-foot level, in the vicinity of the flood, it was probable that they had been caught; but there was just a bare chance that, by fleetness of foot, they might have escaped to the hundred-yard pass—a room where the tunnel was much enlarged to permit the passing of tram-cars. Even though the tunnel was filled with mud, here in the pass they might find air enough to keep them alive for some hours.

And yet there really seemed a mighty slim hope for these Kafir boys should they actually have taken refuge in the pass. You see, the tunnel mouth was already vomiting out the thick, bluish-colored ozone, sending it out in such vast volume that the tunnel itself must be all but filled with it from floor to roof. When that flow should stop—and nobody could tell when that would be—there would surely be at least a hundred yards of mud to dig one's way through before reaching the pass. That would take a precious long time, so long that few of the watchers thought there was any way to save the young men from meeting their Maker.

It happened that the rush ceased sooner than expected. Feeling a sense of guilt to do otherwise, the manager at once set his men to work digging away the mud. Men never worked harder. All the remainder of that day, all through the long night, all the next forenoon, they labored, while the sweat dripped in rivulets down their faces and soaked their scanty clothes. But only the slightest impression had been made upon those tons and tons of solid, slimy earthen matter.

Along about the middle of the afternoon, it was noticed that, for some reason, the mud was slowly settling. It began to flatten out on top, dropping away from the roof, leaving a constantly growing gap between. Reason said that there was not one chance in a thousand that the Kafir boys could still be alive. Yet, the troubled consciences of at least two of the onlookers compelled their heroic natures to respond to this one chance.

Both were young men full of the joy of living, anxious that every other man should enjoy the elixir of life the same as themselves. Color, position, social standing, nationality, meant nothing to these noble fellows. Brown and Brad, both white miners in the De Beers Mine, both jolly, muscular chaps not over thirty, were just the kind to spring forward with an offer to risk their own precious lives in an effort to save the humble lives of two black-skinned natives. However, it was not certain that the company would let them go after the Kafir boys.

The manager of the mine looked at his eager volunteers in blank astonishment. Had the excitement overturned their brain? But no, that could not be; they were too calm, too full of determination and unflinching purpose to have lost their reason. They must be in deadly ear-nest. He now turned his gaze from their faces to the mouth of the tunnel. He saw that barely a foot of space lay between the top of the ooze and the roof. It seemed impossible for a human being to worm his way over such a mess in such cramped quarters and live to tell of the exploit afterwards.

Brown seemed to interpret the manager's thoughts.

"There's room for our bodies, and we can keep our head above the mud, I think," he said.

"We are both good mud turtles," grinned Brad.

"Well, if you will go, go; but remember that I am not responsible if anything happens to you," said the mine official.

Many of their friends tried to dissuade them from what seemed an act of suicide. However, Brown and Brad paid no attention. Equipping their caps with a miner's lamp, they crept into the cold blue mud. It was too thick to permit swimming, and too thin to bear their weights, so they were forced to flounder along in the most toilsome and exhausting manner.

If you have ever waded through snow up to your shoulders you will have a slight idea of the difficulties encountered by these two young Englishmen. That mud was fully ten times messier. To make things worse, there were places in the tunnel where the roof was too low to clear all of their heads, and with lips tightly compressed under the ooze, they had to fight to keep their nostrils and eyes above, while their hands clawed an opening into a wider passage.

As they slowly progressed, a new peril manifested itself. They be-came aware that the air in the narrow channel was becoming fouler and fouler. Soon their lamps went out, whether from a dash of mud or the smothering action of gas they were unable to tell. At last they now found themselves in an inky darkness which seemed as thick as the mass in which they were wallowing. Every moment seemed an eterni-ty. Neither one of them ever expected to see a human face again. How they ever managed to keep on going without strangling in the sea of blue stuff surrounding them is a miracle. Every instant they expected to take the long-looked-for plunge that would end everything but their faith in God.

And yet, the wonderful courage which had prompted their very undertaking of this enterprise kept them fighting, fighting, fighting, on and on. Their arms and legs ached from the intense strain put upon them, till it seemed every nerve and sinew in their bodies was sick in sympathy. Their feet seemed to weigh a hundred pounds each. It was all they could do to raise them each time for another advance; they sighed with weary relief when they could let a foot sink down again. And oh, how sore were their necks! They fancied they could hear the bones creak every time they turned their heads. Their faces had no feeling, being numb with the buffeting of the mud and the thick plaster which had accumulated.

But they fought on. And as they struggled with outstretched limb, close to death, they did not forget the object of their undertaking. From time to time they hallowed, hoping against hope to hear the reply of the Kafir boys somewhere ahead.

At last, their hearts leaped wildly. Could that really be an answering cry they had faintly heard? They stopped, shouted again and listened intently.

"Kai-loo! Kai-loo!"

"That's the Kafirs," spluttered Brown. "They're not far off, either. Keep her up, Brad, old boy."

"Ahead it is," spluttered Brad. "It's no time to turn back now."

With stronger hearts they continued to push forward. Finally, they reached the rising ground of the pass, where, sure enough, they found the two Kafir boys. They had been imprisoned upwards of thirty hours and were in a state of exhaustion fully equal to that of their rescuers.

After a questionable rest, it was decided to begin the backward journey. Fortunately for their purpose, the mud was by this time somewhat lower still, offering more opportunity to breathe, and presenting a lessened resistance to their progress; but for all that, the return, in their weakened condition, was even more terrible than their coming. Forcing the frightened and protesting Kafirs ahead of them, Brown and Brad plunged along the dark tunnel, encouraging the natives sometimes with words of good cheer and at other times with threats of dire punishment, according to need.

Frequently, their last ounce of strength seemed to have departed, and they would pause in the dungeon of slime to take a brief rest. Then on again, driving their jabbering charges before them, they would struggle against the fearful odds. Just when they felt that they could never go on, the waning spark of combat would suddenly kindle once more, and they would flounder ahead for another round of bitter contest.

At last, gasping for breath, eyes bulging from their sockets, bloodshot with strain, they came in sight of the patch of light glimmering at the mouth of the tunnel. Shortly afterwards, friends went in far enough to drag them out. Every part of their bodies was coated thick with mud; their hair was matted with it; their features were unrecognizable by their most intimate comrades. But neither Brown nor Brad cared at all about that. What they had gone after they had got. The two Kafir boys had been saved. Two human beings would continue to enjoy the gift of life.

We might feel that such heroism as this would be largely ignored by the mine owners. Nevertheless, the deed of Brown and Brad was materially appreciated. The mine owners came forth with a substantial sum of money for each of the brave young Englishmen, and a fitting finish was applied when the Royal Humane Society presented them with beautiful silver medals inscribed with a brief story of their exploit. Still, the greatest reward that these men received came as a result of their obedience to the One who said "Inasmuch as you have done it unto the least of my brethren, you have done it unto Me." These men discovered that doing what is right brings its own reward, for God promises peace and contentment of soul to those who dare to do right.

❧ Comprehension Questions

1. Why do some people think that it is necessary for miners to place their lives on the line as they go to work?

2. What was the name of the mine that trapped the two Kafir boys?

3. What techniques did the author use to help you feel the pain and misery of the rescue activities of Brown and Brad?

4. Do you think that the color of a person's skin should dictate whether he is worthy of our assistance during a crisis? Was this an issue with Brown and Brad?

5. In many situations in life, we are only able to serve others if we are willing to get "dirty" and be inconvenienced. Can you explain why this is true?

6. What was the greatest reward Brown and Brad received?

One Minute Longer

by Albert Payson Terhune

Wolf was a collie with a red-gold and white coat. He had a shape more like his long-ago wolf ancestors' than like a domesticated dog's. It was from this ancestral throw-back that he was named Wolf.

He looked not at all like his great sire, Sunnybank Lad, nor like his dainty, thoroughbred mother, Lady. Nor was he like them in any other way, except that he inherited old Lad's staunchly gallant spirit, loyalty, and uncanny brain. No, in traits as well as in looks he was more wolf than dog. He almost never barked, his snarl supplying all vocal needs.

The Mistress or the Master or the Boy—any of these three could romp with him, roll him over, tickle him, or subject him to all sorts of playful indignities. And Wolf entered gleefully into the fun of the romp. But let any human besides these three lay a hand on his slender body, and a snarling plunge for the offender's throat was Wolf's invariable reply to the caress.

It had been so since his puppyhood. He did not fly at accredited guests nor, indeed, pay any heed to their presence, so long as they kept their hands off him. But to all of these, the Boy was forced to say at the very outset of the visit:

"Pat Lad and Bruce all you want to, but please leave Wolf alone. He doesn't care for people. We've taught him to stand for a pat on the head from guests—but don't touch his body."

Then to prove his own immunity, the Boy would proceed to tumble Wolf about, to the delight of them both.

In romping with humans whom they love, most dogs will bite, more or less gently—or pretend to bite as a part of the game. Wolf never did this. In his wildest and roughest romps with the Boy or with the Boy's parents, Wolf did not so much as open his mighty jaws. Perhaps because he dared not trust himself to bite gently. Perhaps because he realized that a bite is not a joke, but an effort to kill.

There had been only one exception to Wolf's hatred for mauling at strangers' hands. A man came to The Place on a business call, bringing along a chubby two-year-old daughter. The Master warned the baby that she must not go near Wolf, although she might pet any of the other collies. Then he became so much interested in the business talk that he and his guest forgot all about the child.

Ten minutes later, the Master chanced to shift his gaze to the far end of the room. And he broke off, with a gasp, in the very middle of a sentence.

The baby was seated astride Wolf's back, her tiny heels digging into the dog's sensitive ribs, and each of her chubby fists gripping one of his ears. Wolf was lying there, with an idiotically happy grin on his face and wagging his tail in ecstasy.

No one knew why he had submitted to the baby's tugging hand except because she *was a* baby, and because the gallant heart of the dog had gone out to her helplessness.

Wolf was the official watchdog of The Place and his name carried dread to the loafers and tramps of the region. Also, he was the Boy's own special dog. He had been born on the Boy's tenth birthday, five years before this story of ours begins; and ever since then, the two had been inseparable chums.

One sloppy afternoon in the late winter, Wolf and the Boy were sprawled, side by side, on the fur rug in front of the library fire. The Mistress and the Master had gone to town for the day. The house was lonely, and the two chums were left to entertain each other.

The Boy was reading a magazine. The dog beside him was blinking in drowsy comfort at the fire. Presently, finishing the story he had been reading, the Boy looked across at the sleepy dog.

"Wolf," he said, "here's a story about a dog. I think he must have been something like you. Maybe he was your great-great-great-great-grandfather. He lived an awfully long time ago—in Pompeii. Ever hear of Pompeii?"

Now, the Boy was fifteen years old, and he had too much sense to imagine that Wolf could possibly understand the story he was about to tell him. But, long since, he had fallen into a way of talking to his dog, sometimes, as if to another human. It was fun for him to note the almost pathetic eagerness wherewith Wolf listened and tried to grasp the meaning of what he was saying. Again and again, at the sound of some familiar word or voice inflection, the collie would prick up his ears or wag his tail, as if in the joyous hope that he had at last found a clue to his owner's meaning.

"You see," stated the Boy in wistful excitement, seeking vainly to guess what was expected of him.

"And," continued the Boy, "the kid who owned him seems to have had a regular knack for getting into trouble all the time. And his dog was always on hand to get him out of it. It's a true story, the magazine says. The kid's father was so grateful to the dog that he bought him a solid silver collar. Solid silver! Get that, Wolfie?"

Wolf did not "get it." But he wagged his tail hopefully, his eyes alight with bewildered interest.

"And," said the Boy, "what do you suppose was engraved on the collar? Well, I'll tell: *This dog has thrice saved his little master from death. Once by fire, once by flood, and once at the hands of robbers.* How's that for a record, Wolf? For *one* dog, too."

At the words *Wolf* and *dog*, the collie's tail smote the floor in glad comprehension. Then he edged closer to the Boy as the narrator's voice presently took on a sadder note.

"But at last," resumed the Boy, "there came a time when a dog couldn't save the kid. Mount Vesuvius erupted. All the sky was pitch-dark, as black as midnight, and Pompeii was buried under lava and ashes. The dog could easily have got away by himself—dogs can see in the dark, can't they, Wolf?—but he couldn't get the kid away. And he wouldn't go without him. You wouldn't have gone without me, either, would you, Wolf? Pretty nearly two thousand years later, some people dug through the lava that covered Pompeii. What do you suppose they found? Of course, they found a whole lot of things. One of them was that dog—silver collar and inscription and all. He was lying at the feet of a child. The child he couldn't save. He was one grand dog—hey, Wolf?"

The continued strain of trying to understand began to get on the collie's high-strung nerves. He rose to his feet, quivering, and sought to lick the Boy's face, thrusting one upraised white forepaw at him in appeal for a handshake. The Boy slammed shut the magazine.

"It's slow in the house here, with nothing to do," he said to his chum, "I'm going up to the lake with my gun to see if any wild ducks have landed in the marshes yet. It's almost time for them. Want to come along?"

The last sentence Wolf understood perfectly. On the instant he was dancing with excitement at the prospect of a walk. Being a collie, he was of no earthly help in a hunting trip; but, on such tramps, as every where else, he was the Boy's inseparable companion.

Out over the slushy snow the two started, the Boy with his light single-barreled shotgun slung over one shoulder, the dog trotting close at his heels. The deep and soggy snow was crusted over, just thick enough to make walking a genuine difficulty for both dog and Boy.

The Place was a bluff that ran out into the lake, on the opposite bank from the mile-distant village. Behind, across the highroad, lay the winter-choked forest. At the lake's northerly end, two miles beyond The Place, were the reedy marshes where wild ducks would congregate. Meanwhile, the Boy continued to plow his way through the biting cold.

The going was heavy and tough. A quarter mile below the marshes the Boy struck out across the upper corner of the lake. Here the ice was rotten at the top, where the thaw had nibbled at it, but underneath it was still a full eight inches thick, easily strong enough to bear the Boy's weight.

Along the gray ice field the two plodded. The skim of water, which the thaw had spread an inch thick over the ice, had frozen in the day's cold spell. It crackled like broken glass as the chums walked over it. The Boy had on big hunting boots. So, apart from the extra effort, the glass-like ice did not bother him. To Wolf, it gave acute pain. The sharp particles were forever getting between the callous black pads of his feet, pricking and cutting him sharply.

Little smears of blood began to mark the dog's course, but it never occurred to Wolf to turn back or to betray by any sign that he was suffering. It was all a part of the day's work—a cheap price to pay for the joy of tramping with his adored young master.

Then, forty yards or so on the other side of the marshes, Wolf beheld an amazing phenomenon. The Boy had been walking directly in front of him, with his gun over his shoulder. With no warning at all, the youthful hunter fell, feet first, out of sight, through the ice.

The light shell of new-frozen water that covered the lake's thicker ice also masked an air hole nearly three feet wide. Into this, as he strode carelessly along, the Boy had stepped. Straight down he had gone, with all the force of his hundred twenty pounds and with all the impetus of his forward stride.

Instinctively, he threw out his hands to restore his balance. The only effect of this was to send the gun flying ten feet away.

Down went the Boy through less than three feet of water (for the bottom of the lake at this point had started to slope upward towards the marshes) and through nearly two feet more of sticky marsh mud that underlay the lake-bed.

His outflung hand struck against the ice on the edges of the air hole, and clung there.

Spluttering and gurgling, the Boy brought his head above the surface and tried to raise himself, by his hands, high enough to wiggle out upon the surface of the ice. Ordinarily, this would have been simple enough for so strong a lad. But the gluelike mud had imprisoned his feet and the lower part of his legs and held them powerless.

Try as he would, the Boy could not wrench himself free of the slough. The water, as he stood upright, was on a level with his mouth. The air hole was too wide for him, at such a depth, to get a good purchase on its edges and lift himself bodily to safety.

Gaining such a finger-hold as he could, he heaved with all his might, throwing every muscle of his body into the struggle. One leg was pulled almost free of the mud, but the other was driven deeper into it. And, as the Boy's fingers slipped from the smoothly wet ice edge, the attempt to restore his balance drove the free leg back, knee-deep into the mire.

Ten minutes of his hopeless fighting left the Boy panting and tired out. The icy water was numbing his nerve and chilling his blood into torpidity. His hands were without sense of feeling, as far up as the wrists. Even if he could have shaken free his legs from the mud, now, he had not strength enough left to crawl out of the hole.

He ceased his uselessly frantic battle and stood dazed. Then he came sharply to himself. For, as he stood, the water crept upward from his lips to his nostrils. He knew why the water seemed to be rising. It was because he was sinking. As soon as he stopped moving, the mud began, very slowly, but very steadily, to suck him downward.

This was not quicksand, but it was a deep mud bed. And only by constant motion could he avoid sinking farther and farther down into it. He had less than two inches to spare, at best, before the water would fill his nostrils; less than two inches of life, even if he could keep the water down to the level of his lips.

There was a moment of utter panic. Then the Boy's brain cleared. His only hope was to keep on fighting—to rest when he must, for a moment or so, and then to renew his numbed grip on the ice edge and try to pull his feet a few inches higher out of the mud. He must do this as long as his chilled body could be scourged into obeying his will.

He struggled again, but with virtually no result in raising himself. A second struggle, however, brought him chin-high above the water. He remembered confusedly that some of these earlier struggles had scarcely budged him, while others had gained him two or three inches. Vaguely, he wondered why. Then turning his head, he realized.

Wolf, as he turned, was just loosing his hold on the wide collar of the Boy's coat. His cut forepaws were still braced against a flaw of ragged ice on the air hole's edge, and all his tawny body was tense.

The Boy noted that; and he realized that the repeated effort to draw his master to safety must have resulted, at least once, in pulling the dog down into the water with the foundering Boy.

"Once more, Wolfie! *Once more!*" chattered the Boy through teeth that clicked together like castanets.

The dog darted forward, caught his grip afresh on the edge of the Boy's collar, and tugged with all his fierce strength, growling and whining ferociously all the while.

Wolf tugs the boy from the ice.

The Boy seconded the collie's tuggings by a supreme struggle that lifted him higher than before. He was able to get one arm and shoulder clear. His numb fingers closed about an up-thrust tree limb which had been washed downstream in the autumn freshets and had been frozen into the lake ice.

With this new purchase and aided by the dog, the boy tried to drag himself out of the hole. But the chill of the water had done its work. He had not the strength to move farther. The mud still sucked at his calves and ankles. The big hunting boots were full of water that seemed to weigh a ton.

He lay there gasping and chattering. Then through the gathering twilight, his eyes fell on the gun, lying ten feet away.

"Wolf!" he ordered, nodding towards the weapon "Get it! *Get* it!"

Not in vain had the Boy talked to Wolf, for years, as if the dog were human. At the words and the nod, the collie trotted over to the gun, lifted it by the stock, and hauled it awkwardly along over the bumpy ice to his master, where he laid it down at the edge of the air hole.

The dog's eyes were cloudy with trouble, and he shivered and whined as with ague. The water on his thick coat was freezing to a mass of ice. But it was from anxiety that he shivered and not from cold.

Still keeping his numb grasp on the tree branch, the Boy balanced himself as best as he could and thrust two fingers of his free hand into his mouth to warm them into sensation again.

When this was done, he reached out to where the gun lay and pulled its trigger. The shot boomed deafeningly through the twilight winter silences. The recoil sent the weapon sliding sharply back along the ice, spraining the Boy's trigger finger and cutting it to the bone.

"That's all I can do," said the Boy to himself. "If anyone hears it, well and good. I can't get at another cartridge. I couldn't put it into the breech if I had it. My hands are too numb."

For several endless minutes he clung there, listening. But this was a desolate part of the lake, far from any road; and the season was too early for other hunters to be abroad. The bitter cold, in any case, tended to make sane folk hug the fireside rather than to venture so far into the open. Nor was the single report of a gun uncommon enough to call for investigation in such weather.

All this the Boy told himself, as the minutes dragged by. Then he looked again at Wolf. The dog, head on one side, still stood protecting above him. The dog was cold and in pain. But being only a dog, it did not occur to him to trot off home to the comfort of the library fire and leave his master to fend for himself.

Presently, with a little sigh, Wolf lay down on the ice, his nose across the Boy's arm. Even if he lacked strength to save his beloved master, he could stay and share the Boy's sufferings.

But the Boy himself thought otherwise. He was not at all minded to freeze to death, nor was he willing to let Wolf imitate the dog of Pompeii by dying helplessly at his master's side. Controlling for an instant the chattering of his teeth, he called. "Wolf!"

The dog was on his feet again at the word, alert, eager.

"Wolf!" repeated the Boy. "*Go!* Hear me? *Go!*" He pointed homeward.

Wolf stared at him hesitant. Again the Boy called in vehement command "Go!"

The collie lifted his head to the twilight sky with a wolf howl hideous in its grief and appeal—a howl as wild and discordant as that of any of his savage ancestors. Then, stooping first to lick the numb hand that clung to the branch, wolf turned and fled.

Across the cruelly sharp film of ice he tore, at top speed, head down, whirling through the deepening dusk like a flash of tawny light.

Wolf understood what was wanted of him. Wolf always understood. The pain in his feet was as nothing. The stiffness of his numbed body was forgotten in the urgency for speed.

The Boy looked drearily after the swift-vanishing figure which the dusk was swallowing. He knew the dog would try to bring help, as has many another and lesser dog in times of need. Whether or not that help could arrive in time, or at all, was a point on which the Boy would not let himself dwell. Into his benumbed brain crept the memory of an old Norse proverb he had read in school:

Heroism consists in hanging on, one minute longer.

Unconsciously, he tightened his feeble hold on the tree branch and braced himself.

From the marshes to The Place was a full two miles. Despite the deep and sticky snow, Wolf covered the distance in less than nine minutes. He paused in front of the gate lodge, at the highway entrance to the drive. But the superintendent and his wife had gone to Paterson, shopping, that afternoon.

Down the drive to the house he dashed. The maids had taken advantage of their employers' day in New York to walk across the lake to the village, to a motion picture show.

Wise men claim that dogs have not the power to think or to reason things out in a logical way. So perhaps it was mere chance that next sent Wolf's flying feet across the lake to the village. Perhaps it was chance and not the knowledge that where there is a village there are people.

Again and again, in the car, he had sat upon the front seat alongside the Mistress when she drove to the station to meet guests. There were always people at the station. And to the station Wolf now raced.

The usual group of platform idlers had been dispersed by the cold. A solitary baggageman was hauling a trunk and some boxes out the express coop to the platform, to be put aboard the five o'clock train from New York.

As the baggageman passed under the clump of station lights, he came to a sudden halt. For out of the darkness dashed a dog. Full tilt, the animal rushed up to him and seized him by the skirt of the overcoat.

The man cried out in scared surprise. He dropped the box he was carrying and struck at the dog, to ward off the seemingly murderous attack. He recognized Wolf, and he knew the collie's reputation.

But Wolf was not attacking. Holding tight to the coat skirt, he backed away, trying to draw the man with him and all the while whimpering aloud like a nervous puppy.

A kick from the heavy-shod boot broke the dog's hold on the coat skirt, even as a second yell from the man brought four or five other people running out from the station waiting room.

One of these, the telegraph operator, took in the scene at a single glance. With great presence of mind he loudly screamed, "Mad dog!"

This as Wolf, reeling from the kick, sought to gain another grip on the coat skirt. A second kick sent him rolling over and over on the tracks, while other voices took up the panic cry of "Mad dog!"

Now, a mad dog is supposed to be a dog afflicted by rabies. Once in ten thousand times, at the very most, a mad-dog hue and cry is justified. Certainly not more often. A harmless and friendly dog loses his master on the street. He runs about, confused and frightened, looking for the owner he has lost. A boy throws a stone at him. Other boys chase him. His tongue hangs out, and his eyes glaze with terror. Then some fool bellows, "Mad dog!"

And the cruel chase is on—a chase that ends in the pitiful victim's death. Yes, in every crowd there is a voice ready to raise that asinine and murderously cruel shout.

So it was with the men who witnessed Wolf's frenzied effort to take aid to the imperiled Boy.

Voice after voice repeated the cry. Men groped along the platform edge for stones to throw. The village policeman ran puffingly upon the scene, drawing his revolver.

Finding it useless to make a further attempt to drag the baggageman to the rescue, Wolf leaped back, facing the ever larger group. Back went his head again in that hideous wolf howl. Then he galloped away a few yards, trotted back, howled once more, and again galloped lakeward.

All of which only confirmed the panicky crowd in the belief that they were threatened by a mad dog. A shower of stones hurtled about Wolf as he came back a third time to lure these dull humans into following him.

One pointed rock smote the collie's shoulder, glancingly cutting it to the bone. A shot from the policeman's revolver fanned the fur of his ruff, as it whizzed past.

Knowing that he faced death, he nevertheless stood his ground, not troubling to dodge the fusillade of stones, but continuing to run lakeward and then trot back, whining with excitement.

A second pistol shot flew wide. A third grazed the dog's hip. From all directions people were running towards the station. A man darted into the house next door and emerged carrying a shotgun. This he steadied on the veranda rail not forty feet away from the leaping dog and made ready to fire.

It was then the train from New York came in. And, momentarily, the sport of "mad-dog" killing was abandoned, while the crowd scattered to each side of the track.

From a front car of the train the Mistress and the Master emerged into a bedlam of noise and confusion.

"Best hide in the station, Ma'am!" shouted the telegraph operator at the sight of the Mistress. "There is a mad dog loose out here. He's chasing folks around, and—"

A flash of tawny light beneath the station lamp, a scurrying of frightened idlers, a final wasted shot from the policeman's pistol— as Wolf dived headlong through the frightened crowd toward a voice he heard and recognized.

Up to the Mistress and the Master galloped Wolf. He was bleeding, his eyes were bloodshot, his fur was rumpled. He seized the astounded Master's gloved hand lightly between his teeth and sought to pull him across the tracks and towards the lake.

The master knew dogs. Especially he knew Wolf. And without a word he suffered himself to be led. The Mistress and one or two inquisitive men followed.

Presently, Wolf loosed his hold on the Master's hand and ran on ahead, darting back every few moment to make certain he was followed.

"Heroism – consists – of – hanging – on – one – minute – longer," the Boy was whispering deliriously to himself for the hundredth time, as Wolf pattered up to him in triumph, across the ice, with the human rescuers a scant ten yards behind.

❧ Comprehension Questions

1. How old was the Boy in the story when Wolf was born?

2. What special story did the Boy read to his dog just prior to the hunting trip?

3. Why was the Boy unable to lift himself out of the water and onto the ice?

4. What old Norse proverb did the Boy frequently quote during his trial in the icy lake?

5. Do you think that it was simply "good luck" when Wolf decided to go to the train station for help?

6. God's providential control over the world includes His control over animals. Can you think of an example from the Scripture that would illustrate this point?

3 Trees

by Sergeant Joyce Kilmer

Sergeant Kilmer served in Europe during World War 1 with the American Expeditionary Force, 165th Infantry (69th New York). He was born December 6, 1886, and died during a major battle near Oaucy, France, on July 30th, 1918. This poem, written a few years before his death, reveals the fact that real fighting men can still be sensitive to the work of God and spiritual things.

> I think that I shall never see
> A poem lovely as a tree.
>
> A tree whose hungry mouth is prest
> Against the earth's sweet flowing breast;
>
> A tree that looks at God all day,
> And lifts her leafy arms to pray;
>
> A tree that may in Summer wear
> A nest of robins in her hair;
>
> Upon whose bosom snow has lain;
> Who intimately lives with rain.
>
> Poems are made by fools like me,
> But only God can make a tree.

4   *Teaching Your Child To Work*

by Michael Farris, Esq.

Michael Farris is the founder and president of the Home School Legal Defense Association, which is based in Virginia. In his position as a skilled attorney, he has successfully represented and defended the Constitutional rights of numerous parents to train their children at home. During a period of thirteen years, Mr. Farris has been used by God to develop and manage a large and successful legal office that has helped thousands of concerned parents realize their dream of teaching their children at home.

As president of a large legal office and corporation, I have responsibility for about forty employees. As I interview potential workers, I have found that there are four qualities which are becoming increasingly scarce. The remarks that follow are designed to encourage teenagers to prepare themselves for the time when they will be called into the work force. This information is also aimed at parents, with the hope that they will teach these precepts to their children with great diligence.

1. RESPECT FOR AUTHORITY

Employers want workers who will respect the principles of a chain of command and who will cheerfully receive a directive as an order. Too many workers believe that their supervisor's directives are merely suggestions which can be followed or not, depending on how the employee feels about the matter. Others will do what their supervisor asks but only with a begrudging attitude. A worker who is willing to follow directions with a smile will shine as a star in the eyes of any employer.

This is an attitude which fathers must instill in their children. If we fail to teach our children to obey, they will never follow directions on the job. If we are tyrants and obtain obedience through undue harshness, then our children will probably become the kind of workers who do what they are told—and no more—and with a sullen attitude.

We need to teach our children to joyfully obey and genuinely respect those in authority over us. Our willingness as fathers to display respect for authority in our own lives is a critical factor in helping our children develop a proper attitude toward authority. Do you show a proper respect for your boss? Do you have a good attitude toward the leadership of your church? How do you talk about the President and other political leaders?

You can respect those in leadership without having to agree with them about everything. If you disagree, you should model the practice of a respectful appeal for your children. If your Governor supports a gay rights bill, for example, calling the Governor bad names in front of your children will not instill the kind of attitude you desire in your children. Instead of bad-mouthing, write a strong letter of appeal to the Governor and let your children read it. You should then pray for your Governor to change his mind. And since the political context allows us to change those in authority over us, you should work diligently to get a better person in office the next election.

2. TAKING INITIATIVE

As an employer, I always value a person who not only does what he is told but sees something else which needs to be done and does it. Taking initiative is a skill and attitude which is much easier to develop as a child than an adult.

If your child is told to wash the dishes, he has the opportunity to show initiative if he not only washes the dishes but also sweeps the floor. A child who learn to walk into a room, see a problem, and resolve it will climb to the upper echelon of any business.

3. STRIVING FOR EXCELLENCE

Too many in our society have forgotten how to be excellent. We are satisfied with being "good enough." When we were in school, the prevailing practice was to produce "acceptable" papers. Now the prevailing attitude on the job is to produce "acceptable" goods and services.

We need to go beyond being "good enough" in the way we do things. Our children should learn to read, understand, critique, and judge literature. They should have a thorough introduction to some of the great books of literature.

Our children should also be able to write well. It is not enough for our children to be able to write clear prose. We should teach our children to write logically and persuasively.

Our children should master basic math and be able to understand and perform some advanced math. Not every child needs calculus. But the ability to perform Algebra and Geometry are benchmarks of acceptable mathematical performance. These two courses are also excellent methods for teaching logic and reasoning. My ninth grade algebra teacher taught me skills I frequently use now to analyze a proposed piece of legislation. Logic, orderly thinking, and reasoning skills are important in many fields outside of the traditional careers associated with math.

There is one academic subject in which we need to go far, far beyond public school standards. We need to provide the best available instruction in the history and geography of our nation. While the public schools are drowning children in the academically meaningless and morally damaging world of "multiculturalism," we should be teaching our children to thoroughly know the history and philosophies of the men and women who founded this country. If American children are not taught the principles of freedom, America will not be free for very long.

4. WILLINGNESS TO WORK HARD

There are too many lazy people. Go to a shopping mall and try to get a clerk to help you. Go to any fast food restaurant. Chances are you will encounter mostly lazy people—people who have no enthusiasm for work.

Let me tell you a secret. I am a lazy person by nature. I do not like to work. It is true that I am very busy and work long hours with my Legal Defense Association. It is true that I help my wife with the home schooling of our eight children. It is true that I do work around the house. It is true that for a year-and-a-half I pastored my church on top of all of my other responsibilities (as a volunteer). I coach a softball team, chair an international human rights organization, and write books.

Obviously, something happened to me along the way to adulthood that allowed me to overcome my natural tendency toward laziness. That "something" was my father. He taught me to work. And I have to admit, it was over my extreme protests. I fought him every step of the way.

I was forced to mow the lawn, paint the house, re-roof the house, dig ditches for our irrigation system, and dig up some awful stuff in the yard called "quack grass." Since my father was employed by the public schools and received only one paycheck at the beginning of the summer, our family almost always ran out of money later in the summer. When that happened, our whole family went out and picked fruit. We picked peaches, cherries, plums, pears, strawberries and raspberries. I remember having to help significantly from age eight on. And I hated it. I cried and I screamed—literally.

I look back today and believe that my father did me an enormous amount of good by forcing me to work and work hard. I don't want to give you the impression that we never played, because we did. I remember with considerable fondness the great fun our family would have when we would finish a day's work in the summer and go to the city pool for family hour. And I was much older before I worked all summer long. In my younger years, it was only for a two-to-three week period that I worked anything approximating full time. But compared to many kids today, I was compelled to work hard.

I wasn't given any realistic choice to live a lazy life. As a consequence, my natural tendency toward laziness was eventually overcome by my father's diligence. I still have a heart that is easily tempted by laziness. But as a child, I was trained up in the way I should go and now that I am old I have a very hard time departing from my training and returning to my natural state.

I believe that fathers have special responsibilities to prepare their children for adulthood. Obviously, neither parent has exclusive duties with younger or older children. Both parents need to be involved throughout the child's life. But fathers do have special responsibilities as a child approaches maturity.

Fathers have a duty to see that their children are properly prepared for a career. When children are at home, the father has the clear biblical mandate to be the provider. However, God never intended for children to receive provisions from their dads for an entire lifetime. God intended that somewhere along the line, fathers would stop simply giving their children a fish and teach them how to fish for themselves. There are many facets of your responsibility to train your children for a career. The first step is to teach your child good work habits. Ultimately, young people need to take responsibility for their own attitudes and actions after they have been given a proper foundation and direction.

5 Henry V of Monmouth

by Charlotte M. Yonge

The young King Henry V was full of noble and godly thoughts. He was most devout in going to church, tried to make good Bishops, gave freely to the poor, and was so kind, and merry in all his words and ways, that everyone respected him. Still, he thought it was his duty as the King of England to go and make war in France. He had been taught to believe the kingdom belonged to him, and it was in so wretched a state that he thought he could do it good.

Henry V before battle.

The poor French king, Charles VI, was mad. Chaos ruled the day as people were always fighting, till the streets of Paris were often red with blood, and the whole country was miserable. Henry hoped to set all in order for them, and gathering an army together, crossed to Normandy. He called on the people to own him as their king, and never let any harm be done to them, for he hung any soldier who was caught stealing or misusing anyone. He took the town of Hafleur on the coast of Normandy, but not till after a long siege, when his camp was in so wet a place that there was much illness among his men. The store of food was nearly used up, and he was obliged to march his troops across to Calais, which you know belonged to England, to get some more. But on the way, the French army came up to meet him—a very grand, splendid-looking army, commanded by the king's eldest son the dauphin. Just as the English kings' eldest son was always Prince of Wales, the French kings' eldest son was always called Dauphin of Vienne, because Vienne, the country that belonged to him, had a dolphin on its shield.

The French army was very large—quite twice the number of the English—but, though Henry's men were weary and half-starved, and many of them sick, they were not afraid but believed their king when he told them that there were enough Frenchmen to kill, enough to run away, and enough to make prisoners. At night, however, the English had solemn prayers, and made themselves ready, and the king traveled from tent to tent to see that each man was in his place; while, on the other hand, the French were feasting and revelling, and settling what they would do to the English when they had made them prisoners. They were close to a little village which the English called Agincourt, and, though that is not quite its right name, it is what we have called the battle ever since.

The French, owing to the quarrelsome state of the country, had no order or obedience among them. Nobody would obey any other, and when their own archers were in the way, the horsemen began cutting them down as if they were the enemy. Some fought bravely, but it was of little use; and by night all the French were routed, and King Henry's banner waved in victory over the field. He went back to England in great glory, and all the aldermen of London came out to meet him in red gowns and gold chains, and among them was Sir Richard Whittington, the great silk mercer.

Henry was so modest that he would not allow the helmet he had worn at Agincourt, all knocked about with terrible blows, to be carried before him when he rode into London, and he went straight to church to give thanks to God for his victory.

He soon went back to France, and went on conquering it till the queen came to an agreement with him that he should marry her daughter Catherine. The queen of France also established that, though poor, crazy Charles VI should reign to the end of his life; when he died Henry and Catherine should be king and queen of France. So Henry and

Catherine were married, moved their home to England with great joy and pomp. King Henry left his brother Thomas, Duke of Clarence, to take care of his army in France. For, of course though the queen had made this treaty for her insane husband, most brave, honest Frenchmen could not but feel it a wicked and unfair thing to give the kingdom away from her son, the Dauphin Charles.

The Dauphin was not a good man, and had consented to the murder of his cousin, the Duke of Burgundy, and this had turned some against him; but still he was badly treated, and the bravest Frenchmen could not bear to see their country given up to the English. So, though he took no trouble to fight for himself, they fought for him, and got some Scots to help them; and by and by news came to Henry that his army had been beaten, and his brother killed.

He came back again in haste to France and his presence made everything go well again, but all the winter he was besieging the town of Meaux, where there was a very cruel robber who made all the roads to Paris unsafe, and by the time he had taken it his health was much injured. His queen came to him, and they kept a very grand court at Paris, at Whitsuntide; but soon after, when Henry set out to join his army, he found himself so ill and weak that he was obliged to turn back to the Castle of Vincennes, where he grew much worse. He called for all his friends and begged them to be faithful to his little baby son, whom he had never even seen. He spoke especially to his brother John, Duke of Bedford, to whom he left the charge of all he had gained.

King Henry had tried to be a good Christian man, he had meant to do right, yet he often caused great misery. So he was not afraid to face death, and he died when only thirty-four years old, while he was listening to the 51st Psalm. Everybody grieved for him—even the French—and nobody had ever been so good and dutiful to poor old King Charles, who sat in a corner lamenting for his good friend Henry. The old insane king was so broken-hearted that he died, only three weeks later, and was buried the same day, at St. Denys's Abbey, near Paris, while Henry was buried at Westminster Abbey, near London.

6 *Henry V Before Battle*

by William Shakespeare

William Shakespeare (1564–1616) an English author, wrote numerous plays that have been widely produced and read.

This scene is in the English camp just before the battle of Agincourt. Henry V, the young and warlike English king, had asserted a claim to the French crown and had invaded France with a few thousand men. In the battle of Agincourt he defeated a French force which far outnumbered his. The Earls of Westmoreland, Warwick, and Salisbury, the Dukes of Bedford, Exeter, and Gloucester of Gloster, and John Talbot Earl of Shrewsbury, were English noblemen in the army of King Henry. The Dukes of Bedford and Gloster were the king's brothers. The battle of Agincourt was fought October 25, 1415.

WESTMORELAND.

Oh, that we now had here
But one ten thousand of those men in England
That do no work today!

KING HENRY.

What's he that wishes so?
My cousin Westmoreland? No, my fair cousin:
If we are marked to die, we are enough
To do our country loss; and if to live,
The fewer men, the greater share of honor.
God's will! I pray thee, wish not one man more.
By Jove, I am not covetous for gold,
Nor care I who doth feed upon my cost;
Such outward things dwell not in my desires:
But if it be a sin to covet honor,
I am the most offending soul alive.
No faith, my coz, wish not a man from England:
God's peace! I would not lose so great an honor
As one man more, methinks, would share from me,
For the best hope I have. Oh, do not wish one more!
Rather proclaim it, Westmoreland, through my host,
That he which hath no stomach to this fight,

Let him depart; his passport shall be made
And crowns for convoy put into his purse:
We would not live in that man's company
That fears his fellowship to die with us.
This day is called the feast of Crispian:
He that outlives this day, and comes safe home,
Will stand a tiptoe when this day is named,
And rouse him at the name of Crispian.
He that shall live this day, and see old age,
Will yearly on the vigil feast his neighbors,
And say, "Tomorrow is Saint Crispian:"
Then will he strip his sleeve and show his scars,
And say "These wounds I had on Crispian's day."
Old men forget; yet all shall be forgot,
But he'll remember with advantages
What feats he did that day: then shall our names,
Familiar in his mouth as household words,
Harry the king, Bedford and Exeter,
Warwick and Talbot, Salisbury and Gloster,
Be in their flowing cups freshly remembered.
This story shall the good man teach his son;
And Crispin Crispian shall ne'er go by,
From this day to the ending of the world,
But we in it shall be remembered;
We few, we happy few, we band of brothers;
For he today that sheds his blood with me
Shall be my brother; be he ne'er so vile,
This day shall gentle his condition:
And gentlemen in England now abed
Shall think themselves accursed they were not here,
And hold their manhoods cheap whiles any speaks
That fought with us upon Saint Crispian's day.

SALISBURY.

My sovereign Lord, bestow yourself with speed:
The French are bravely in their battles set,
And will with all expedience charge on us.

KING HENRY.

All things are ready, if our minds be so.

WESTMORELAND.

     Perish the man whose mind is backward now!

KING HENRY.

     Thou dost not wish more help from England coz?

WESTMORELAND.

     God's will! my liege, would you and I alone,
     Without more help, might fight this royal battle out!

KING HENRY.

     Why, now thou has unwished five thousand men;
     Which likes me better than to wish us one.
     You know your places: God be with you all!

❦ Comprehension Questions

1. What one thing did good King Henry V covet?

2. Do you think that King Henry V understood how fearful and perplexed his troops were before the battle? Explain your answer.

3. The feast of Crispian was celebrated to honor two brothers, Crispian and Crispianus, who were martyred for attempting to spread Christianity throughout France. Why do you think King Henry V drew attention to the feast of Crispian during his speech?

4. Did Westmoreland have a change of heart after hearing the words of his king?

5. It is often God's will that His servants must fight the battles of life against great odds. Why is it foolish for Christians to be fearful of God's enemies just because their resources seem limited compared to their adversaries? Read Judges chapter seven prior to answering this question.

7   *Recessional*

by Rudyard Kipling

Born in India and educated in England, Kipling (1865–1936), became well known as a writer after his return to India in 1882. After traveling around the world, he married an American and settled in Vermont. In 1896 he returned to England. This poem calls England to remember the God of their fathers.

God of our fathers, known of old—
  Lord of our far-flung battle line—
Beneath Whose awful Hand we hold
  Dominion over palm and pine—
Lord God of Hosts, be with us yet,
  Lest we forget — lest we forget!

The tumult and the shouting dies—
  The captains and the kings depart—
Still stands Thine ancient Sacrifice,
  A humble and a contrite heart.
Lord God of Hosts, be with us yet,
  Lest we forget — lest we forget!

Far-called, our navies melt away—
  On dune and headland sinks the fire—
Lo, all our pomp of yesterday
  Is one with Nineveh and Tyre!
Judge of the Nations, spare us yet,
  Lest we forget — lest we forget!

If, drunk with sight of power, we loose
  Wild tongues that have not Thee in awe—
Such boasting as the Gentiles use
  Or lesser breeds without the Law—
Lord God of Hosts, be with us yet,
  Lest we forget — lest we forget!

For heathen heart that puts her trust
  In reeking tube and iron shard,
All valiant dust that builds on dust,
  And guarding calls not Thee to guard—
For frantic boast and foolish word,
  Thy mercy on Thy people, Lord!

8 Patrick Henry: The Orator of the Revolution

by Charles Morris

In 1765, there was an important meeting of the House of Burgesses of Virginia, as the law-making body of the colony was called. They had come together to debate upon a great question, that of the Stamp Act passed by the British Parliament for the taxation of the colonies. Most of the members were opposed to it, but they were timid and doubtful, and dreadfully afraid of saying or doing something that might offend the king. They talked all around the subject, but were as afraid to come close to it as if it had been a chained wolf.

They were almost ready to adjourn, with nothing done, when a tall and slender young man, a new and insignificant member whom few knew, rose in his seat and began to speak upon the subject. Some of the rich and aristocratic members looked upon him with indignation. What did this nobody mean in meddling with so weighty a subject as that before them, and which they had already fully debated? But their indignation did not trouble the young man.

He began by offering a series of resolutions, in which he maintained that only the Burgesses and the Governor had the right to tax the people, and that the Stamp Act was contrary to the constitution of the colony and therefore was void. This was a bold resolution. No one else had dared to go so far. It scared many of the members, and a great storm of opposition arose, but the young man would not yield.

He began to speak and soon there was flowing from his lips a stream of eloquence that took every one by surprise. Never had such glowing words been heard in that old hall. His force and enthusiasm shook the whole Assembly. Finally wrought up to the highest pitch of indignant patriotism, he thundered out the memorable words: "Caesar had his Brutus, Charles the First his Cromwell, and George the Third—" "Treason! Treason!" cried some of the excited members, but the orator went on—"many profit by their example. If this be treason make the most of it." His boldness carried the day; his words were irresistible; the resolutions were adopted; Virginia took a decided stand; and

Patrick Henry, the orator, from that time took first rank among American speakers. A zealous and daring patriot, God had made this man's words a power among the people.

Who was this man that had dared hurl defiance at the king? A few years before he had been looked upon as one of the most insignificant of men, a failure in everything he undertook, an awkward, ill-dressed, slovenly, lazy fellow, who could not even speak the king's English correctly. He was little better than a tavern lounger, most of his time being spent in hunting and fishing, in playing the flute and violin, and in telling amusing stories. He was adept in the latter and made himself popular among the common people.

He had tried farming and failed. He had made a pretense of studying law, and gained admittance to the bar, though his legal knowledge was rather slight. Having almost nothing to do in the courts, he spent most of his time helping about the tavern at Hanover Court-House, kept by his father-in-law. Henry was largely dependent upon this relative to help his family, for he had married early, with little means of supporting his wife.

One day, there came up a case in court which all of the leading lawyers had refused. It was called the "Parsons' Cause," and had to do with the claim of the ministers of the Established Church to collect dues from all the people, whatever their religious faith. A refusal to pay these had brought on the suit. The parsons had engaged one of the ablest lawyers of the county town on their side, and none of the lawyers seemed willing to take the opposite side.

What was the surprise of the people when the story went around that Patrick Henry had offered himself on the defendant's side! His taking up the case was a joke to most of them, and a general burst of laughter followed the news. What did this fellow know about the law? He was a good talker, no doubt, in his low Virginia dialect, but what kind of a show would he make in pleading a case before a learned judge! The case of the people seemed desperate indeed when entrusted to such hands as these.

When the young lawyer appeared in court, smiles went around among the lawyers and the audience. The idea of this awkward, backward, slovenly, untrained man attempting to handle such an important case! It seemed utterly absurd, and the opposing lawyers felt that they would make short work of him. They had the law on their side, their plaintiffs' case was a good one, their opponent was a mountebank, the defendants would be made to pay.

It is likely enough that Patrick Henry felt much the same way. His powers had never been tried except before a bar-room audience, and he could not have had much confidence in them. Doubtless he would have been glad enough, now it was too late, to get out of the court and back in the friendly tavern of his father-in-law.

When he rose to speak he faltered and hesitated. It looked as if he would break down utterly. But he had spoken before his friends; he was not quite a tyro in oratory; as he went on his timidity vanished and his confidence returned. He warmed up to his subject and a change seemed to come over him. His form straightened, his face filled out, his eyes blazed, the words poured from his mouth, clear, forcible sentences that carried everybody away with admiration and astonishment. There was not much statute law in what Patrick Henry said, but there was much of the eternal principles of right and justice. What right in equity had these plaintiffs to make the people pay for what they did not want and what they refused to accept? The argument was masterly and irresistible. It was poured forth in a flood of burning eloquence. The plaintiffs could not bear the storm of his accusations. They left the court in confusion. The specious plea of the opposing lawyers was quite overslaughed. The jury, carried away by his argument, returned the plaintiffs a verdict of one penny damages; and the people filled with enthusiasm, lifted the young advocate on their shoulders and carried him out of the court-house in triumph.

Patrick Henry was a made man. He no longer had to lounge in his office waiting for business. Plenty of it came to him. He set himself for the first time to an earnest study of the law, he improved his dialect and his command of language, the dormant powers of his mind rapidly unfolded, and two years after pleading his first case, he was elected a member of the House of Burgesses. We have seen how, in this body, he "set the ball of the Revolution rolling."

The idle tavern orator suddenly found himself launched into greatness. With all his careless habits and rural manners, he was a man of honor and integrity. Those who knew him respected him. For the first time he had learned what was in him, and he worked hard to make the best of his powers. Not many years passed after that great scene in the country court before Patrick Henry was transformed into a new man, one of culture, learning, and of extraordinary powers of oratory.

It was the time for such a man to make his force felt. The country was in a critical state. The people were on all sides demanding their rights, and would soon be demanding their liberty. Excitement spread everywhere. Fearless leaders were needed, men full of the spirit of patriotism. Patrick Henry had shown that he was both. In his spirit-stirring oration before the House of Burgesses he had put himself on record for all time. His defiance of the king stamped him as a warrior who had thrown his shield away and thence-forward would fight only with the sword.

The patriot leaders welcomed him. He worked with Thomas Jefferson and others upon the Committee of Correspondence, which sought to spread the story of political events through the colonies. The Virginia Assemblies which were broken up by the governor and called together again by the people welcomed him as a member. He was sent to Philadelphia as a member of the First Continental Congress, and his voice was eloquently heard in that body. In fact, he became one of the most active and ardent of the American patriots.

Of Patrick Henry's early speeches we know nothing beyond that intense blaze of eloquence with which he electrified the House of Burgesses. The first speech of his on record was that noble one given before the convention held at Richmond in March 1775. But this was an effort almost without a parallel in the annals of oratory. He had presented resolutions before the convention in favor of an open appeal to arms. To this, the more timid spirits made strong opposition. The fight at Lexington had not yet taken place, but Henry's prophetic gaze saw it coming. In a burst of flaming eloquence, he laid bare the tyranny of Parliament and king, declared that there was nothing left but to fight, and ended with an outburst thrilling in its force and intensity:

"There is no retreat but in submission and slavery! Our chains are forged! Their clanking may be heard on the plains of Boston! The war is inevitable—and let it come! I repeat, sir, let it come! It is in vain to extenuate the matter. Gentlemen may cry, Peace, peace—but there is no peace! The war is actually begun! The next gale that sweeps from the north will bring to our ears the clash of resounding arms! Our brethren are already in the field! Why stand we here idle? What is it that gentlemen wish? What would they have? Is life so dear, or peace so sweet, as to be purchased at the price of chains and slavery? Forbid it, Almighty God! I know not what course others may take; but as for me, give me liberty or give me death!"

Where was the idle fisher and fiddler, who had amused himself in telling stories to tavern loungers? Was this the man, this burning orator, whose voice was capable of moving great audiences like a cyclone, and the echo of whose words still thrills our hearts? Certainly in the career of Patrick Henry we have a remarkable example of mental progress. He was asleep in the early days, an idling dreamer. When he awoke he made the world rock with his voice. The kind Providence and grace of God was pleased to raise up a humble vessel to call men to the truth and to liberty.

As for Virginia, it listened to his fervid appeal, and when the news of Lexington reached its soil its sons were ready to spring to arms. Henry helped to gather a force of ardent patriots and led them to prevent the royal governor from carrying away the military stores of the state. He was elected Governor of Virginia in 1776, and held the office till 1779, actively aiding the popular cause. He was Governor again in 1784 and 1785.

In 1788, when the Federal Constitution had been formed and the States were called upon to adopt it, Henry, as a member of the Virginia Convention, appeared in a new role. He was bitterly opposed to the Constitution, which he said had "an awful squinting towards monarchy," and he opposed its adoption in a number of speeches of extraordinary eloquence. Fortunately, he did not succeed, the demand for a stronger Union being too great for even his powers of oratory.

He died June 6, 1799, with the reputation of being the greatest of American orators. John Randolph of Roanoke, himself one of Virginia's famous orators, has said that Patrick Henry was Shakespeare and Garrick in one, with their genius applied to the actual business of life. But the true seed of Henry's genius was his relationship with Jesus Christ. His soul was aflame with a passion for righteousness. Therefore, his tongue could not keep itself from its God ordained mission of helping to establish a nation that had no other King but Jesus.

❧ Glossary

mountebank a charlatan or quack

tyro a beginner in learning something

overslaugh to pass over a person by preferring or promoting another

fervid impassioned or fervent

9   *The Power of the Jury*

by Michael J. McHugh

In the year 1775, a young Christian attorney by the name of Patrick Henry rode into the small town of Culpeper, VA. There, in the middle of the town square was a minister tied to a whipping post, his back laid bare and bloody with the bones of his ribs showing. He had been scourged mercilessly with whips without the benefit of as much as a token appearance before a jury of his peers.

This incident disturbed Henry so deeply that he sought to find out the exact nature of this minister's crime. A reply came from one of the spectators that this man of God had defied a judge's order to stop preaching without a license. This minister was one of twelve men who were locked in jail because they refused to take a license. These men were fully persuaded of the fact that they possessed an inalienable right, granted by God alone, to preach the Word of God and that it would be sinful and treasonous for them to attempt to give any body of men the power to control that which belongs only to God.

In short, they refused to accept the legal premise of a man-made law that asserted that preaching the Word of God was a **privilege** granted by civil government.

Three days later, this preacher was scourged to death because he refused to bow the knee to an ungodly edict of men. This was the incident which sparked Patrick Henry to speak the famous words which later became the rallying cry of the American Revolution. "What is it that Gentlemen wish? What would they have? Is life so dear, or peace so sweet, as to be purchased at the price of chains and slavery? Forbid it Almighty God! I know not what course others may take, but as for me, give me liberty or give me death!"

Securing the God-given right of the individual is just as much a concern in modern American society as it was in the days of Patrick Henry. But what you may ask, if any, means did our founding fathers leave us to help the common man preserve his individual liberties?

In principle, our early statesmen left us a three-fold system by which an informed citizenry can control those acting in the name of government. Before we look at this system, however, we need to become thoroughly grounded in the true authority structure that our country is based upon:

1. God created man and gave him eternal laws to live by…

2. Man (that's you) created the Constitution…

3. The written agreement (or covenant) called the Constitution created our government and established its boundaries of authority.

4. Government is only empowered to enforce and administrate those laws that are consistent with its constitutionally enumerated authority, and even then, such laws must be consistent with the eternal laws of God as summarized in the Ten Commandments.

The system of government as structured by our founding fathers was to insure that the base of power was to remain in "We the People." Our nation was to be a constitutional Republic that respected each citizen as an individual created in the image of God with certain inalienable rights. The Constitution was designed to be the great tireless protector of the people.

However, if this were our only means of safeguarding our freedoms, then we would be no better off than those in a democracy, for elected officials often fail to keep their promises to faithfully uphold the Constitution.

Sadly, due to the ignorance of many Americans and the numerous acts of treason perpetrated by power hungry politicians, judges, and bureaucrats, the foundation of our Republic has been gradually weakened. As a result, America has begun to function like a democracy instead of a Republic.

A democracy places the liberties of the people in constant peril, for it is a one-vote system. This simply means that the rights of the people are always one vote away from extinction. If the majority can be persuaded or beguiled into forfeiting their freedoms, then those freedoms are taken from all the people. The principal of "majority rule" often makes it impossible for those in the minority to retain their God-given liberties.

Our constitutional Republic, on the other hand, has a three-vote system to check tyranny. Our first vote is at the polls on election day when we pick those who are to represent us in the seats of government. Few Americans realize, however, that they possess two additional powers that are the most effective means by which a common citizen can control those appointed to serve them in government.

The second power or vote is available when citizens serve on a Grand Jury. Before anyone can be brought to trial for a capital or infamous crime by those acting in the name of government, permission must be obtained from people serving on the Grand Jury! A grand jury's purpose is to protect individuals from an overzealous or politically motivated prosecutor.

The third power or vote, which is even more valuable, comes when a citizen acts as a jury member during a courtroom trial. It is in this setting that each juror has more power than the President, all of Congress, and all of the judges combined! Congress can legislate (make law), the President or some bureaucrat can make an order or issue regulations, and judges may instruct or make a decision, but no juror can ever be punished for voting "Not Guilty." Any juror can choose to disregard the mandates of Congress or the instructions of any judge or attorney in rendering his vote. If only one juror should vote "not guilty" for any reason, there is no conviction and no punishment can be handed out. Therefore, those acting in the name of government must come before the common man to get permission to enforce a law. How sad it is that the average American citizen is ignorant of, or sadly neglects the opportunities that are inherent in the exercise of the office of juror. One juror can stop tyranny with a "not guilty" vote. He can also nullify bad laws in any case that he hears by "hanging the jury."

One of the principal reasons why our founding fathers decided to include in the Constitution the right of citizens to receive a trial by a jury of his peers, as well as the concept of a Grand Jury, is for the protection of the weak against the strong. This is the principal, although not the sole motive for the establishment of all legitimate government.

When a government becomes oppressive, it is only the weaker minority that loses its liberties. The stronger party, in all societies, is free by virtue of its superior strength. The strong never oppress themselves. Legislation, therefore is commonly the work of the stronger party; and if, in addition to the sole power of legislation, they control the means of enforcing their laws they have all power in their hands, and the weaker parties are the subjects of legislative tyranny. Unless the minority party can gain access to a veto of some kind, they have no effective means to stop the power of government regulations that are designed to silence and destroy them. The trial by jury is the only institution that gives the weaker party any veto upon the power of a strong centralized government. Consequently, the jury is the sole institution that gives a principled minority any effective voice in the government, or any meaningful safeguard against oppression. The jury is the final check and balance upon government to insure that "We The People" retain the ultimate power to establish justice and rule the nation.

Unchecked authority is the foundation of tyranny, for fallen man cannot be trusted with absolute power. It is the juror's duty to use the jury room as a vehicle to stem the tide of oppression and tyranny. A faithful juror can prevent bloodshed by peacefully removing power from those who have abused it. Regardless of the pressures or abuse that jury members may face from other parties in the court, they must never yield their sacred vote to the conscience of another. The juror is not there as a fool, merely to agree with the majority, but as an officer of the court and a qualified judge in his own right.

Our nations first Chief Justice, John Jay, was very outspoken regarding the power of the jury. In the Supreme Court case of Georgia v. Brailsford (1794), Chief Justice Jay gave the following instructions to the jury: ... It may not be amiss here, gentlemen, to remind you of the good old rule, that on questions of fact it is the province of the jury, on questions of law, it is the province of the Court to decide. But it must be observed, that, by the same law which recognizes this reasonable distribution of jurisdiction, you have, nevertheless, a right to take upon yourselves to judge of both, and to determine the law as well as the fact in controversy. Both objects are lawfully within your power of decision."

John Adams, our second president, had this to say about the juror: "It is not only his right, but his duty ... to find the verdict according to his own best understanding, judgment, and conscience, though in direct opposition to the direction of the court." Our third president, Thomas Jefferson, put it like this: "I consider trial by jury as the only anchor yet imagined by man by which a government can be held to the principles of its constitution."

If jurors all throughout the United States begin and continue to bring in verdicts of *not guilty* in such cases where a man-made statute is defective or oppressive, these statutes will become as ineffective as if they had never been written. Therein lies the opportunity for the accomplishment of "Liberty and Justice for All," by the direct consent of the governed who sit upon the jury. This view also elevates the significance of the jury in terms of its ability to provide a viable "check and balance" on Congressional legislators at the state and federal levels.

Ye shall do no unrighteousness in judgment: thou shalt not respect the person of the poor, nor honor the person of the mighty: but in righteousness shalt thou judge thy neighbour."

—Leviticus 19:15

10 The Story of Martin, the Cobbler

by Leo N. Tolstoy

Born of a noble family in Russia, Leo Nikolaevich Tolstoy (1828–1910) became an orphan at the age of nine. After attending the University of Kazan he led an ungodly life in Moscow before entering the army. After travel in Western Europe (1857) he married. In the 1870s he underwent a religious change which redirected his life. This story is translated from *Where Love Is, There God Is Also*.

In a certain city of Russia dwelt Martin Avdyeeich, the cobbler. He lived in a cellar, a wretched little hole with a single window. The window looked up toward the street, and through it, Martin could just see the passers-by. It is true that he could see little more than their boots, but few indeed were the boots in that neighborhood which had not passed through his hands at some time or other. While Martin was still a journeyman, his wife had died, but she left him a little boy. No sooner had the little one begun to grow up and be a joy to his father's heart than he, too, died. Then Martin grew so despondent that he began to murmur against God.

Lo! one day there came to him an aged peasant pilgrim. Martin fell a-talking with him and began to complain of his great sorrow. "As for living any longer, thou man of God," said he, "I desire it not." But the man said to him, "Thy speech, Martin, is not good. It is because thou wouldst fain have lived for thy own delight that thou dost now despair."

"But what then *is* a man to live for?" asked Martin.

The old man answered, "For God, Martin! He gave thee life, and for Him therefore must thou live. When thou dost begin to live for Him, thou wilt grieve about nothing more, and all things will come easy to thee."

Martin was silent for a moment, and then he said, "And how must one live for God?"

"Christ hath shown us the way. Buy the Gospels and read. There thou wilt find out how to live for God. There everything is explained."

These words made the heart of Martin burn within him, and he went the same day and bought for himself a New Testament, printed in very large type, and began to read. He set out thinking to read it only on holidays; but as he read, it did his heart so much good that he took to reading it every day. The more he read, the more clearly he understood what God wanted of him, and how it was that he must live for God; and his heart grew lighter and lighter continually.

Henceforth, the whole life of Martin was changed. Formerly, whenever he had a holiday, he would go to the tavern to drink brandy now and again. He had done with all that now. His life became quiet and joyful. With the morning light he sat down to his work, worked all day, then took down his lamp from the hook, placed it on the table, took down his Book from the shelf and began to read.

It happened once that Martin was up reading till very late. He was reading St. Luke's Gospel and so he came to that place where the rich Pharisee invites our Lord to be his guest. He read all about how the woman who was a sinner anointed his feet and washed them with her tears. And Jesus said to Simon, "Seest thou this woman? I entered into thine house; thou gavest me no water for my feet; but she has washed my feet with tears and wiped them with the hairs of her head. Thou gavest me no kiss, but this woman, since the time that I came in, hath not ceased to kiss my feet." Martin took off his glasses, laid them on the book and fell a-thinking.

"Am I not always thinking of myself like Simon? Am I not always thinking of drinking tea, and keeping myself as warm and cozy as possible, without thinking at all about the guest? Simon thought about himself, but did not give the slightest thought to his guest. But who was his guest? The Lord Himself. Suppose He were to come to me, should I receive Him as Simon did?"

Martin leaned both his elbows on the table and, without perceiving it, fell a-dozing.

"Martin!"—it was as though the voice of someone spoke close to his ear.

Martin started up from his nap. "Who's there?"

He turned around, he looked at the door, but there was no one. Again he dozed off. Suddenly he heard quite plainly, "Martin, Martin, I say! Look tomorrow into the street. I am coming."

Martin awoke, rose from his chair and began to rub his eyes. He did not know himself whether he had heard these words asleep or awake.

At dawn the next day, he arose, prayed to God, lit his stove, got ready his gruel and cabbage soup, filled his samovar, put on his apron and sat down by his window to work. There he sat and thought of nothing but the things of yesternight. He thought at one time that he must have gone off dozing and then again he thought he really must have heard that voice. He looked out of his window as much as at his work, and whenever a strange pair of boots passed by, he bent forward and looked out of the window, so as to see the face as well as the feet of the passer-by. There passed close to the window an old soldier, one of Nicholas' veterans, in tattered old boots with a shovel in his hands. The old fellow was called Stepanuich, and lived with the neighboring shop keeper who gave him a home out of charity. Stepanuich stopped before Martin's window to sweep away the snow.

"I'm not growing wiser as I grow older," thought Martin, "I make up my mind that Christ is coming to me, and lo! 'tis only Stepanuich clearing away the snow." He looked through the window again, and there he saw that Stepanuich had placed the shovel against the wall, and was warming himself a bit.

"It is quite plain that the old fellow has scarcely strength enough to scrape away the snow," thought Martin to himself. "Suppose I make him drink a little tea! The samovar is just on the boil." He put down his awl, got up, placed the samovar on the table, put some tea in it, and tapped on the window with his fingers. Stepanuich turned round and came to the window. Martin beckoned to him, and then went and opened the door.

"Come in and warm yourself," cried he. "You're a bit chilled, eh?"

"Christ reward you! Yes!" said Stepanuich. He came in, shook off the snow, and began to wipe his feet so as not to soil the floor.

"Come in and sit down," said Martin. "Here, take a cup of tea." He filled two cups and gave one to his guest, but as he drank, he could not help glancing at the window from time to time.

"Dost thou expect anyone?" asked his guest.

"Do I expect anyone? Well, honestly, I hardly know. I am expecting and I am not expecting. Whether it was a vision or no, I know not. I was reading yesterday about our Lord Jesus Christ, how He came down to earth, how He went to Simon the Pharisee, and Simon did not receive Him at all. But suppose, I thought, if He came to me, would I receive Him? So thinking, I fell asleep. Then, much to my surprise, I heard my name called. I started up. A voice was whispering at my very ear. 'Look out tomorrow,' it said, 'I am coming.' And so it befell twice. Now look! wouldst thou believe it? The idea stuck to me—I scold myself for my folly, and yet I look for Him, our friend, Christ!"

Stepanuich shook his head and said nothing, but he drank his cup dry and put it aside. Then Martin took up the cup and filled it again.

"Drink some more," he said. "Twill do thee good. Now it seems to me that when Jesus went about on earth, He sought unto the simple folk most of all. Those disciples of His too, He chose most of them from amongst our brother laborers, sinners like unto us. 'He who would become the first among you,' he says, 'let him be the servant of all.' "

Stepanuich forgot his tea. He was an old man, soft-hearted and tearful. He sat and listened and the tears rolled down his cheeks. "I thank thee Martin Avdyeeich," said he. "I fared well at thy hands, and thou hast refreshed me both in body and soul."

"Thou wilt show me a kindness by coming again," said Martin. Stepanuich departed, and Martin sat down again by the window to work. He had some back-stitching to do, but he was looking for Christ and could think of nothing but Him and His work. Two soldiers passed by, one in boots of Martin's own making. A baker with a basket also passed. Then there came alongside the window a woman in worsted stockings and roughly made shoes. Martin saw that she was a stranger, poorly clad, and that she had a little child with her. She was leaning up against the wall with her back to the wind, trying to wrap the child up, but she had nothing to wrap it in, for she wore thin, summer clothes, and thin enough they were. From his corner, Martin heard the child crying and the woman trying to comfort him, but she could not. Then he got up, went out of the door onto the steps and cried, "My good woman! My good woman!"

The woman heard him and turned around.

"Why dost thou stand out in the cold there with the child? Come inside! In the warm room thou wilt be better able to tend him. This way!"

The woman was amazed to see an old fellow in an apron, with glasses on his nose calling to her. She came towards him. They went down the steps into the room together.

"There," said Martin, "Sit down, friend, nearer to the stove, and warm and feed thy little one."

He spread the cloth on the table, got a dish, put some cabbage soup into the dish, and placed it on the table.

"Seat thyself and have something to eat," said he, "and I will sit down a little with the youngster. I have had children of my own and know how to manage them."

The woman sat down at the table and began to eat, and Martin sat down on the bed with the child. He smacked his lips at him again and again. And all the time the child never left off shrieking. Then Martin hit upon the idea of shaking his fingers at him, so he snapped his fingers up and down, backwards and forwards, and the child stared at the fingers and was silent and presently he began to laugh. Martin was delighted. The woman went on eating and told him who she was and whence she came. "I am a soldier's wife," she said. "My husband they drove away from me to the army and nothing has been heard of him since. I took a cook's place but they could not keep me and the child. It is now three months since I have been drifting about without any fixed resting place. I have eaten away my all. I am chilled to death and he is quite tired out."

"Have you no warm clothes?" asked Martin.

"Ah, kind friend, this is indeed warm-clothes time, but yesterday I sold my last shawl for a few cents."

Martin went to the wall cupboard, rummaged about a bit, and then brought back with him an old jacket.

"Look," said he, "'tis a shabby thing, 'tis true, but it will do to wrap up in."

The woman looked at the old jacket, then she gazed at the old man, and taking the jacket, fell a-weeping. "Christ requite thee, dear little father," said she. "It is plain that it was He who sent me by thy window, and He who made thee look out of the window and have compassion on me."

Martin smiled lightly and said, "Yes, He must have done it." Then he told his dream to the soldier's wife also, and how he had heard a voice promising that Christ should come to him that day.

"All things are possible," said the woman. Then she rose up, put on the jacket, and wrapped it round her little one, and began to curtsy and thank Martin once more.

"Take this and buy back your shawl," said Martin, giving her a two grivenka piece. So the woman thanked him again and went away.

Martin sat down and worked on and on, but he did not forget the window, and whenever it was darkened, he immediately looked up to see who was passing. Soon he saw how an old woman, a huckster, had taken her stand there. She carried a basket of apples, and across one shoulder bore a sack full of shavings. She must have picked them up near some new building, and was taking them home with her. It was plain that the shavings were very heavy, so she placed the apple basket on a small post and started to shift the sack from one shoulder to the other. As she did so, and urchin in a ragged cap suddenly turned up, goodness knows from whence, grabbed at one of the apples in the basket and would have made off with it, but the wary old woman turned quickly around and gripped him by the sleeve. The lad fought and tried to tear himself loose, but the old woman seized him with both hands, knocked his hat off and tugged hard at his hair. The lad howled and the woman reviled him. Martin did not stop to put away his awl; he pitched it on the floor and rushed into the street.

"I didn't take it!" said the boy. "What are you whacking me for?!"

Martin tried to part the two. He seized the lad by the arm and said: "Let him go, little mother! Forgive him for Christ's sake."

"I'll forgive him so that he shan't forget the taste of fresh birch-rods. I mean to take the rascal to the police station."

Martin began to entreat with the old woman.

"Let him go, little mother; he will not do so any more."

The old woman let him go. The lad would have bolted, but Martin held him fast.

"Beg the little mother's pardon," said he, "and don't do such things any more. I saw thee take the apple."

Then the lad began to cry and beg pardon.

"Well, that's all right if thou art sorry! Now there's an apple for thee." Martin took one out of the basket and gave it to the boy. "I'll pay thee for it, little mother," he said to the old woman.

"Thou wilt ruin boys that way, the blackguards," grumbled the woman. "If I had the rewarding of him, he would not be able to sit down for a week!"

"Oh, little mother, little mother," cried Martin, "that is one way of looking at things but it is not God's way. God bade us forgive if we would be forgiven."

The old woman shook her head and sighed. "Boys will be boys, I suppose. Well, God be with him," she said.

But just as she was about to hoist the sack again on to her shoulder, the lad rushed forward and said:

"Give it here, and I'll carry it for thee, granny! It's all in my way."

The old woman shook her head, but she did put the sack on the lad's shoulder. And so they trudged down the street together, side by side. Martin followed them with his eyes till they were out of sight, then he went in and sat down to work again. Soon it grew dark; he was scarcely able to see the stitches, and the lamp-lighter came by to light the street lamps. So Martin put away his tools, swept up the cuttings, placed the lamp on the table, and took down the Gospels from the shelf. He wanted to find the passage where he had last evening place a strip of morocco leather by way of a marker. But just as he opened the book, he recollected his dream of yesterday evening.

No sooner did he call it to mind than it seemed to him as if some persons were moving about and shuffling with their feet behind him. He looked round and saw—yes, someone was really there, but who he could not exactly make out. Then a voice whispered in his ear, "Martin, Martin, does thou not know me?"

"Who are thou?" cried Martin.

" 'Tis I," cried the voice, "lo, 'tis I!" And forth from the dark corner stepped Stepanuich. He smiled; it was as though a little cloud was breaking and he was gone.

"It is I!" cried the voice again, and forth from the corner stepped a woman with a little child. The woman smiled, the child laughed, and they also disappeared. "And it is I!" cried the voice. The old woman and the lad with the apple stepped forth. Both of them smiled and they also disappeared.

The heart of Martin was glad; he began to read the Gospels at the place where he had opened them. And at the top of the page he read these words:

"I was an-hungered and thirsty and ye gave Me to drink. I was a stranger and ye took Me in." At the bottom of the page he read further.

"Inasmuch as ye have done it to the least of these, My brethren, ye have done it unto Me."

And Martin understood that his dream had not deceived him, and that the Saviour had really come to him that day and he had really received Him.

❧ Comprehension Questions

1. What type of work did Martin do for a living?

2. What advice did Martin receive from the old peasant pilgrim that dramatically changed his life?

3. Why is it against the law of Christ to be self-centered?

4. Martin learned to view human problems as God-ordained opportunities for serving Christ. How would our world change if more people viewed human needs in this light?

5. In what way did Christ reward Martin for his faithful service to Him?

6. The Bible teaches us that God is a Giver. He loves to give good gifts to the least of men. Do you think that all individuals who claim to be children of God have a duty to reflect the giving nature of their Lord? Please explain your answer.

⚜ Glossary

samovar   a metal urn, used especially in Russia, for heating water in making tea

11   *Daniel Boone: Wilderness Scout*

by Stewart Edward White

When we think of American pioneers we recall automatically certain names—Daniel Boone, Davy Crockett, Kit Carson, perhaps Simon Kenton. Of course, there were hundreds, yes thousands of others, who met the same dangers, exhibited at least approximate skills, and fought the same adversaries. But the names of most of them are unknown, and of the rest only the special student is aware. Often, the more obscure men have performed specific deeds that common legend ascribes to better known names.

Early Pioneers head West.

Columbus, as we know, was really not the first to discover America. Common belief has it that Daniel Boone, "discovered" Kentucky; but actually, he first entered Kentucky lured by the glowing tales of a man named Finley who had, with others, preceded him. Did you ever hear of Finley? But we have all heard of Boone.

This is because the truly famous men have possessed some quality that the others did not. It mattered little what special deeds they performed. Others must have performed similar feats, or the West would never have been conquered. Certain deeds became renowned, not so much because they were thrilling, but because of the men who did them.

Thus Daniel Boone's name is inseparably connected with the occupation of "the dark and bloody ground" because he was Daniel Boone.

He was one of the many great Indian fighters of his time. Boone lived for years with a rifle in one hand and a tomahawk in the next. He lost brothers and sons under the scalping knife. He was a master woodsman, capable of finding his way through a hundred miles of unbroken forest. When he was outdoors, he could maintain himself alone, not merely for a day or a week but for a year or more without other resources than his rifle, his tomahawk, and his knife; and this in the face of the most wily of foes.

He was muscular, strong, and enduring; the victor in many a hand-to-hand combat; conqueror of farms cut from the forest; performer of long journeys afoot, at speeds that would seem incredible to a college athlete. He was a dead shot with the rifle, an expert hunter of game. Other men, long since forgotten, were all these things as well.

But Daniel Boone was reverent in the belief that he was ordained by God to open the wilderness. He was brave with a courage remarkable for its calmness and serenity. Calmness and serenity, indeed, seem to have been his characteristics in all his human relations. Those who knew him remark frequently on this, speak of the fact that where everyone else was an Indian hater, Boone never cherished rancor against them, so that as honorable antagonists they always met, both in peace and war.

He was trustworthy, so that when wilderness missions of great responsibility were undertaken, he was almost invariably the one called. He was loyal to the last drop of his blood. He was ready ever to help others. These are simple, fundamental qualities, but they are never anywhere too common; they are rarely anywhere combined in one man; and in those rough times of primitive men they sufficed, when added to his wilderness skill and determination, to make him the leading and most romantic figure.

If the Boy Scouts would know a man who, in his attitude toward the life to which he was called, most nearly embodied the precepts of their laws, let them look on Daniel Boone. Gentle, kindly, modest, peace-loving, absolutely fearless, a master of Indian warfare, a mighty hunter, strong as a bear, and active as a panther. His life was lived in daily danger, almost perpetual hardship and exposure; yet he died in his bed at nearly ninety years of age.

Mercy

12

By William Shakespeare

From "Merchant of Venice"

The quality of mercy is not strained;
It droppeth as the gentle rain from heaven
Upon the place beneath: it is twice blest,—
It blesseth him that gives and him that takes:
'Tis mightiest in the mightiest; it becomes
The throned monarch better than his crown:
His sceptre shows the force of temporal power,
The attribute to awe and majesty,
Wherein doth sit the dread and fear of kings;
But mercy is above this sceptred sway,—
It is enthroned in the hearts of kings,
It is an attribute to God himself;
And earthly power doth then show likest God's,
When mercy seasons justice.

❦ Comprehension Questions

1. The words of Christ state: "Blessed are the merciful, for they shall obtain mercy." How does this verse apply to the writing listed above?

2. Explain why a crown of mercy or righteousness is more noble than a crown of gold for earthly kings.

3. What did Shakespeare try to teach the reader about the principle of seasoning justice with mercy?

Shakespeare's birthplace in Stratford-on-Avon, England.

13

Dorothea Dix: Helper of the Insane

by Charles Morris

The treatment of the insane in the past centuries was a frightful example of "man's inhumanity to man." Their condition was pitiable in the extreme. No one had a conception of the proper way of dealing with these unfortunates, and they were treated more like wild beasts in a menagerie than human beings; iron cages, chains, clubs, and starvation being used as methods of restraint, while their medical care was crude and barbarous. This "care" was usually limited to purging, bleeding, and electric shock treatments.

It was often ignorance rather than malice that led to this merciless treatment. When in 1792 Dr. Pinel in France declared that such methods were barbarous and fit only to make patients worse, no one was ready to believe him. And when he proved that mercy was tenfold better than severity, it came as a new revelation. About the same time a similar system began to make its way in England. The system of restraint by straitjackets, etc., was continued till later, and in the United States, the old methods held their own until well into the nineteenth century. The change to a more merciful treatment of these weaker vessels was largely brought about by the efforts of one woman, a philanthropist of the highest type.

This woman, Dorothea Lynde Dix, was born April 4, 1802, in Hampden, Maine, the daughter of an itinerant physician, who died while she was quite young. She had her own way to make, and at fourteen years of age was teaching a child-school. In 1821, she taught an older school, and in 1831, opened a select school for young ladies in Boston. Frail and delicate, she broke down completely in 1836. Fortunately, she had inherited an estate which made her independent. She now went to Europe for her health, spending a year or two there.

During her period of teaching she had given much time to the care and instruction of the neglected inmates of the State's prison at Charlestown, and on her return from Europe became deeply interested in the condition of the paupers, prisoners, and lunatics, especially the latter, of Massachusetts. She was not alone in this. Others were awakening to the sorry condition of these unfortunates, and a benevolent doctor gave her much aid and encouragement in the investigation which she undertook.

Her inquiry into the condition of the insane in the State roused at once her pity and indignation; her deepest sympathies were awakened, and she began an investigation of the subject which had the merit of being thorough and untiring. Practical in character, she made a complete study of the question as it existed in other lands, and in 1841, began her earnest investigation of the methods of dealing with the insane in America. What she discovered was heart-breaking to one of her sympathetic nature.

At that time, there were very few insane asylums in the country. Lunatics were placed with the paupers in almshouses and the prisoners in jail, all being herded indiscriminately together, and treated with brutal inhumanity. Filth prevailed, heat was lacking in bitter weather, there was no separation of the innocent, the guilty, and the insane. Chains were used for the restraint of those who might easily have been managed by kindness.

Miss Dix's investigation led to a hearing before the legislature of Massachusetts, in which she vividly depicted the state of affairs and earnestly called for an amelioration of the horrors she had found. Her testimony illuminated the shocking condition of things, and revealed that the situation was the result of neglect and indifference. The methods of medieval times had by no means died out even in intellectual Massachusetts, ignorance of the true condition of the almshouses and prisons having much to do with it. Miss Dix was determined that the plea of ignorance should no longer prevail.

Her testimony was full of disturbing facts and earnest appeals. We can here quote only one of its most startling passages: "I proceed, gentlemen, to call your attention to the present state of insane persons confined within the commonwealth; in cages, closets, cellars, stalls, pens; chained, naked, beaten with rods, and lashed into obedience."

This general statement was borne out by detailed accounts of the horrible things she had seen in many instances. As a mild example may be mentioned the recital of one almshouse keeper, who said that one of his insane inmates had been troublesome and disposed to run away, but was now satisfied and docile. His docility proved to be due to an iron ring around his neck and a chain fastening him to the wall.

The testimony was a revelation to the legislature. A bill for measures of relief was quickly introduced and carried by a large majority, and with that legislation began the era of wise and merciful treatment of the insane in Massachusetts. By two years of hard work, Miss Dix had set in motion a plan to regenerate the condition of paupers and lunatics in that old commonwealth.

Her research in Massachusetts carried her over the borders into other States, in which she found like conditions prevailing, and her inquiry was gradually extended until it covered the whole United States. She traversed the entire country east of the Rocky Mountains, made investigations everywhere, and found the same sickening conditions which Massachusetts had revealed. At that time, very few States had any public asylum for the insane, and an important field of her labors was to have these established. Her first success in this was in New Jersey, an asylum being founded in Trenton in 1845 as a result of her earnest representations. This was but the beginning; many other States followed, and the herding of the indigent and the insane together in almshouses began to be a thing of the past.

Miss Dix spared no efforts in her indefatigable labors. She went from legislature to legislature, interviewing members, pleading, demanding, repeating the results of her inquiries, winning votes, everywhere commanding respect and attention, everywhere gaining favorable legislation. And this was not alone in the United States, for more than once she crossed the ocean and found conditions still existing in Europe that badly needed improvement.

The plea of State poverty was one of the difficulties she met at home, and this she sought to overcome by an appeal to Congress. Large grants of the public lands were being made for the endowment of schools, and she begged for a similar grant in aid of her lifework. Her first application was made in 1848, when she asked for 5,000,000 acres. She later on increased this demand to 12,250,000 acres, 10,000,000 being for the benefit of the insane and the remainder for the deaf and dumb.

It was a difficult task she had undertaken. Congress was then occupied with exciting questions that threatened to lead to civil war, and it was hard to enlist its attention to an act of pure beneficence. Sadly, Miss Dix failed to take her case to the Christian Church and wealthy Christian businessmen. Her socialistic upbringing would not permit her to see that the state should not be taking a leading role in the development of charitable institutions or clinics. Such duties are the responsibility of private citizens, religious organizations, families, and private charitable foundations. Once acts of local charity are given over to the control of central state bureaucracies, the legitimate providers of social welfare, (i.e. family, church, and private foundations) are encouraged to retreat from their God-given responsibilities to care for the downcast and poor.

Nevertheless year after year, Miss Dix kept up her struggle, only to meet defeat and disappointment. More than once, her bill was passed by the Senate but killed in the House. Again, the House supported it and the Senate defeated it. Not until 1854 did she succeed in getting a favorable vote from both houses to fund her projects.

It was with the highest gratification that she heard of her success, her triumph. The unfortunates for whom she had so long worked and pleaded would now be amply cared for, and the disgrace on the nation which had so long existed would come to an end. Her heart was filled with joy, and congratulations poured in upon her. Alas! the bill had the President still to pass, and her heart sank into the depths when President Pierce vetoed the bill on the ground of its being alien to the Constitution, which indeed it was.

In God's providence, Miss Dix was defeated. It was hopeless to seek to revive the measure during the years of excitement that followed, but she continued her work with success among the States until the outbreak of the Civil War rendered useless all labors in this direction. The Lord overruled her well intended, but unbiblical, plans for State-controlled care for the mentally ill and moved her in a different direction.

She now sought Washington and offered her services in a new role of benevolence, as a nurse for wounded soldiers. In this the zeal and ability in management she displayed were such that on the tenth of July, 1861, Secretary Cameron appointed her Superintendent of Women Nurses. As such she established excellent regulations, which were strictly carried out, but not without controversies with others in authority. Miss Dix had a somewhat autocratic manner, which was likely to cause offense and lead to opposition, but her instincts were well-intended. She meant it all for good. She continued her service until the end of the war, carefully inspecting the hospitals, overseeing the work of the nurses, and maintaining a high state of discipline among them. For this she accepted no salary, and provided amply for the health of those working under her.

When the war ended, Miss Dix returned to her labors on behalf of the insane and kept them up until advancing age reduced her powers. She resided at Trenton, New Jersey, the seat of the first asylum instituted through her efforts, and died there July 18, 1887. Her life is a solid testimony of what one woman can do to bless the lives of the weak and helpless among us.

14   *The Men to Make a State*

by G. W. Doane

1. THE MEN, TO MAKE A STATE, MUST BE INTELLIGENT MEN

I do not mean that they must know that two and two make four; or, that six percent a year is half a percent a month. I take a wider and a higher range. I limit myself to no mere utilitarian intelligence. This has its place. And this will come almost unsought. The contact of the rough and rugged world will *force* men to it in self-defense. The lust of worldly gain will drag men to it for self-aggrandizement. But men that are made this way, will never make a state. The intelligence which this endeavor demands, will take a wider and a higher range. Its study will focus on how God rules man. It will make history its chief experience. It will read hearts. It will know men. It will, however, first know *itself*.

A free state, like our own, has a fearful dependence upon its citizens being prepared to intelligently exercise their right to vote. Voting calls for wisdom, and discretion, and intelligence, of no ordinary standard. It takes in, at every exercise, the interests of all the nation. Its results reach forward through time into eternity. Its discharge must be accounted for among the dread responsibilities of the great day of judgment. Who will go to it blindly? Who will go to it passionately? Who will cast their vote as a pawn, a tool, a slave? How many *do*! *These* are not the men to make a state.

2. THE MEN, TO MAKE A STATE, MUST BE HONEST MEN

I do not simply mean men that would never *steal*. I do not mean men that would never cheat in making change. I mean men with a single *face*. I mean men with a single *eye*. I mean men with a single *tongue*. I mean men that consider always what is *right*; and do it at whatever cost. I mean men who can live, like Oliver Cromwell, on little or much; and whom, therefore, no king on earth can *buy*.

Men that are in the market for the highest bidder; men that make politics their *trade* and look to office for a *living*; men that will crawl, where they cannot climb; *these* are not the men to make a state.

3. THE MEN, TO MAKE A STATE, MUST BE RELIGIOUS MEN

States are from God. States are dependent upon God. States are accountable to God. To leave God out of states, is to be Atheists. I do not mean that men must be pietists. I do not mean that men must wear long faces. I do not mean that men must talk of *conscience*, while they take your *spoons*. One shrewdly called hypocrisy, the tribute which vice pays to virtue. These masks and vizors, in like manner, are the forced concession which a moral nature makes to him, whom, at the same time it dishonors. I speak of men who feel and intimately know their Creator. I speak of men who feel and own their sins. I speak of men who think the Cross no shame. I speak of men who have it in their heart as well as on their brow. The men that are accountable to no one but themselves and own no future, the men that trample on the Bible, the men that never pray are *not* the men to make a *state*.

Noah Webster wrote in 1823:

> In selecting men for office, let principle be your guide. Regard not the particular sect or denomination of the candidate—look at his character. It is alleged by men of loose principles, or defective views of the subject, that religion and morality are not necessary or important qualifications for political stations. But the Scriptures teach a different doctrine. They direct that rulers should be men who rule in the fear of God, able men, such as fear God, men of truth, hating covetousness. It is to the neglect of this rule that we must ascribe the multiplied frauds, breaches of trust, peculations and embezzlements of public property which astonish even ourselves; which tarnish the character of our country and which disgrace government. When a citizen gives his vote to a man of known immorality, he abuses his civic responsibility; he sacrifices not only his own responsibility; he sacrifices not only his interest, but that of his neighbor; he betrays the interest of his country.

4. THE MEN, TO MAKE A STATE, ARE MADE BY FAITH

A man that has no faith, is so much *flesh*. His heart a *muscle*; nothing more. He has no *past*, for *reverence*; no *future*, for *reliance*. He lives. So does a clam. Both die. Such men can never make a state. There must be *faith*, which furnishes the fulcrum that Communists in the Soviet Union could not find, for the long lever that should move the world. There must be faith to look through clouds and storms up to the sun that shines as cheerily on high as on creation's morn. There must be faith that can lay hold on Heaven, and let the earth swing from beneath it, if God will. There must be faith that can afford to sink the *present* in the *future*; and let *time* go, in its strong grasp upon *eternity*. This is the way that men are made, to make a state.

5. THE MEN, TO MAKE A STATE, ARE MADE BY SELF-DENIAL

The willow dallies with the water, and is fanned forever by its coolest breeze, and draws its waves up in continual pulses of refreshment and delight; and is a *willow*, after all. An acorn has been loosened, some autumn morning, by a squirrel's foot. It finds a nest in some rude cleft of an old granite rock, where there is scarcely earth to cover it. It knows no shelter, and it feels no shade. It squares itself against the storms. It shoulders through the blast. It *asks* no favor, and *gives* none. It grapples with the rock. It crowds up towards the sun. It is an oak. It has been seventy years an oak. It *will* be an oak for *seven times* seventy years; unless you need a man-of-war to thunder at the foe that shows a flag upon the shore, where freemen dwell: then you take no willow in its daintiness and gracefulness; but that old, hardy, storm-stayed and storm-strengthened oak. So are the men made that will make a state.

6. THE MEN, TO MAKE A STATE, ARE THEMSELVES MADE BY OBEDIENCE

Obedience is the health of human hearts: obedience to God; obedience to father and to mother, who are, to children, in the place of God; obedience to teachers and to masters, who are in the place of father and mother; obedience to spiritual pastors, who are God's ministers; and to the powers that be, which are ordained of God. Obedience is but self-government in action: and he can never govern men who does not govern first *himself*. Only such men *can* make a state.

15

Charles Goodyear:
The Prince of the Rubber Industry

by Charles Morris

The story of Charles Goodyear provides numerous examples of how to persevere under disappointments and difficulties. No human being ever kept up his spirit longer under trials and troubles than this great discoverer, winning success where thousands would have failed. The story of his life is that of the India-rubber industry. His labors in this took more than ten years of the prime of his life. For it he suffered poverty, imprisonment, and ridicule, and, though he produced one of the great modern industries, he failed to gain an adequate return in money for his great sacrifice. Great wealth did not come to him as a result of his discovery, and he had largely to be content with the satisfaction of helping mankind.

The sap of the India-rubber tree long held out a promising lure to inventors. It formed a waterproof material which could readily be molded into almost any shape, and in the first half of the last century, many companies were organized for the manufacture of shoes and other rubber goods. But there was one great problem—the rubber was fit for use in winter, but it would not bear the summer's heat, softening and becoming useless.

For example, distributors of India-rubber life-vests were of the opinion that their product was hopelessly flawed. They would make a large quantity of goods during the winter and sell them for good prices, but in the summer many of these melted down and were returned as ruined. The rubber would grow sticky in the sun and stiff in the cold. Many efforts had been made to overcome this by mixing other materials with it, but all in vain, and ruin seemed to stare all rubber manufacturers in the face. The man who saved them from this fate was Charles Goodyear, a merchant of Philadelphia, but a native of New Haven, Connecticut, in which city he was born on the 29th of December, 1800.

At the time mentioned, around 1834, he was engaged in the hardware business of A. Goodyear & Sons in the Quaker city. At this period, a very large business had sprung up in the rubber trade, in spite of its disadvantages, and he grew interested in it as a possible source of profit. When in New York one day, he bought one of the India-rubber life-preservers made by the Roxbury Rubber Co., the manufacturers previously mentioned. Having the taste for invention as a true son of Connecticut, he took this home, examined it carefully, and fancied that he could improve upon it. He soon devised a plan, which he took to the Roxbury Company and asked them to adopt. They declined to do so, telling him the story of their difficulties in terms of financial limitations.

"Your plan is a good one," he was told, "but business conditions will not let us take on new expenses. If you can only find some way to make India-rubber stand the heat of summer and the cold of winter, both our fortunes will be made. Anything less than that will be of no use to us."

Here was an idea, thrown out as a mere suggestion, but it was one that sank deep into Charles Goodyear's mind. But he was poorly fitted to work it out. A chemical process was needed, and he knew almost nothing of chemistry. In fact, he had little education of any kind. Money was lacking, and he was scantily provided with that. The failure of some business houses about this time made his father's firm bankrupt, and he, as a member of the firm, was arrested and imprisoned for debt.

Those were the years in which a debtor could be put in prison, and during the several years following, Goodyear spent much of his time in jail. He had a family, he was in poor health, he needed to do something that would make him a living, but he had grown so infatuated with the idea of discovering the secret of a marketable India-rubber that he could think of nothing else.

Rubber was abundant enough in those days, and he was able easily to get it even when in prison. He was constantly engaged in experiments with it, whether in prison or out. His friends, who aided him at first, soon grew tired of encouraging him in what they deemed his infatuation. His ignorance of chemistry was a real problem for him, and though he explained his difficulty to the chemists of his city, none of them were able to help him.

If Charles Goodyear lacked money, there was one thing he had in abundance—perseverance. He never gave up. Persuasion, argument, ridicule, had no effect upon him. He tried endless experiments, made India-rubber fabrics of various kinds, and, with a native taste for art, ornamented some of them. It was this that led to his first step towards success.

He had bronzed the surface of some rubber drapery, and, finding his bronze too heavy, poured aqua fortis on it to eat some of it away. The acid did its work too well, removing all the bronze and discoloring the fabric, so that he threw it away as spoiled. Thinking over it some days later, he picked up the discarded piece and examined it again, and was delighted to find it much improved in quality, it bearing heat far better than any he had tried before. Here was something learned. He hastened to patent his new process, and, gaining some money, he engaged in the manufacture of rubber treated with aqua fortis.

But his troubles were not yet at an end. People had grown sick of India-rubber, which had ruined many firms that had engaged in it, and no investors cared to touch it. As for Goodyear himself, many began to think that he had become so possessed with his idea that he was little better than a crazy man. His enthusiasm for his rubber was such that he wore whole suits made of it, coat, cap, shoes, and all, and made himself a walking advertisement. He talked of it so incessantly that people felt like running away from him. It was "rubber, rubber, rubber," all day long, till many considered him a nuisance.

All this time he was suffering from poverty, and the pawnbroker and he grew much too well acquainted. His family suffered as well, and hunger ruled in the Goodyear household. After a time, he persuaded some of the members of the old Roxbury company to invest in his new discovery, and a new factory was started, which for a time did a large business. Then it was found that the aqua fortis hardened the surface only, and that the rest of the rubber would not bear the heat. At once the business fell off, the Roxbury men withdrew their funds, and the inventor sank into destitution again.

His friends now did their utmost to persuade him to give up his fruitless work. His wife and children did the same. But they advised and persuaded in vain. He would not yield. Through it all he was working blindly, handicapped by his small knowledge of chemistry, and still he continued his random experiments day and night.

Success began to shine through an assistant of his who had tried the effect of mixing gum with sulphur. This was a new process, not tried before by Goodyear, and he studied it thoroughly, working at it for months, but with very unsatisfactory results. Yet the end was near at hand. Providence helped him where science had failed. One day in 1839, a mass of gum and sulphur he had mixed happened to touch a red-hot stove. To his surprise and delight, its character was changed by the heat and it would not melt. He tried and tested it in every way he could think of, and always with the same result. He had penetrated the mystery. The great secret was his! All that was needed was to mix the gum with sulphur and expose it to great heat. It would afterwards stand both heat and cold.

For five years the indefatigable investigator had been steadily at work, in prison and out, in poverty and hunger, under every discouragement, enduring the ridicule of the public, the reproaches of friends and family, the insults of those who touched their heads significantly when they looked at him. He had at last won out, as the saying is; the great discovery of vulcanized rubber was his, and fortune at length seemed to lie in his path.

Yet it did not come quickly. Six years more of severe labor and hard trials were before him. He did not propose to act hastily again, as he had with his former discovery. He spent these years in new experiments, working out one thing after another, perfecting this point and that, taking out a patent on everything achieved, until he had sixty patents in all, covering every step he had made.

Unfortunately, his patents were confined to America. Other parties secured in England and France the rights which should have been his, litigation was needed at home to protect his rights, and his profits from his valuable discovery were far smaller than they should have been. But honors came to him from many sources. From the Crystal Palace Exhibition of 1851 he received the Grand Council medal, and at the Paris Exposition of 1855 the emperor gave him the Grand Medal of Honor and the Cross of the Legion of Honor. But disease had attacked the discoverer. Returning to America in 1858, he went to work energetically to perfect his processes, but his ills had become chronic, and death came two years later on July 1, 1860.

Nevertheless, he lived to see his material applied to nearly five hundred uses, and to give employment, in England, Germany, France, and the United States, to sixty thousand persons... Art, science, and humanity are indebted to him for a material which serves the purposes of them all, and serves them as no other known material could.

The next time you jump into your car on a hot summer day, you may begin to appreciate the work of this inventor from years gone by. Without his tireless efforts, and God-blessed skills, your rubber tires would not carry you one block in the heat of the day!

⚜ Glossary

aqua fortis   nitric acid

vulcanize   to treat rubber with sulphur or its compounds and subject it to heat in order to make it nonplastic and increase
its strength and elasticity

16 *Crossing the Bar*

by Alfred Tennyson

The English poet Alfred Tennyson was born August 6, 1809 and died in October 1892. This short poem or lyric was written by Tennyson at the age of eighty-one. Tennyson himself tells us in his memoirs that this piece about facing death "came in a moment." The same evening that he wrote this poem, he read it aloud to his son who excitedly exclaimed, "It is the crown of your life's work." A few weeks before his death, Tennyson said to his son, "Mind you put 'Crossing the Bar' at the end of my poems." This last request was always honored by his son, who helped to publish several editions of his father's poetry.

Sunset and evening star,
   And one clear call for me,
And may there be no moaning of the bar,
   When I put out to sea.

But such a tide as moving seems asleep,
   Too full for sound and foam,
When that which drew from out the boundless deep
   Turns again home.

Twilight and evening bell,
   And after that the dark!
And may there be no sadness of farewell,
   When I embark;

For tho' from out our bourne of time and place
   The flood may bear me far,
I hope to see my Pilot face to face
   When I have crossed the bar.

 *Glossary*

bourne   boundary

17 *How Did You Die?*

by Edmund Vance Cooke

Edmund Cooke was born June 5, 1866 and died December 18, 1932.
This poem was first published in 1903.

Did you tackle that trouble that came your way
  With a resolute heart and cheerful?
Or hide your face from the light of day
  With a craven soul and fearful?

Oh, a trouble's a ton, or a trouble's an ounce,
  Or a trouble is what you make it.
And it isn't the fact that you're hurt that counts,
  But only how did you take it?

You are beaten to earth? Well, well, what's that?
  Come up with a smiling face.
It's nothing against you to fall down flat,
  But to lie there–that's disgrace.

The harder you're thrown, why the higher you bounce;
  Be proud of your blackened eye!
It isn't the fact that you're licked that counts;
  It's how did you fight and why?

And though you be done to death, what then?
  If you battled the best you could;
If you played your part in the world of men,
  Why, the Critic will call it good.

Death comes with a crawl, or comes with a pounce,
  And whether he's slow or spry.
It isn't the fact that you're dead that counts,
  But only, how did you die?

18 First Prayer in Congress

by Rev. Jacob Duche

The Second Continental Congress was opened with a special prayer by Rev. Jacob Duche on September 7, 1777. This prayer was written down and circulated to every member of the Congress as well as to the common people. The United States Congress has been opened with prayer for many generations, and this godly tradition still exists at the present time.

O Lord, our Heavenly Father, high and mighty King of kings, and Lord of lords, who dost from Thy throne behold all the dwellers of the earth, and reignest with power supreme and uncontrolled over all the kingdoms, empires, and governments, look down in mercy, we beseech Thee, on the American States, who have fled to Thee from the rod of the oppressor, and thrown themselves on Thy gracious protection, desiring to be henceforth dependent only on Thee. To Thee they have appealed for the righteousness of their cause; to Thee do they now look up for that countenance and support which Thou alone canst give. Take them, therefore, Heavenly Father, unto Thy nurturing care. Give them wisdom in council and valor in the field.

Defeat the malice of our adversaries; convince them of the unrighteousness of their course, and, if they still persist in sanguinary purposes, oh! let the voice of Thine own unerring justice, sounding in their hearts, constrain them to drop the weapons of war from their unnerved hands in the day of battle. Be Thou present, O God of wisdom, and direct the councils of this honorable assembly. Enable them to settle things on the best and surest foundations, that the scenes of blood may be speedily closed, and order, harmony, and peace may be effectually restored, and truth and justice, religion, and piety prevail and flourish among Thy people. Preserve the health of their bodies and the vigor of their minds; shower down upon them and the millions they here represent, such temporal blessing as Thou seest expedient for them in this world, and crown them with everlasting glory in the world to come. All this we ask in the name and through the merits of Jesus Christ, Thy Son, our Saviour. Amen.

Booker T. Washington

by Charles Morris

Near the end of the days of slavery, on a plantation in Franklin County, Virginia, was born a negro boy who was destined to lift himself, by moral and mental strength, into the ranks of the great men of the world. He was an outstanding representative of a race that numbers more than thirty million people in the United States. Freed from slavery only a century ago, not yet freed from ignorance, the negro race has had little opportunity to develop the powers it possesses. Frederick Douglas, an able and brilliant orator of the times before the Civil War, was the only man of negro blood to raise himself to a national reputation before the coming of Booker T. Washington, of whose striking career it is our purpose now to speak.

Born in a tumble-down log cabin on an old Virginia plantation, the young Washington came into a world in which he was expected to play so small a part that no record was kept even of the year of his birth. All he knew was that it was some time during the year 1858 or 1859. His father, a white man, he never knew. He knew no name except Booker, by which he was called during his few years of slave life on the plantation. A mere toddler as he was, only six or seven years old when the war ended and freedom came, he was kept busy at odd jobs, cleaning the yard, carrying water to the men, and taking corn to the mill. Years later, Washington recalled the times he would fall from his horse with his bag of corn and sit in tears by the wayside until someone came along to lift him up again.

Schooling was not thought of for most youngsters with black skin, though the little slave boy already felt a thirst for knowledge. He tells us how he would carry the books of his young mistress when she went to the school-house, closed against all of his color, but which seemed to him like a paradise to which he was denied entrance.

The slaves, he tells us, knew well the purpose of the war. They had a system of wireless telegraphy of their own, by which they often heard of events in the field before their masters. The fact that "Massa Linkum" had set them free was quickly spread among them. When the war ended, and they could move about without hindrance, many former slaves began to leave the plantations to test their new liberty.

Booker's reputed father, who had been a slave on a neighboring plantation, made his way to West Virginia, where he got work in the mines and soon sent for his wife and children. Here little Booker was put to work in a salt furnace. His childish desire to learn grew intense as time passed on. The art of reading seemed something magical to the child, who had an alert brain under his sable skin; and, after he finally obtained a book, he poured over it intently, with no one to help, for all around were as ignorant as himself. All he succeeded in doing was to learn the alphabet from it; the joining of the letters into words was beyond his childish powers.

Some time later a young negro opened a school in the vicinity, but to Booker's keen disappointment, his father would not let him go, insisting that he should keep at work. Determined to open the closed door of knowledge, he managed to get some lessons at night from the teacher, and appealed so earnestly that his father finally consented to his going to day school for a few months, if he would work in the furnace until nine o'clock in the morning and for two hours in the afternoon after school had closed.

Little Booker was willing to do anything to gain an education. His thirst for knowledge had grown with his years, and there was no danger but that he would be a diligent student. But his first day at school brought him distressing difficulty. When the teacher called the roll he learned that every boy there had at least two names. He felt a deep sense of shame at the fact that he had only one. He had never been called anything but Booker, and knew of no other name. But a native shrewdness made him equal to the situation. When the teacher asked for his name he calmly replied that it was Booker Washington, appropriating the name of the Father of the Country without a qualm of conscience. Later on his mother told him that his real name was Booker Taliaferro, but he clung to the name he had adopted, and has ever since been known as Booker T. Washington.

From the salt furnace, the boy was transferred to a coal mine, a change, in his opinion, much for the worse; but a few months later he got a place as servant in the house of Mrs. Ruffner, the wife of the mine owner. Mrs. Ruffner had the reputation for being a hard mistress, with whom no servant would stay more than a few months, but Booker soon found that the trouble was more with the servants than with the mistress. What she demanded was that they should keep things clean and do their work promptly and systematically. When her new butler learned what she wanted he did his best to please her, and instead of a harsh taskmaster found her considerate and just. He would have stayed in this position, for he had made Mrs. Ruffner a kind of friend, but for a new desire that stirred his soul.

One day, while in the coal mine, he had heard two miners talking about a great school for colored people somewhere in Virginia. He heard also that worthy students could work out part of their board and be taught a useful trade. The news filled him with an intense eagerness to go to this wonderful school, and in the fall of 1872, when he was thirteen or fourteen years old, he determined to get there if it was possible.

His mother strongly opposed the idea, and gave her consent only after long pleading. But the colored people of the vicinity favored it. Education seemed to them like an inestimable treasure. Some of them helped the boy with a little money, and at length, with a very slender purse, he set out on his long journey to Hampton, five hundred miles away.

He had expected to ride there, but his first day's journey in the stage coach showed him that his funds would not carry him a fifth of the way, and he changed riding for walking, except when he could beg a ride. He reached the city of Richmond at length. His pockets were empty, and Hampton still far away. No lodging was to be had for a wandering colored urchin, and that night he slept under a raised part of the board sidewalk. The next day, he earned a little money by helping unload a vessel at the wharves, and this he kept at for several days, still sleeping under the boards. Years afterwards, when he visited Richmond as a distinguished man, he sought out this spot in the streets and looked with pathetic interest upon his first sleeping place in Virginia's capital city. When he reached Hampton at length, he had just fifty cents with which to get an education in the famous institute.

A sorry picture was the vagrant student when he presented himself tremblingly before the head teacher of the institute. Ill-clad, begrimed, hungry-looking, he waited with sinking heart while others were admitted, but no attention paid to him. At length, after a weary probation, the teacher looked him over disapprovingly, and put a broom into his hands, telling him to sweep one of the recitation rooms. Now young Booker's severe training under Mrs. Ruffner served him well. He swept and dusted that room so thoroughly that when the teacher, a Yankee housewife, came in she could not find a speck of dust hiding anywhere. "I guess you will do to enter this institution," she said.

The boy had swept his way into her good graces. She offered him a position as janitor, which enabled him to pay his board, and was ever afterwards his good friend. General Armstrong, that faithful friend of the blacks who was at the head of the institution, was so pleased with the earnestness and intelligence of the boy, one of the youngest under his care, that he induced a friend to pay the $70 a year for the little lad's tuition, and thus he was fairly launched upon the highroad of education.

That Booker worked hard we may be assured. His diligence, fidelity, and studiousness won him friends on all sides. He obtained work outside during the vacations, and after two years paid a visit home, only to see his mother die. She had been a good mother to him, and he mourned her loss.

His term at Hampton ended in 1875, but his connection with the institution did not cease, for after a time he was made a teacher in the night-school and also put in charge of the Indian inmates. The opportunity of his life, for which he had been unwittingly preparing, came in 1881, while he was still a night-school teacher at Hampton. An application had come to General Armstrong for some one to take charge of a colored normal school at Tuskegee, Alabama. The kindly superintendent, who knew well the capability of his night-school teacher, offered him the position, and Booker, with some natural hesitation, agreed to try.

Tuskegee was a town of about two thousand population, nearly half of them colored. It was situated in the Black Belt of Alabama, negroes being plentiful and education sparse. The legislature had voted an annual appropriation of $2000 to pay the running expenses of the school, but when the new teacher reached Tuskegee, he was disappointed to find that no buildings and no equipment had been provided. There were plenty of scholars, but that was all.

Booker went to work with a will, determined to make the most of his chance. The best place he could get for a school-house was an old shanty near the colored Methodist church, and here he opened with thirty students, ranging from fifteen to forty years of age, most of them having already served, in some fashion, as school-teachers. The roof was so leaky that when it rained one of the students had to hold an umbrella over him as he taught.

After three weeks Miss Olivia A. Davidson came to the school as a co-teacher—a bright girl, with new ideas, who afterwards became Mr. Washington's wife. Booker Washington was a born man of business from the start. After he had been in Tuskegee for three months, an abandoned plantation nearby was offered for sale for the low sum of $500. He determined to obtain it if possible, and succeeded in borrowing from the treasurer of the Hampton Institute $250 for the first payment. The remaining sum was raised by various measures in time to make the final payment and secure the property.

The mansion house of the plantation had been burned down. The buildings remaining consisted of a cabin which had been used as the dining-room, a kitchen, a stable, and an old hen-house. The latter two were used for school purposes, and the others as residences. The first animal obtained was an old, blind horse. It was the pioneer in a troop of animals and cows, about seven hundred hogs, and many sheep and goats, while the original tumble-down buildings have been replaced by a large number of well built structures, nearly all erected by the students themselves.

The new principal was a man of ambitious views and genius for affairs. His first daring undertaking was to build a $6000 schoolhouse without a dollar of capital. But he had already won a reputation for ability and integrity and help came in. The necessary lumber was supplied by a dealer in the vicinity who insisted on sending it and waiting for pay. Contributions came from many sources, and the building was completed and paid for. By this time, the strenuous and self-sacrificing efforts of the young teacher and the remarkable results he was achieving with the smallest means were becoming known and appreciated throughout the country, and aid began to come in from many sources. He made in subsequent years frequent lecturing tours in the North, describing with simple eloquence the character and needs of his work, and obtaining in this way the annual amount necessary for its administration.

His purpose was to develop at Tuskegee an educational and industrial school, teaching the essential elements of education while making each student familiar with some trade. In this regard he had such significant success that he is looked upon as having established a standard for progress that affected an entire generation of black Americans. Booker T. Washington purposed to make his students capable, self-supporting, and self-respecting, a design which has been carried out to a highly gratifying extent, while the present school at Tuskegee has given birth to various offsprings in which the same methods are pursued.

All the ordinary trades are taught in the institution, especially the various branches of farming. Twenty-five separate industries are carried on by the students, the object being to train the colored youth in self-supporting occupations. Washington believed that the race problem will be solved when the negro becomes a valuable workman and financially independent, and he did noble work in the effort to bring this about.

The leaky cabin with which he began is now superseded by forty or more handsome and well adapted buildings, large and small, all but four of which have been erected by student labor, even to the making of the bricks and sawing of the planks. The thirty students with whom he began have increased to over eleven hundred, and his solitary labors have been replaced by the work of some eighty instructors. The old shanty of 1881 has grown in the short space of twenty years to an extensive group of edifices, and his fragment of meeting-house ground to a broad estate of 2,460 acres, the whole valued at over $6,000,000. This looks like a magical result from the work of the ragged and penniless boy who made his way on foot to the Hampton Institute in 1872. It is rather obvious that Booker T. Washington was an extraordinary man.

This was the state of affairs in 1900. Since then the development has continued, and the endowment fund has been greatly increased through generous gifts. Andrew Carnegie, the well-known millionaire philanthropist from the early 1900s, said this concerning Mr. Washington: "To me he seems one of the greatest of living men, because his work is unique, the modern Moses who lead his race and lifts it through education to even better and higher things than a land overflowing with milk and honey. History is to tell of two Washingtons, one white and the other black, both fathers of their people."

Carnegie was not alone in this opinion. There are many who look upon Booker T. Washington as one of the greatest men of American history. He has won the respect and admiration of the South as well as of the North. He went far to win the South by his highly effective address at the opening of the Atlanta Exposition of 1895. *The Boston Transcript* said of this speech: "It seems to have dwarfed all the other proceedings and the Exposition itself. The sensation it has caused in the press has never been equalled." Its purpose was to show how the whites and blacks could live together in harmony in the South.

Since then, Tuskegee has become a place of pilgrimage for our Presidents on their journeys through the land. President McKinley visited it, with the general approbation of the people, and in 1905 President Roosevelt did the same. In history, there are few examples of so remarkable a career as that of this Moses of the negro race.

20 *The Great Lover*

by Rupert Brooke

Rupert Brooke was born in England in 1887 and died in 1915. He was prominent among a notable host of youthful poets who died in World War 1. "The Great Lover" shows how intently this poet pursued the joys that are a part of everyday life. Although Rupert Brooke was ultimately unable to "cheat drowsy Death," he did leave an enduring challenge to all human beings to appreciate the little blessings that God tucks into the corners of our lives.

I have been so great a lover: filled my days
  So proudly with the splendour of Love's praise,
The pain, the calm, and the astonishment,
  Desire illimitable, and still content,
And all dear names men use, to cheat despair,
  For the perplexed and viewless streams that bear
Our hearts at random down the dark of life.
  Now, ere the unthinking silence on that strife
Steals down, I would cheat drowsy Death so far,
  My night shall be remembered for a star
That outshone all the suns of all men's days.
  Shall I not crown them with immortal praise
Whom I have loved, who have given me, dared with me
  High secrets, and in darkness knelt to see
The inerrable godhead of delight?
  Love is a flame;—we have beaconed the world's night.
A city:—and we have built it, these and I.
  An emperor:—we have taught the world to die.
So for their sakes I loved, ere I go hence,
  And the high cause of Love's magnificence,
And to keep loyalties young, I'll write those names
  Golden for ever, eagles, crying flames,
And set them as a banner, that men may know,
  To dare the generations, burn, and blow
Out of the wind of Time, shining and streaming...

These I have loved:
  White plates and cups, clean-gleaming,
Ringed with blue lines; and feathery, fairy dust;
  Wet roofs, beneath the lamp-light; the strong crust
Of friendly bread; and many-tasting food;
  Rainbows; and the blue bitter smoke of wood;

And radiant raindrops couching in cool flowers;
    And flowers themselves, that sway through sunny
hours,
Dreaming of moths that drink them under the moon;
    Then, the cool kindness of sheets, that soon
Smooth away trouble; and the rough male kiss
    Of blankets; grainy wood; live hair that is
Shining and free; blue-massing clouds; the keen
    Unpassioned beauty of a great machine;
The benison of hot water; furs to touch;
    The good smell of old clothes; and other such—
The comfortable smell of friendly fingers,
    Hair's fragrance, and the musty reek that lingers
About dead leaves and last year's ferns...

Dear names,
    And thousand other throng to me! Royal flames;
Sweet water's dimpling laugh from tap or spring;
    Holes in the ground; and voices that do sing;
Voices of laughter, too; and body's pain,
    Soon turned to peace; and the deep-panting train;
Firm sands; the little dulling edge of foam
    That browns and dwindles as the wave goes home;
And washen stones, gay for an hour; the cold
    Graveness of iron; moist black earthen mould;
Sleep; and high places; footprints in the dew;
    And oaks; and brown horse-chestnuts, glossy-new;
And new-peeled sticks; and shining pools on grass;—
    All these have been my loves. And these shall pass,
Whatever passes not, in the great hour,
    Nor all my passion, all my prayers, have power
To hold them with me through the gate of Death.
    They'll play deserter, turn with the traitor breath,
Break the high bond we made, and sell Love's trust
    And sacramented covenant to the dust.
—Oh, never a doubt but, somewhere, I shall wake,
    And give what's left of love again, and make
New friends, now strangers...

But the best I've known,
    Stays here, and changes, breaks, grows old, is blown
About the winds of the world, and fades from brains
    Of living men, and dies.

Nothing remains.
   O dear my loves, O faithless, once again
This one last gift I give: that after men
   Shall know, and later lovers, far-removed,
Praise you, "All these were lovely"; say, "He loved."

🕯 *Comprehension Questions*

1. The poet gives quite an extensive list of things that he has loved in this poem. What things would you include if you wrote this poem?

2. Rupert Brooke confesses that the earthly things that he loves will play the traitor and fly away some day when he dies. He points out that all of this is outside of his control. Read Ecclesiastes 8:4-8, and explain why it is foolish to try to base our happiness upon the temporal things of this world.

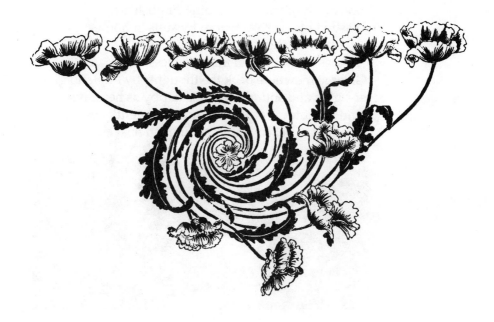

21 *The Soldier*

by Rupert Brooke

Written in 1914 while the author was fighting in a foreign land with the British army, this poem was exhibited by the British Museum as a memorial to a whole generation of Englishmen who fought for their country and paid the ultimate price. Brooke revealed quite clearly that he learned to appreciate the beauties and simple comforts of human existence.

> If I should die, think only this of me:
>   That there's some corner of a foreign field
> That is for ever England. There shall be
>   In that rich earth a richer dust concealed;
> A dust whom England bore, shaped, made aware,
>   Gave, once, her flowers to love, her ways to roam,
> A body of England's, breathing English air,
>   Washed by the rivers, blest by suns of home.
> And think, this heart, all evil shed away,
>   A pulse in the eternal mind, no less
>   Gives somewhere back the thoughts by England given;
> Her sights and sounds; dreams happy as her day;
>   And laughter, learnt of friends; and gentleness,
>   In hearts at peace, under an English heaven.

❧ *Comprehension Questions*

1. List three things that the author believed were precious about his homeland.

2. Write a short poem about the blessings of your homeland.

3. A child of God passes from this world with the sure hope and joy that he will enter a new and glorious home. After death, what need will Christians have to cling to earthly homelands?

22

Excerpt from Robinson Crusoe

by Daniel DeFoe

This selection is taken from *Robinson Crusoe*, the well known masterpiece by English author Daniel DeFoe (1660–1731). The story, suggested by the experiences of a sailor named Alexander Selkirk, narrates the adventures of a man shipwrecked on an uninhabited island. DeFoe also wrote *A History of the Plague* and many other books.

When I came down from my makeshift apartment in the tree, I looked about me again, and the first thing I found was the boat, which lay, as the wind and the sea had tossed her up, upon the land, about two miles on my right hand. The weather was clear, as the storm had finally moved on.

I walked as far as I could upon the shore to have got to her; but found a neck, or inlet, of water, between me and the boat, which was about half a mile broad; so I came back for the present, being more intent upon getting at the ship, where I hoped to find something for my present subsistence.

A little after noon, I found the sea very calm and the tide ebbed so far out that I could come within a quarter of a mile of the ship; and here I found a fresh renewing of my grief; for I saw, evidently, that if we had kept on board, we had all been safe; that is to say, we had all got safe on shore, and I would not have been so miserable as to be left entirely destitute of all comfort and company, as I now was.

This forced tears from my eyes again, but as there was little in that, I resolved, if possible, to get to the ship; so I pulled off my clothes, for the weather was hot to extremity, and took to the water. But when I came to the ship, my difficulty was still greater to know how to get on board; for as she lay aground, and high out of the water, there was nothing within my reach to lay hold of.

I swam round her twice, and the second time I spied a small piece of rope, which I wondered I did not see at first, hanging down the fore-chains so low, as that with great difficulty I got hold of it, and by the help of that rope got up into the forecastle of the ship.

Here I found that the ship was bulged, and had a great deal of water in her hold; but that she lay so on the side of a bank of hard sand, or rather earth, that her stern lay lifted up upon the bank, and her head low, almost to the water.

By this means all her quarter was free, and all that was in that part was dry; for you may be sure my first work was to search and to see what was spoiled and what was free: and, first, I found that all the ship's provisions were dry and untouched by the water; and, being very well disposed to eat, I went to the bread room, and filled my pockets with biscuit, and ate it as I went about other things, for I had no time to lose. Now I wanted nothing but a boat to furnish myself with many things which I foresaw would be very necessary to me.

It was in vain to sit still and wish for what was not to be had, and this extremity roused my application. We had several spare yards, and two or three large spars of wood, and a spare topmast or two in the ship. I resolved to fall to work with these, and flung as many of them overboard as I could manage for their weight, tying every one with a rope, that they might not drive away.

When this was done, I went down the ship's side, and pulling them to me, I tied four of them fast together at both ends, as well as I could, in the form of a raft, and laying two or three short pieces of plank upon them crossways, I found I could walk upon it very well, but that it was not able to bear any great weight, the pieces being too light; so I went to work, and with the carpenter's saw I cut a spare topmast into three lengths, and added them to my raft, with a great deal of labor and pains. But the hope of furnishing myself with necessaries encouraged me to go beyond what I should have been able to do upon another occasion.

My raft was now strong enough to bear any reasonable weight. My next care was what to load it with, and how to preserve what I laid upon it from the tossing sea; but I was not long considering this.

I first laid all the planks or boards upon it that I could get, and having considered well what I most wanted, I first got three of the seamen's chests, which I had broken open and emptied, and lowered them down upon my raft; the first of these I filled with provisions, viz., bread, rice, three Dutch cheeses, five pieces of dried goats' flesh, which we lived much upon, and a little remainder of European corn, which had been laid by for some fowls which we had brought to sea with us, but the fowls were killed. There had been some barley and wheat together, but, to my great disappointment, I found afterward that the rats had eaten or spoiled it all.

The tide had now begun to flow, though very calm; and I had the mortification to see my coat, shirt, and waistcoat, which I had left on shore upon the sand, swim away; as for my breeches, which were only linen and open-kneed, I swam on board in them.

However, this put me upon rummaging for clothes, of which I found enough but took no more than I wanted for present use, for I had other things which my eye was more upon; as, first, tools to work with on shore; and it was after long searching that I found the carpenter's chest, which was, indeed, a very useful prize to me, and much more valuable than a ship-lading of gold would have been at that time. I got it down to my raft, even whole as it was, without losing time to look into it, for I knew in general what it contained.

My next care was for some ammunition and arms. There were two very good fowling pieces in the great cabin, and two pistols; these I secured first, with some powder-horns and a small bag of shot, and two old rusty swords. I knew there were three barrels of powder in the ship, but knew not where our gunner had stowed them; but with much search I found them, two of them dry and good, the third had taken water. Those two I got to my raft, with the arms.

And now I thought myself pretty well freighted and began to think how I should get to shore with them, having neither sail, oar, nor rudder; and the least capful of wind would have overset all my navigation.

I had three encouragements: first, a smooth, calm sea; secondly, the tide rising, and setting in to the shore; thirdly, what little wind there was blew me toward the land. And thus, having found two saws, an ax, and a hammer; and with this cargo I put to sea.

For a mile or thereabouts my raft went very well, only that I found it drive a little distant from the place where I had landed before, by which I perceived that there was some indraft of the water, and consequently I hoped to find some creek or river there which I might make use of as a port to get to land with my cargo.

As I imagined, so it was: there appeared before me a little opening of the land, and I found a strong current of the tide set into it, so I guided my raft, as well as I could, to keep in the middle of the stream. I tried to keep from having a second shipwreck, which if I had, I think it verily would have broken my heart; for, knowing nothing of the coast, my raft ran aground at one end of it upon a shoal, and not being aground at the other end, it tipped a little so that all my cargo began to slip off toward that end that was afloat.

I did my utmost, by setting my back against the chests, to keep them in their places, but could not thrust off the raft with all my strength; neither durst I stir from the posture I was in, but holding up the chests with all my might I stood in that manner near half an hour, in which time the rising of the water brought me a little more upon a level.

A little after, the water still rising, my raft floated again, and I thrust her off, with the oar I had, into the channel; and then driving up higher, I at length found myself in the mouth of a little river, with land on both sides, and a strong current or tide running up. I looked on both sides for a proper place to get to shore, for I was not willing to be driven too high up the river, hoping, in time, to see some ship at sea, and therefore resolved to place myself as near the coast as I could.

At length, I spied a little cove on the right shore of the creek, to which, with great pain and difficulty, I guided my raft, and at last got so near, as that, reaching ground with my oar, I could thrust her directly in; but here I almost dipped all my cargo into the sea again; for that shore lying pretty steep, that is to say, sloping, there was no place to land. If my raft ran on shore, it would lie so high on one side, that it would endanger my cargo again.

All that I could do was to wait till the tide was at the highest, keeping the raft with my oar like an anchor, to hold the side of it fast to the shore, near a flat piece of ground, which I expected the water would flow over; and so it did. As soon as I found water enough, for my raft drew about a foot of water, I thrust her upon the flat piece of ground, and there fastened or moored her, by sticking my two broken oars into the ground, one on one side near one end: and thus I lay till the water ebbed away, and left my raft and all my cargo safe on shore.

My next work was to view the country, and seek a proper place for my habitation, and where to stow my goods, to secure them from whatever might happen. Where I was I yet knew not: whether on the continent, or on an island; whether inhabited, or not inhabited; whether in danger of wild beasts, or not. There was a hill, not above a mile from me, which rose up very steep and high, and which seemed to overtop some other hills, which lay as in a ridge from it, northward.

I took out one of the fowling pieces and one of the pistols and a horn of powder; and thus armed I traveled for discovery up to the top of that hill; Where, after I had, with great labor and difficulty, got up to the top, I saw my fate, to my great affliction. I was on an island. There was no land to be seen, except some rocks, which lay a great way off, and two small islands, less than this, which lay about three leagues to the west.

I found also that the island I was in was barren, and, as I saw good reason to believe, uninhabited, except by wild beasts, of whom, however, I saw none; yet I saw abundance of fowls, but knew not their kinds; neither, when I killed them, could I tell what was fit for food, and what not.

At my coming back, I shot at a great bird, which I saw sitting upon a tree, on the side of a great wood. I believe it was the first gun that had been fired there since the creation of the world. I had no sooner fired, but from all parts of the wood there arose innumerable number of fowls of many sorts, making a confused screaming and crying, every one according to his usual note; but not one of them of any kind that I knew. As for the creature I killed, I took it to be a kind of a hawk, its color and beak resembling it, but it had no talons or claws more than common. Its flesh was carrion and fit for nothing.

Contented with this discovery, I came back to my raft, and fell to work to bring my cargo on shore, which took me up the rest of the day: what to do with myself at night I knew not, nor indeed where to rest; for I was afraid to lie down on the ground, not knowing but some wild beast might devour me; though, as I afterward found, there was really no need for those fears.

However, as well as I could, I barricaded myself round with the chest of boards that I had brought on shore, and made a kind of hut for that night's lodging. As for food, I yet saw not which way to supply myself except that I had seen two or three creatures, like hares, run out of the wood where I shot the fowl.

I now began to consider that I might yet get a great many things out of the ship which would be useful to me, and particularly some of the rigging and sails, and such other things as might come to land; and I resolved to make another voyage on board the vessel, if possible. And as I knew that the first storm that blew must necessarily break her all in pieces, I resolved to set all other things apart, till I got everything out of the ship that I could get.

Then I called a council, that is to say, in my thoughts, whether I should take back the raft; but this appeared impracticable: so I resolved to go as before, when the tide was down; and I did so, only that I stripped before I went from my hut, having nothing on but a checkered shirt , a pair of linen drawers, and a pair of pumps on my feet.

I got on board the ship as before, and prepared a second raft; and having had experience of the first, I neither made this so unwieldy, nor loaded it so hard, but yet I brought away several things very useful to me; as, first, in the carpenter's stores, I found two or three bags of nails and spikes, a great screw jack, a dozen or two of hatchets, and, above all, that most useful thing called a grindstone.

All these I secured together, with several things belonging to the gunner; particularly, two or three iron crows, and two barrels of musket bullets, seven muskets, and another fowling piece, with some small quantity of powder more, a large bag full of small shot, and a great roll of sheet lead; but this last was so heavy, I could not hoist it up to get it over the ship's side.

Besides these things, I took all the men's clothes that I could find, and a spare fore-topsail, a hammock, and some bedding; and with this I loaded my second raft, and brought them all safe on shore, to my very great comfort.

I was under some apprehensions lest, during my absence from the land, my provisions might be devoured on shore; but when I came back, I found no sign of any visitor; only there sat a creature like a wild cat upon one of the chests, which, when I came toward it, ran away a little distance, and then stood still. She sat very composed and unconcerned, and looked full in my face, as if she had a mind to be acquainted with me.

I presented my gun to her, but, as she did not understand it, she was perfectly unconcerned at it, nor did she offer to stir away upon which I tossed her a bit of biscuit, though I was not very free of it, for my store was not great; however, I spared her a bit, I say, and she went to it, smelled of it, and ate it, and looked, as pleased, for more; but I thanked her, and could spare no more: so she marched off.

Having got my second cargo on shore,—though I was fain to open the barrels of powder, and bring them by parcels, for they were too heavy, being large casks,—I went to work to make me a little tent, with the sail and some poles, which I cut from that purpose; and into this tent I brought everything that I knew would spoil either with rain or sun; and I piled all the empty chests and casks up in a circle round the tent, to fortify it from any sudden attempt either from man or beast.

When I had done this, I blocked up the door of the tent with some boards within, and an empty chest set up on end without; and spreading one of the beds upon the ground, laying my two pistols just at my head, and my gun at length by me, I went to bed for the first time, and slept very quietly all night, for I was very weary and heavy; for the night before I had slept little, and had labored very hard all day, as well to fetch all those things from the ship as to get them on shore.

I had the biggest magazine of all kinds now that ever was laid up, I believe, for one man; but I was not satisfied still, while the ship sat upright in the posture, I thought I ought to get everything out of her that I could; so every day, at low water, I went on board, and brought away something or other; but particularly the third time I went, I brought away as much of the rigging as I could, as also all the small ropes and rope twine I could get, with a piece of spare canvas, which was to mend the sails upon occasion, and the barrel of wet gunpowder.

In a word, I brought away all the sails first and last; only that I was fain to cut them in pieces, and bring as much at a time as I could, for they were no more useful to be sails, but as mere canvas only.

But that which comforted me still more was, that, last of all, after I had made five or six such voyages as these, as thought I had nothing more to expect from the ship that was worth my meddling with: I say, after all this, I found a great hogshead of bread, and a box of sugar, and a barrel of fine flour; this was surprising to me, because I had given over expecting any more provisions, except what was spoiled by the water. I soon emptied the hogshead of that bread, and wrapped it up, parcel by parcel, in pieces of the sails, which I cut out; and, in a word, I got all this safe on shore also.

The next day, I made another voyage, and now having plundered the ship of what was portable and fit to hand out, I began with the cables, and cutting the great cable into pieces such as I could move, I got two cables and hawser on shore, with all the iron work I could get; and having cut down the spritsailyard and the mizzenyard, and everything I could, to make a large raft, I loaded it with all those heavy goods and came away.

This raft was so unwieldy and so overladen that after I entered the little cove, where I had landed the rest of my goods, not being able to guide it so handily as I did the other, it overset, and threw me and all my cargo into the water; as for myself, it was no great harm, for I was near the shore; but as to my cargo, it was a great part of it lost, especially the iron, which I expected would have been of great use to me.

However, when the tide was out, I got most of the pieces of cable ashore and some of the iron, though with infinite labor; for I was fain to dip for it into the water—a work which fatigued me very much. After this, I went every day on board, and brought away what I could get.

I had been now thirteen days ashore, and had been eleven times on board the ship, in which time I had brought away all that one pair of hands could well be supposed capable to bring, though I believe verily, had the calm weather held, I should have brought away the whole ship, piece by piece; but preparing, the twelfth time, to go on board, I found the wind began to rise. However, at low water, I went on board.

Though I thought I had rummaged the cabin so effectually as that nothing could be found, yet I discovered a locker with drawers in it, in one of which I found two or three razors, and one pair of large scissors, with some ten or a dozen of good knives and forks; in another I found about thirty-six pounds in money, some European coin, some Brazil, some pieces of eight, some gold, and some silver.

I smiled to myself at the sight of this money: "O drug!" I exclaimed. "what are thou good for? Thou art not worth much to me, no, not the taking off the ground; one of those knives is worth all this heap: I have no manner of use for thee; e'en remain where thou art, and go to the bottom, as a creature whose life is not worth saving."

However, upon second thoughts, I took it away; and wrapping all this in a piece of canvas, I began to think of making another raft; but while I was preparing this, I found the sky overcast, and the wind began to rise, and in a quarter of an hour it blew a fresh gale from the shore.

It presently occurred to me that it was in vain to pretend to make a raft with the wind off shore; and that it was my business to be gone before the tide of flood began, or otherwise I might not be able to reach the shore at all. Accordingly, I let myself down into the water, and swam across the channel which lay between the ship and the sands, and even that with difficulty enough, partly with the weight of the things I had about me, and partly the roughness of the water; for the wind rose very hastily, and before it was quite high water it blew a storm.

But I was able to reach my little tent, where I lay hard all that night, and in the morning, when I looked out, behold, no more ship was to be seen. I was a little surprised, but recovered myself with this satisfactory reflection, viz., that I had lost no time, nor abated no diligence, to get everything out of her that could be useful to me, and that, indeed, there was little left in her that I was able to bring away, if I had had more time.

❧ Glossary

quarter the after part of a ship's side, between the beam and the stern

forecastle the upper deck of a ship in front of the foremast

fowling piece a type of shotgun for hunting wild fowl

magazine a place of storage, or military supply depot

23 *How to Tell Bad News*

by Mrs. M. Zschokke

This scene takes place in a suburb of New York in 1929. Two men, one of them a wealthy land owner, and the other a hired servant discuss events. The rich man, Mr. Hogan, has just made the mistake of asking how things are going on at home.

MR. HOGAN.   Good morning, steward, good morning. How are things going on at home?

STEWARD.   Bad enough, your Honor: the magpie's dead.

MR. HOGAN.   Poor Mag! so he's gone. How did he die?

STEWARD.   Over-ate himself, sir.

MR. HOGAN.   Did he, indeed? greedy villain! Why, what did he get that he liked so well?

STEWARD.   Horse-flesh, sir: he died of eating horse-flesh.

MR. HOGAN.   How did he get so much horse-flesh?

STEWARD.   All your father's horses, sir.

MR. HOGAN.   What! are they dead too?

STEWARD.   Ay, sir; they died of overwork.

MR. HOGAN.   Why were they overworked?

STEWARD.   Carrying water sir.

MR. HOGAN.   Carrying water! and what are they carrying water for?

STEWARD.   Well, sir, to put out the fire.

MR. HOGAN.   Fire! what fire?

STEWARD.   O, sir, your father's house is burned to the ground.

MR. HOGAN.   My father's house is burned down! How did it start to burn?

STEWARD.   I think it must have been the torches.

MR. HOGAN.   Torches! what torches?

STEWARD.	At your mother's funeral.
MR. HOGAN.	Alas! alas! my mother's funeral.
STEWARD.	Yes, poor lady, she never looked up after it.
MR. HOGAN.	After what?
STEWARD.	The loss of your father.
MR. HOGAN.	What! my father gone too?
STEWARD.	Yes, poor gentleman; he took to his bed as soon as he heard of it.
MR. HOGAN.	Heard of what?
STEWARD.	The bad news, sir, if it please your Honor.
MR. HOGAN.	What! more miseries? more bad news? O no: you can add nothing more.
STEWARD.	Yes, sir: the bank has failed, and you are not worth a dollar in the world. I made bold, sir, to come and tell you about it, for I thought you would like to hear the news.
MR. HOGAN.	Thank you, steward, for your helpful report regarding my bank account and for the other incidentals that you happened to share. You certainly have an interesting way of telling bad news!

❧ *Comprehension Questions*

1. Do you think the steward did a good job of breaking the bad news to Mr. Hogan?

2. How could he have done a better job of getting this information conveyed?

3. How should Christians react to "bad news" when they receive it? Please read Job chapter one before answering this question.

24 *What Makes a Woman*

by Albert N. Raub

Not costly dress nor queenly air;
 Not jeweled hand, complexion fair;
Not graceful form nor lofty tread,
 Nor paint, nor curls, nor splendid head:
Not pearly teeth nor sparkling eyes,
 Not voice that nightingale outvies;
Not breath as sweet as eglantine,
 Not gaudy gems nor fabrics fine;
Not all the stores of fashion's mart,
 Not yet the blandishments of art;
Not one, nor all of these combined,
 Can make one woman true, refined.

'Tis not the body that we prize,
 But that which in the body lies.
These outward charms that please the sight
 Are naught unless the heart be right.
She, to fulfill her destined end,
 Must with her beauty goodness blend;
She must make it her incessant care
 To deck herself with jewels rare;
Of priceless gems must be possessed,
 In robes of richest beauty dressed;
Yet these must clothe the inward mind,
 In purity the most refined.

She who hath all these virtues combined
 Can man's rough nature well refine;
She will have all she needs in this frail life
 To fit her for mother, sister, wife.
He who possesses such a friend,
 Should cherish well till death doth end.
Woman, so fine, the mate should be
 To sail with man o'er life's rough sea;
And, when the stormy cruise is o'er,
 Attend him to fair Canaan's shore.

—From *Normal Fifth Reader*, 1878

Nothing But Leaves

by Albert N. Raub

Nothing but leaves! The Spirit grieves
Over a wasted life:
O'er sins committed while conscience slept;
Promises made but never kept;
Folly, and shame, and strife;
Nothing but leaves.

Nothing but leaves! No gathered sheaves
Of life's fair ripening grain;
We sow our seeds, lo! tares and weeds,
Words, idle words, for earnest deeds;
We reap with toil and pain,
Nothing but leaves.

Nothing but leaves! Sad memory weaves
No veil to hide the past;
And as we trace our weary way,
Counting each lost and misspent day,
Sadly we find at last
Nothing but leaves.

Ah! who shall thus the Master meet,
Bearing but withered leaves?
Ah! who shall at the Saviour's feet,
Before the awful judgment-seat,
Lay down for golden sheaves
Nothing but leaves?

—From *Normal Fifth Reader*, 1878

❦ Comprehension Questions

1. Write a paragraph that explains the major point of this poem.

2. What does the poet mean by the phrase "idle words, for earnest deeds"?

3. Read Psalm 126 and write a paragraph that explains how this Psalm relates to the poem.

4. Read Proverbs chapter 31 and write down all of the virtuous characteristics that are attributed to the godly woman.

26 *William McKinley*

by Charles Morris

Every great man begins as a boy, and so we must begin with McKinley in his boyhood days. He was one of the kind of boys we like to read about. The stories of his life as a fisher, a skater, a blackberry picker, and of the boy who had his boyish battles to fight and win, are such to make every boy's and man's heart warm with memories of similar experiences. Niles, Ohio, was McKinley's birthplace. He was born there on January 29, 1843. The house in which he was born has recently been cut in two, and the section which includes the room of his birth has been moved a mile away, to a pretty spot known to the people of Niles as Riverside Park.

It was a poor little two-story frame house, but was far better than the log-huts in which some of our Presidents were born. McKinley's parents were not rich, but they had enough to live on, and he had plenty of time for play and for school-life. He was a good student and a good boy. His pious mother read her Bible to him till he knew much of it by heart, and he joined the Methodist Church when he was fifteen years old. He was a member of this Church all the rest of his life.

One would think he was born to be a fine public speaker by the way he argued and debated in his school-boy days. He was always ready. At Poland, where he lived when he grew older, there was a literary society and debating club, and of it he was, for some time, president. The story is told that the boys and girls saved up their spending money until they had enough to buy a carpet for the meeting room of the club. They purchased at a neighboring carpet store what they thought a very handsome one. Its groundwork was green, and it was ornamented with great golden wreaths. The society decided that no boots should ever soil that sacred carpet, and the girl members volunteered to knit slippers for all the members to wear. Unfortunately, the slippers were not ready for the first meeting, and so all the members who attended, and the visitors, too, were required to put off their shoes from their feet and listen to the debate in stockings. The debaters did the same, and young McKinley presided over the meeting in his stocking feet.

McKinley received a good education. He went to the common school at Niles, to the academy at Poland, and to Alleghany College at Meadville, in Pennsylvania. However, at college, he soon became sick and had to go home; and then he became a school-teacher himself, for his father had lost much of his money, and the boy had to help the family along.

All this was before the great War Between the States had begun. When Fort Sumter was fired on, and the people everywhere were getting ready to fight, young McKinley was just past his eighteenth year. He was a short, slender, pale-faced boy, but he was full of fight, and away he marched to the war with the first company of Ohio volunteers. His regiment was the 23rd Ohio Volunteers, whose major was Rutherford B. Hayes. You will remember his name among our list of Presidents. So this regiment had one future President among its officers and one in its ranks. That was something to be proud of, if it had been known. In the ranks, Mr. McKinley was a good soldier, obeyed all orders, and was always pleasant to his comrades. And he had plenty of soldiering among the West Virginia mountains, where he became worn out with marching, fighting and going through all sorts of rough work.

Let us get on with the boy soldier's story. He had been made a sergeant for his good work in West Virginia. He was made a lieutenant for his good work at the terrible battle of Antietam. This is how it came about.

McKinley was commissary sergeant of his regiment. That is, he had charge of the food supplies. He did not have to fight, but was two miles back from the fighting line. Most boys would have thought that a good place to stay, but the boy sergeant did not think so. He thought only of the poor fellows in the ranks, fighting all day under the burning sun. How parched and hungry they must be! What would they not give for a cup of hot coffee!

As soon as he thought of this, he got hold of some of the stragglers in the rear and set them to making coffee. There were plenty of them, as there are in all battles. Then he filled two wagons with steaming cans of hot coffee and with food, and drove off with his mule teams for the line of battle. One of the wagons broke down, but the other kept on. He was ordered back but nothing could stop him, and on to the lines he went at full speed.

One of the officers says: "It was nearly dark when we heard tremendous cheering from the left of our regiments. As we had been having heavy fighting right up to this time, our division commander, General Scammon, sent me to find out the cause, which I very soon found to be cheers for McKinley and his hot coffee. You can readily imagine the rousing welcome he received from both officers and men. When you consider the fact of his leaving his post of security and driving into the middle of a bloody battle with a team of mules, it needs no words of mine to show the character and determination of McKinley, a boy of, at this time, not twenty years of age."

When the Governor of Ohio heard the story of McKinley and his hot coffee for the fighting boys, he made him a lieutenant. Don't you think he well deserved it?

There are other stories of McKinley's gallant conduct. One of them comes from the time of the fighting in the Shenandoah Valley in July 1864. Here the confederate General Early attacked General Crook and his men with so strong a force that Crook was driven back. General Hastings tells us how the young lieutenant in the face of death, at the command of General Hayes, his commander, rode into the thick of the battle through a rain of shot and bursting shells, and brought out the regiment safely. This deed made a captain of the brave lieutenant.

The fighting was over. The country was at peace. Everybody was getting back to work again. What would the young major do? He had his living to make. He had tried teaching and fighting, and now he thought he would like to be a lawyer, as he was so good a talker. So he entered a law office and began to study as hard as he had fought. In two years he was ready to practice, and hung out his sign in Canton, Ohio. This place was his home for the rest of his life, and here he was buried when he died.

Here is the story of how he got his first case. One day as he sat waiting for clients and thinking they would never come, Judge Glidden, who had been his law instructor, came into his office and said: "McKinley, here are the papers in a case of mine. It comes up tomorrow. I have got to go out of town, and I want you to take charge of it for me."

McKinley declared that he could not do justice to the case at so short a notice. "I never tried a single case yet, Judge," said he.

"Well, begin on this one, then," was the Judge's reply. And it was finally settled that McKinley should do so. He sat up all night working on the case, tried it the next day, and won it. A few days later, Judge Glidden entered his office and handed him $25. McKinley did not wish to take it.

"It is too much for one day's work," he said.

"Don't let that worry you," replied Glidden, good-naturedly. "I charged $100 for this case, and I can well afford a quarter of it to you."

He became a good public speaker and was in great demand. His first office was as district attorney of his county. In due time the rising lawyer got married and settled down as a family man. His wife was Miss Ida Saxton, a beautiful and intelligent girl, the daughter of a rich banker from Canton. McKinley loved her dearly, and never did two people pass happier lives together, for it was a case of true love all through. Mrs. McKinley was an invalid nearly all her life, and he was always kind and devoted to her.

Major McKinley was elected to Congress in 1876, nine years after he began to practice law. General Hayes, who had been the first major of his old regiment, was now President. He and McKinley were as warm friends now as when they had been in the army together.

McKinley was fourteen years in Congress, and in every one of those years he made his mark in some way or other. In 1890 he was defeated in the election for Congress but he was too well known and too much liked to stay defeated long. If the country did not want him the State did, and the next year he was elected Governor of Ohio by a good majority. In 1893, he was re-elected by over 80,000 votes. The soldier-boy was coming on well, wasn't he?

He made a good Governor, but he met with a sad misfortune through his kindness of heart. For he put his name on the notes of an old friend, and when this man soon after failed in business, McKinley found that he had been sadly cheated. He had signed for only $15,000, but his seeming friend had made him liable for nearly $100,000.

This was like the story of Jefferson in his old days. Every cent he owned would have gone if some friends had not raised the money to pay his debt, as Jefferson's friends did for him. McKinley said he would not take any money, but he could not help himself. All the notes were paid as they came due and he never knew who paid them, so he could not return the money. In that way, his kind friends got the better of him.

And now came the time when the people of the whole country wanted McKinley. Ohio was not big enough to hold a man like him any longer. In 1896, a new President was to be chosen, and McKinley was the people's favorite and was elected by a very large number of votes.

It was not a quiet chair to which President McKinley came. If you recall the lives of some of the other Presidents, you will find that they had no great troubles to meet. But McKinley had to face war and insurrection and all the difficult questions these brought on, and that was a good deal for a man who had grown to love peace and quiet.

The map of your country will show you in the ocean just south of Florida, the long, narrow island of Cuba. It is so close to us that it really should have belonged to the United States, but Spain had owned it ever since it was discovered by Columbus more than four hundred years before.

Spain had no right to own any island, for she did not know how to treat the people. The Cubans were treated so badly that they began to fight for liberty. Then the Spaniards treated them worse than ever, causing thousands of them to starve to death. That was more than Americans could stand. McKinley asked Spain to stop her cruelty. When she would not, the people of the United States so sympathized with the poor Cubans that armies and fleets were sent to fight the Spaniards in Cuba. President McKinley did not want war. He did all he could to keep it off. But when he found that Spain would not listen to reason there was nothing left to do but to teach the Spaniards a lesson.

Only a few great battles were fought. Admiral Dewey won a great naval victory in the Philippines and then there were battles in Cuba. You know how the war ended. Cuba was taken from Spain and made a free nation. Puerto Rico, in the West Indies, and the Philippine Islands, in the Pacific Ocean, were given over to this country. Then there came another war in the Philippines, an outbreak of the people, which lasted much longer than the war in Cuba. There was also a great rebellion in China, and the United States Minister at Peking, the capital of China, was in great danger from the rebels, and troops had to be sent to rescue him.

All this made plenty of work for the President. He did not please everybody with what he did, but no one can do that. He dealt ably and wisely with all the questions that came up, and in 1900, when there was another presidential election, he was more popular than ever. He was chosen by the whole Republican Convention, and was elected with the great majority of 137 electoral votes.

It was a time of splendid prosperity during President McKinley's first term. Business was booming, commerce was active, thousands were growing rich, millions were living well and were happy and contented. That was one good reason for wanting him again. But the country was not to keep him long, for a dreadful event was close at hand, as I have now to tell.

The second inauguration of President McKinley took place on

March 4, 1901. All looked promising. The war in the Philippines was nearly at an end, the country was growing greater and grander, business was better than ever, nobody dreamed of a great coming tragedy. The President and his wife took a long journey that spring through the South and West, from Washington to San Francisco. The people of all towns and cities turned out in multitudes to see and hear him. It was plain that he was a great public favorite. One would have thought he had not an enemy in the land.

In September he went to Buffalo, in New York State, to see the great Fair that was being held there, in which the best and most beautiful things in America were being shown. Here, too, the people greeted him like a beloved friend. On the 6th, that he might meet them the more closely, a reception was held in the Temple of Music, where they would have an opportunity to shake hands with their President.

Perhaps some of my readers may have read about the tragic event that happened that day, at the Fair. At any rate, in the Temple of Music, there was a long line of people taking the President's hand and looking into his kindly, smiling face. Some of them may even have heard the fatal sound when a desperate villain fired a pistol at the President, and have seen the good man turn pale and fall back. "Let no one hurt him," he gasped as the guards rushed furiously at the murderer.

After that there was a week of terrible anxiety in the country. Two bullets had struck the President, but for a time doctors thought he would get well, and the people were full of hope. Then he suddenly began to sink, and on Friday, just one week from the time he was shot, death was very near. His wife was brought in and wept bitterly as she begged the doctors to save him.

"Good bye, all; good bye," whispered the dying man. "It is God's way. His will be done."

These were his last words. A few hours afterward he was dead.

So passed away this great and noble-hearted Christian, the third of our martyred Presidents and one of the kindest and gentlest of them all. He was buried with all the ceremony and all the demonstrations of respect and affection the country could give. At the time his body was lowered into the grave, for five minutes the whole people came to rest, all business ceased, and a solemn silence overspread the land from sea to sea. Then the stir began again, and once more the world roared on. It never stops long, even for the greatest of men.

—From *Heroes of Progress*, 1903

27 *History of our Flag*

by Rev. Alfred P. Putnam

Extracts from a sermon preached in 1870 at Roxbury, Massachusetts, from the text "And in the name of our God we will set up our banners. (Psalm 20:5)"

The history of our glorious flag is of exceeding interest, and brings back to us a throng of sacred and thrilling associations. The banner of St. Andrew was blue, charged with a white cross, in the form of the letter X, and was used in Scotland as early as the eleventh century. The banner of St. George was white, charged with the red cross, and was used in England as early as the first part of the fourteenth century. By a royal proclamation, dated April 12, 1700, these two crosses were joined together upon the same banner, forming the ancient national flag of England.

It was not until 1801 that the present national flag of England, so well known as the Union Jack, was completed. But it was the ancient flag of England that constituted the basis of our American banner. Various other flags had indeed been raised at other times by our colonial ancestors. But they were not particularly associated with, or, at least, were not incorporated into, and made a part of, the destined "Stars and Stripes." It was after Washington had taken command of the fresh army of the Revolution at Cambridge that, on January 2, 1776, he unfolded before them the new flag of thirteen stripes of alternate red and white, having upon one of its corners the red and white crosses of St. George and St. Andrew, on a field of blue. And this was the standard which was borne into the city of Boston when it was evacuated by the British troops, and was entered by the American army.

Uniting, as it did, the flags of England and America, it showed that the colonists were not yet prepared to sever the tie that bound them to the mother country. By that union of flags they claimed to be a vital and substantial part of the empire of Great Britain, and demanded the rights and privileges which such a relation implied. Yet it was by these thirteen stripes that they made known the union also of the thirteen colonies, the stripes of white declaring the purity and innocence of their cause, and the stripes of red giving forth defiance to cruelty and opposition.

On the 14th day of June 1776, it was resolved by Congress, "That the flag of the thirteen United States be thirteen stripes, alternate red and white, and that the Union be thirteen white stars in the blue field." This resolution was made public September 3, 1776, and the flag that was first made and used in pursuance of it was that which led the Americans to victory at Saratoga. Here the thirteen stars were arranged in a circle, as we sometimes see them now, in order better to express the idea of the union of the states.

In 1794, there having been two more new states added to the Union, it was voted that the alternate stripes, as well as the circling stars, be fifteen in number, and the flag, as thus altered and enlarged, was the one which was borne through all the contests of the war of 1812. But it was thought that the flag would at length become too large if a new stripe was added with every freshly admitted state. It was therefore enacted, in 1818, that a permanent return should be made to the original number of thirteen stripes, and that the number of stars should henceforth correspond to the growing number of states.

Thus the flag would symbolize the Union as it might be at any given period of its history, and also as it was at the very hour of its birth. It was at the same time suggested that these stars, instead of being arranged in a circle, be formed into a single star—a suggestion which we occasionally see adopted. In fact, no particular order seems now to be observed with respect to the arrangement of the constellation. It is enough if only the whole number be there upon that azure field—the blue to be emblematical of perseverance, vigilance, and justice, each star to signify the glory of the state it may represent, and the whole to be the eloquent symbol of a Union that must be "one and inseparable."

What precious associations cluster around our flag! Not alone have our fathers set up this banner in the name of God over the well-won battlefields of the Revolution, and over the cities and towns which they rescued from despotic rule; but think where also their descendants have carried it, and raised it in conquest or protection! Through what clouds of dust and smoke has it passed—what storms of shot and shell—what scenes of fire and blood! Not only at Saratoga, at Monmouth, and at Buena Vista and Chapultepec. It is the same glorious old flag which, inscribed with the dying words of Lawrence—"Don't give up the ship"—was hoisted on Lake Erie by Commodore Perry just on the eve of his great naval victory—the same old flag which our great chieftain bore in triumph to the proud city of the Aztecs, and planted upon the heights of her national palace. Brave hands raised it above the eternal regions of ice in the arctic seas, and have set it up on the summits of the lofty mountains in the distant west.

Where has it not gone, the pride of its friends and the terror of its foes? What countries and what seas has it not visited? Where has not the American citizen been able to stand beneath its guardian folds and defy the world? With what joy and exultation seamen and tourists have gazed upon its stars and stripes, read in it the history of their nation's glory, received from it the full sense of security, and drawn from it the inspirations of patriotism! By it, how many have sworn loyalty to their country!

What bursts of magnificent eloquence it has called forth from Webster and from Everett! What lyric strains of poetry from Drake and Holmes! How many heroes its folds have covered in death! How many have lived for it, and how many have died for it! How many, living and dying, have said, in their enthusiastic devotion to its honor, like that young wounded sufferer in the streets of Baltimore, "O, the flag! the Stars and Stripes!" And wherever that flag has gone, it has been the herald of a better day—it has been the pledge of freedom, of justice, of order, of civilization, and of Christianity. Tyrants only have hated it, and the enemies of mankind alone have trampled it to the earth. All who sigh for the triumph of truth and righteousness, love and salute it.

❦ Comprehension Questions

1. Describe the banner of St. George.

2. How many stars and stripes did the United States flag have during the War of 1812?

3. Do you think that the author could write the same article regarding our flag's glorious history if he wrote it today?

4. Do you think that the old glory that was associated with our nation and its flag had any connection with our public support of Christianity in past generations?

5. What do you think the Biblical phrase "Blessed is the nation whose God is the Lord" has to do with the history of our nation's flag?

28

Governor Edward Winslow's Letter

This letter was written from Plymouth Town in New England by its first governor, Edward Winslow, on December 11, 1621. The letter was sent to a friend of Rev. Winslow who lived in Great Britain. This individual was hoping to immigrate to New England, and join the pilgrims in the New World.

Dear Friend,—

Although I received no letter from you by this ship, yet forasmuch as I know you expect the performance of my promise, which was to write you truly and faithfully of all things, I have therefore, at this time, sent unto you accordingly, referring you for further satisfaction to our more large relations.

You shall understand that in this little time that a few of us have been here, we have built seven dwelling houses and four for the use of the plantation, and have made preparation for divers others.

We set the last spring some twenty acres of Indian corn, and sowed some six acres of barley and pease; and according to the manner of Indians, we manured our ground with herrings, or rather shads, which we have in great abundance, and take with great ease at our doors.

Our corn did prove well; and God be praised, we had a good increase of Indian corn, and our barley indifferent good, but our pease not worth the gathering, for we feared they were too late sown. They came up very well, and blossomed; but the sun parched them in the blossom.

Our harvest being gotten in, our governor sent four men on fowling, that so we might, after a special manner, rejoice together after we had gathered the fruit of our labors. The four, in one day, killed as much fowl as with a little help beside, served the company almost a week. At which time, amongst other recreations, we exercised our arms, many of the Indians coming among us, and among the rest their greatest king, Massasoit, with some ninety men, whom for three days we entertained and feasted; and they went out and killed five deer, which they brought to the plantation, and bestowed upon our governor, and upon the captain and others. And although it be not always so plentiful as it was at this time with us, yet by the goodness of God we are so far from want, that we often wish you partakers of our plenty...

We have often found the Indians very faithful in their covenant of peace with us, very loving, and ready to pleasure us. We often go to them, and they come to us…Yea, it hath pleased God so to possess the Indians with a fear of us and love to us, that not only the greatest king amongst them, called Massasoit, but also all the princes and peoples round about us, have either made suit to us, or been glad of any occasion to make peace with us; so that seven of them at once have sent their messengers to us to that end… They are a people without any religion or knowledge of any God, yet very trusty, quick of apprehension, ripe-witted, just…

Now, because I expect you coming unto us, with other of our friends, I thought good to advertise you of a few things needful. Be careful to have a very good bread room to put your biscuits in. Let not your meat be dry-salted; none can better do it than the sailors. Let your meal be so hard trod in your cask that you shall need an adz or hatchet to work it out with. Trust not too much on us for corn at this time, for we shall have little enough till harvest.

Build your cabins as open as you can, and bring good store of clothes and bedding with you. Bring every man a musket or fowling piece. Let your piece be long in the barrel, and fear not the weight of it, for most of our shooting is from stands.

I forbear further to write for the present, hoping to see you by the next return. So I take my leave, commending you to the Lord for a safe conduct unto us, resting in him.

Your loving friend,
Edward Winslow

Psalm 19

by David, King of Israel

The heavens declare the glory of God;
and the firmament showeth his handiwork.
Day unto day uttereth speech,
and night unto night showeth knowledge.

There is no speech nor language,
where their voice is not heard.
Their line is gone out through all the earth,
and their words to the end of the world.

In them hath he set a tabernacle for the sun,
which is as a bridegroom coming out of his chamber,
and rejoiceth as a strong man to run a race.
His going forth is from the end of the heaven,
and his circuit unto the ends of it:
and there is nothing hid from the heat thereof.

The law of the Lord is perfect, converting the soul:
the testimony of the Lord is sure, making wise the simple.
The statutes of the Lord are right, rejoicing the heart:
the commandment of the Lord is pure,
enlightening the eyes.

The fear of the Lord is clean, enduring for ever:
the judgments of the Lord are true
and righteous altogether.
More to be desired are they than gold,
yea, than much fine gold:

sweeter also than honey and the honeycomb.
Moreover by them is thy servant warned:
and in keeping of them there is great reward.

Who can understand his errors?
Cleanse thou me from secret faults.
Keep back thy servant also from presumptuous sins;
let them not have dominion over me:
then shall I be upright,
and I shall be innocent from the great transgression.

Let the words of my mouth,
and the meditation of my heart,
be acceptable in thy sight,
O Lord, my strength, and my redeemer.

🌿 Comprehension Questions

1. Provide two examples of how the heavens declare the glory of God.

2. Explain why people who refuse to believe in the Genesis account of Creation actually rob God of His rightful glory as Creator.

3. When God established the world, He ordained various laws to insure that His creation would run properly. Explain why God's people should be thankful that the Lord provided mankind with laws and rules for daily living.

The Little Word "Only"

This selection warns against the danger of spending oneself into bankruptcy through covetousness, impulse buying, and not being able to say *no*.

MRS. THRIFTY. What brings you so early, Mrs. Debtor?

MRS. DEBTOR. I have a favor to ask of you, Mrs. Thrifty.

MRS. THRIFTY. A favor! If it is in my power to oblige you, I shall be very glad to do it.

MRS. DEBTOR. It's only a trifle. Will you please be so kind as to lend me five dollars?

MRS. THRIFTY. Only five dollars?

MRS. DEBTOR. Only five dollars. I've seen a dress in the town,—such a lovely dress! lilac, with white flowers. To be sure, I can't say I need it; but it is such a beautiful dress! And it is so very cheap! Just think: it costs only five dollars!

MRS. THRIFTY. Only five dollars?

MRS. DEBTOR. Yes indeed! Perhaps I may even get it for a little less, but I must have it.

MRS. THRIFTY. Indeed?

MRS. DEBTOR. I am sorry to trouble you; but I expect the money from my estate tomorrow, and then I will repay you.

MRS. THRIFTY. Then you have had something left you by your father?

MRS. DEBTOR. Yes, I have; but it was so little it is hardly worth mentioning.

MRS. THRIFTY. How much was it, Mrs. Debtor?

MRS. DEBTOR. Only five hundred dollars.

MRS. THRIFTY. Only five hundred dollars?

MRS. DEBTOR. That's all, Mrs. Thrifty.

MRS. THRIFTY. I will lend you the money with pleasure; but I must ask you to hear a story which may bring you an income of five hundred dollars a year if you can understand it well.

MRS. DEBTOR.   Indeed? Do let me hear it.

MRS. THRIFTY.   Did you know the goldsmith's widow that lived in the mansion over yonder?

MRS. DEBTOR.   O yes! I knew her. She has just died with few friends and even less money.

MRS. THRIFTY.   She once had a great deal of money, Mrs. Debtor; but a little word made her a beggar.

MRS. DEBTOR.   A word! How can that be?

MRS. THRIFTY.   Yes, a word,—a single word, a very little word.

MRS. DEBTOR.   What one word can do all that?

MRS. THRIFTY.   I will tell you. In the first place, she always thought every thing very cheap. If she came home in the afternoon from the shopping mall, she was always in high spirits. The perfumes had cost only ten dollars and the necklace just the same. She was in high glee when she had spent only twenty or thirty dollars.
(How much does the dress cost, neighbor?)

MRS. DEBTOR.   The dress! The dress! They only want five dollars for it.

MRS. THRIFTY.   Yes, that's it. My memory fails me at times.
The good woman had the weakness of thinking any money only a trifle. She sold her garden for only five hundred dollars, and her house for only fifty thousand. She was glad when she had got rid of them. But you know, neighbor, that she soon had nothing left. That awful word *only*! Yes, that one word brought her to bankruptcy.

MRS. DEBTOR.   The word *only*. O, now I see what you mean!

MRS. THRIFTY.   How much shall I lend you, neighbor?

MRS. DEBTOR.   Come to think of it, Mrs. Thrifty, I shall let the dress go. The story about the widow is very sad. Good day. Please do not hold this silly idea against me.

MRS. THRIFTY.   Certainly not. If I can at any time oblige you, I shall be very glad. Good day.

—Swinton's *Fourth Reader*

❧ *Comprehension Questions*

1. Read Proverbs 15:16 and Ecclesiastes 4:6. Write a paragraph that explains how these verses apply to the story you just read.

2. Why is it important to distinguish between things that we really need versus things we merely want?

3. How does the old proverb "A fool and his money are soon parted" apply to the story you read?

31

The Unknown Citizen

by W. H. Auden

The remarks listed below were inscribed on an imitation marble monument erected by the State Central Planning Commission for one of its citizens. The memorial monument was temporarily erected in the year 2009. The honorary citizen was affectionately known as JS/07/M/666.

He was found by the Bureau of Statistics to be
One against whom there was no official complaint
And all the reports on his conduct agree
That, in the modern sense of an old-fashioned word, he was a saint,
For in everything he did he served the Greater Community.
Except for the War till the day he retired
He worked in a factory and never got fired,
But satisfied his employers, Fudge Motors Inc.
Yet he wasn't a scab or odd in his views,
For his Union reports that he paid his dues,
(Our report on his Union shows it was sound)
And our Social Psychology workers found
That he was popular with his mates and liked a drink.
The Press are convinced that he bought a paper every day
And that his reactions to advertisements were normal in every way.
Policies taken out in his name prove that he was fully insured,
And his health-card shows he was once in a hospital but left it cured.
Both Producers Research and High-Grade Living declare
He was fully sensible to the advantages of the Installment Plan
And had everything necessary to the Modern Man,
A phonograph, a radio, a car and a frigidaire.
Our researchers into Public Opinion are content
That he held the proper opinions for the time of year;
When there was peace, he was for peace; when there was war, he went.
He was married and added five children to the population,
Which our Eugenist says was the right number for a parent of
                    his generation,
And our teachers report that he never interfered with their education.
Was he free? Was he happy? The question is absurd:
Had anything been wrong, we should certainly have heard.

❦ Comprehension Questions

1. History teaches us that men will either be ruled by God or by tyrants. Why is it dangerous and idolatrous for people to entrust government leaders with unlimited powers?

2. Do you agree with the statement "Absolute power corrupts absolutely"? Does this principle apply to all men? Does it apply to God?

3. The author of this short selection is trying to wake up people who are in the habit of thinking they are free simply because they still have some of the material blessings of modern society, (i.e. color television, phone, car). Do you think that people in the United States need to wake up to the fact that they are bartering away their freedoms for the sake of security? If so, why?

32

Abraham and the Fire-worshiper

Scene—The inside of a tent, in which the patriarch Abraham, and a Persian traveler, a Fire-worshiper, are sitting awhile after supper.

FIRE-WORSHIPER. [*Aside.*]

What have I said or done, that by degrees
Mine host hath changed his gracious countenance,
Until he stareth on me, as in wrath!
Have I between wake and sleep, lost his wise love?
Or sit I thus too long, and he himself—
Would he mind if I went to bed? I will speak to that.

[Aloud]

Impute it, O my great and gracious lord,
Unto my feeble flesh, and not my folly,
If mine old eyelids droop against their will,
And I become as one that hath no sense
Ev'n to the milk and honey of thy words.—
With my lord's leave, and his good servant's help,
My limbs would creep to bed.

ABRAHAM. *[Angrily leaving his seat.]*
In this tent, never.
Thou art a thankless and an impious man.

FIRE-WORSHIPER. *[Rising in astonishment.]*
A thankless and an impious man! Oh, sir,
My thanks have all but worshiped thee.

ABRAHAM. And who have you forgotten?
Like the fawning dog I have seen you eat.
From the foot-washing to the meal, and now
To this thy sudden and dog-like wish for bed,
I've noted thee; and never hast thou breathed
One syllable of prayer or praise or thanks,
To the great God who made and feedeth all.

FIRE-WORSHIPER. Oh, sir, the God I worship is the Fire,
The god of gods; and seeing him not here,
In any symbol, or on any shrine,
I waited till he blessed mine eyes at morn,
Sitting in heaven.

ABRAHAM. Oh, foul idolater!
And darest thou still to breathe in Abraham's tent?
Forth with thee, wretch: for he that made thy god,
And all thy tribe, and all the host of heaven,
The invisible and only dreadful God,
Will speak to thee this night, out in the storm,
And try thee in thy foolish god, the fire,
Which with his fingers he makes lightnings of.
Hark to the rising of his robes, the winds,
And get thee forth, and wait for him.

[*A violent storm is heard rising.*]

FIRE-WORSHIPER. What! unhoused!
And on a night like this! me, poor old man
A hundred years of age!

ABRAHAM. [*Urging him away.*]
Not reverencing
The God of ages, thou forfeits any reverence due thy
age.

FIRE-WORSHIPER. Thou hadst a father!—think of his gray hairs,
Houseless, and cuffed by such a storm as this.

ABRAHAM. God is thy father, and thou own'st not him.

FIRE-WORSHIPER. I have a wife, as aged as myself,
And if she learns of my death, she'll not survive it,
No, not a day; she is so used to me;
So propped up by her other feeble self.
I pray thee, strike us not both down.

ABRAHAM. [*Still urging him.*]
God made
Husband and wife, and must be owned of them,
Else he must needs disown them.

FIRE-WORSHIPER. We have children—
One of them, sir, a daughter, who next week
Will all day long be going in and out,
Upon the watch for me. Spare, O spare her!
She's a good creature, and not strong.

ABRAHAM. Mine ears
Are deaf to all things but thy blasphemy,
And to the coming of the Lord and God,
Who will this night condemn thee.

[*Abraham pushes him out; and remains alone speaking.*]

For if ever
God came at night-time upon the world,
'Tis now this instant. Hark to the huge winds,
The cataracts of hail, and rocky thunder,

Splitting the quarries of the stony clouds,
Beneath the touching of the foot of God.
That was God's speaking in the heavens,— that last,
An inward utterance coming by itself.
What is it shaketh thus thy servant, Lord,
Making him fear, that in some loud rebuke
To this idolater, whom thou abhorrest,
Terror will slay himself? Lo, the earth quakes
Beneath my feet, and God is surely here.

[*A dead silence; and then a still small voice.*]

THE VOICE.   Abraham!

ABRAHAM.   Where art thou, Lord? and who is it that speaks
So sweetly in mine ear, to bid me turn
And dare to face thy presence?

THE VOICE.   Who but He
Whose mightiest utterance thou hast yet to learn?
I was not in the whirlwind, Abraham;
I was not in the thunder, or the earthquake;
But I am in the still small voice.
Where is the stranger whom thou tookest in?

ABRAHAM.   Lord, he denied thee, and I drove him forth.

THE VOICE.   Then didst thou what God himself would not.
For I have grieved while he did deny me, and have
Put up with this foolish sinner for one-hundred years,
And couldst thou not endure him one sole night,
And such a night as this?

ABRAHAM.   Lord! I have sinned,
And will go forth, and if he be not dead,
Will call him back, and tell him of thy mercies
Both to himself and me.

THE VOICE.   Behold and learn how I can turn hearts
And give salvation in spite of foolish words.

[*The voice retires while it is speaking; and a fold of the tent is
turned back, disclosing the Fire-worshiper, recently converted, who is calmly sleeping, with his head on the back of a*

house-lamb.]

ABRAHAM. O loving God! the lamb itself's his pillow,
    And on his face is a sign he has spoken to you,
    And in his sleep he smileth. I, mean time,
    Poor and proud fool, with my presumptuous hands,
    Not God's, was dealing judgments on his head,
    Which God himself had cradled!—Oh, methinks
    There's more in this than prophet yet hath known,
    And the Messiah some day,
    Will bring all his wandering sinners home.

❧ Comprehension Questions

1. What primary message do you think this fictional story contained?

2. Why is it important to distinguish between stories that contain a biblical moral and actual Bible stories that are a part of the Scriptures?

3. Why do Christians need to "season" their words with grace when they present the truths of Scripture to an unbeliever?

⚜ Glossary

countenance appearance, esp. the expression of the face

blasphemy irreverent utterance or action concerning God or sacred things

fawning a servile demeanor, esp. in dogs, as they show happiness by licking someone's hand or wagging their tail

33 *How to Become a Dynamic Speaker*

by Bob and Rose Weiner

Bob and Rose Weiner have authored numerous books and articles on behalf of a national youth ministry from Florida, known as Maranatha Ministries. They are both respected speakers who provide a wealth of practical information to those who sit under their instruction or read their writings

Christians are called to be the greatest communicators in the world. Christianity is known historically as the "great confession." Although the word "confession" is usually thought of in negative terms as acknowledging and avowing sin or wrongdoing, confession in the positive sense means to publicly declare a belief in something, or adherence to that belief.

A *confessor* is defined by Webster's (1828) dictionary as "one who makes a profession of his faith in the Christian religion." The word is appropriately used to denote one who avows his religion in the face of danger, and adheres to it in defiance of persecution and torture. It was formerly used as synonymous with the word "martyr."

History and the Bible are full of resplendent examples of those whose unforgettable words and fiery speeches changed the course of nations and the destinies of peoples. Whose heart doesn't thrill as the words of Patrick Henry echo down the corridors of time, "Is life so dear, or peace so sweet as to be purchased at the price of chains and slavery? Forbid it, Almighty God! I know not what course others may take, but as for me, *give me liberty, or give me death!*" How many Americans have read this speech and have secretly desired to say something so stirring and profound!

On May 29, 1765, when Patrick Henry gave his famous oration against the Stamp Act, a young man who attended William and Mary college had taken a break from his intensive studies to hear the debates in the House of Burgesses. He writes, "I attended the debate (standing) at the door of the lobby of the House of Burgesses and heard the splendid display of Mr. Henry's talents as a popular orator. They were great indeed; such as I have never heard from any other man."

As the young man listened to Henry denounce the abuses against the American colonies, a flame began to kindle in his soul. Such a mighty surge of fervor for the cause of liberty, freedom, and justice raced through his entire being, that the light from that flame burned brightly the rest of his life. The young man was Thomas Jefferson. He later referred to that day as the most important day of his life. It was the day that fixed his destiny.

Who cannot be inspired by the words that Daniel Webster proclaimed as he asserted the significance of the Declaration of Independence: "We may die colonists; die slaves; die; it may be on the scaffold. Be it so... If it be the pleasure of Heaven that my country shall require the poor offering of my life, the victim shall be ready at the appointed hour of sacrifice, come when that hour may. But while I do live, let me have a country, or at least the hope of a country and that a free country ... All that I have and all that I am, and all that I hope in this life, I am now ready here to stake upon it... Independence now and Independence forever!"

The words of an immigrant of another era, although his name is forgotten, still speak: "I am an American. My ancestors died in the mines of Siberia: another was crippled for life by twenty blows from the taskmaster, another was killed defending his home during the massacres ... But then the dream came—the dream of America. In the light of the Liberty torch, my father became a man and my mother became a woman for the first time. 'See,' said my father, pointing to the flag that fluttered near, 'that flag of stars and stripes is yours; it is the emblem of the promised land. It means, my son, the hope of humanity. Live for it... Die for it!' "

George Whitefield, one of the master communicators during the first Great Awakening, upon being barred from preaching in the churches in England, responded by proclaiming, "Bless God, the fields are open!" So Whitefield moved his preaching to the open air where tens of thousands of people gathered to hear him proclaim the gospel. The result was the salvation of multiplied thousands and the reformation of the nation of England.

There is one thing which all of these men had in common that made them master communicators and enabled them to speak such ennobling and immortal words, influencing their generation as well as those after them. That is, they were alive with an idea which they believed was important. When a man or woman becomes absorbed with an idea, when one is carried away with a great emotion or conviction, that person will stand out from the crowd. His tongue becomes "the pen of a ready writer" and he is bursting from within to speak and proclaim his message.

When a man or woman is aflame with an idea, the desire to plunge into a speech is at its maximum. The power of great ideas is what gave strength and courage to men such as Henry, Whitefield, and Webster. It is the power of great ideas which have inspired people and nations to confidence and whole-hearted effort during danger and hardship.

Being alive with a great idea and desire to see America reformed earned former President Ronald Reagan the title given to him by the press as "the great communicator." The secret of President Reagan's ability to communicate did not lie in the fact that he was a former actor with the whole world for his stage—as the media would have us believe. He was, on the contrary, a man inflamed with ideas and convictions which have proven to have the power to move the heart of Americans and to change the climate of the nation from one preparing for scarcity to one preparing for victory.

Those who are possessed of great ideas are undaunted by hunger, pain, persecution, torture, or the threat of death. They are willing to give their lives for the cause they so ardently proclaim. They are heroes who, as watchmen set upon the watchtowers of freedom, refuse to be silent day or night.

If we fear God properly, we won't fear anything else. Let us remember Shadrach, Meshach, and Abednego who, because of their fear of God, refused to bow down and worship the golden image that King Nebuchadnezzar of Babylon had set up.

When the king threatened them with the fiery furnace, they said, "O Nebuchadnezzar, we do not need to give you an answer concerning this. If it be so, our God whom we serve is able to deliver us from the furnace of blazing fire; and He will deliver us out of your hand, O king. But even if he does not, let it be known to you, O king, that we are not going to serve your god or worship the golden image which you have set up" (Dan. 3:16–18). These were men whose souls were on fire with a great idea that enabled them to stand up in the face of death, refusing to bow down.

Daniel was also like them. When he knew that King Darius had signed the document that forbade the worship of any god besides himself, he entered his house and prayed by his open window. Three times a day, he prayed and gave thanks to God as he had done previously. Daniel did not fear the edict of the king for he had the proper fear of God; he was therefore bold, daring, and courageous. As a result, he was thrown into a den of hungry lions. The Lord sent an angel by night to protect him and he was delivered unharmed.

Daniel was a man on fire with an idea that he refused to let go of even in the face of death. This was the source of his courage, his boldness, and his bravery.

The early Christians, apostles of Jesus, the Christian martyrs, the great revivalists and statesmen throughout history, have been men and women aflame with ideas from God. They have through their great confessions, changed the destinies of men and of nations.

Jesus has given to all His followers the great commission to go into all the world and make disciples of all nations, teaching them everything that He taught. To fulfill this great commission it is imperative that Christians become masters of communication. John Naisbitt, in his book, *Megatrends*, which explains ten new directions which are reshaping our society, states that we are moving from an industrial to an information society. Those who will be the masters of the new age must be masters of communication.

A speaker—or "communicator"—becomes great when he is able to stretch his mind to understand great ideas to the extent that his soul catches fire. The real challenge to the speaker, then, is not stage fright or trying to overcome that weak-in-the-knees feeling, but it is the challenge to recognize, appreciate, understand, and dedicate himself to his ideas, his message.

Spurgeon, a well-known British preacher of the 19th century, exhorted his students: "Extemporary speech without study is a cloud without rain. Out of nothing comes nothing. If we can study and do not...we have no right to call in a divine agent to make up the deficits of our idleness or eccentricity."

"The God of providence has promised to feed His people with temporal food; but if we came together to a banquet, and no one had prepared a single dish, because all had faith in the Lord that food would be given in the selfsame hour, the festival would not be eminently satisfactory but folly would be rebuked by hunger...

"All sermons ought to be well considered and prepared by the preachers; and as much as possible, every minister should, with much prayer for heavenly guidance, enter fully into his subject, exert all his mental faculties in original thinking, and gather together all the information within his reach.

"...His sermon should be his mental life-blood, the out-flow of his intellectual and spiritual vigour... they should be diamonds well cut and well set—precious, intrinsically, and bearing the marks of labor.

God forbid that we should offer to the Lord that which costs us nothing."

M. Bautain, in his work on extempore speaking, remarks, "You will never be capable of speaking properly in public unless you acquire such mastery of your own thought as to be able to decompose it into its parts, to analyze it into its elements and then at need to recompose, re-gather and concentrate it again. The pen is the scalpel which dissects the thoughts and never, except when you write down what you behold internally, can you expect to understand yourself, and make others understand you."

Many Christians mistake the teaching of Jesus which says, "…They will lay their hands on you and will persecute you, delivering you to the synagogues and prison, bringing you before kings and governors for My name's sake. It will lead to an opportunity for your testimony. So make up your minds not to prepare beforehand to defend yourselves; for I will give you utterance and wisdom which none of your opponents will be able to resist or refute" (Luke 21:12–15).

It is important to notice that in this scripture Jesus is not telling His disciples to avoid preparing to speak publicly… He is referring to a time of persecution in which they may be called up before authorities to defend themselves. He is exhorting His disciples to take no thought for their own personal defense. He will give them the words to say at that same hour.

On the other hand, the scriptures everywhere exhort men to ask, to seek, to knock, to cry out for understanding. Proverbs exhorts us: "My son, if you will receive my sayings, and treasure my commandments within you, make your ear attentive to wisdom, incline your heart to understanding, if you seek her as silver, and search for her as for hidden treasures; then you will discern the fear of the lord and discover the knowledge of God. For the Lord gives wisdom; from His mouth come knowledge and understanding… for wisdom will enter your heart and knowledge will be pleasant to your soul; discretion will guard you, understanding will watch over you…" (Proverbs 2: 1–6, 10–11).

So never forget that in order to overflow, to speak extemporaneously, you must be full. Out of the abundance of the heart the mouth will speak. Get in the habit of thinking and feeding your mind with much food for thought. Store your mind very richly, work hard at every available moment.

Don't forget that to waste time all week and then to cast yourself upon the Lord for His aid is presumption. We cannot expect the Lord to cover up for our self-indulgency. When you are called upon to speak without prior knowledge, then you may with fullest confidence cast yourself upon the Lord and depend upon the Spirit of God to help you.

According to Spurgeon, "The divine mind beyond a doubt comes into contact with the human intellect, lifts it out of its weakness and distraction, makes it soaring and strong and enables it both to understand and to express divine truth in a manner far beyond its unaided powers. Such interpositions are not meant to supersede our efforts or slacken our diligence, but are the Lord's assistance in an emergency. In every situation, we should cultivate a childlike reliance upon the Holy Ghost."

Having established the need for study, preparation, and musing to enable us to expand our minds to understand great ideas and cause our souls to be aflame with our message, we will consider some practical methods of preparation and delivery.

SOME BASIC PRINCIPLES

Clearness in speaking is fundamental. The speaker should be content, not when his meaning may be understood, but when his meaning cannot be misunderstood. Therefore, every speech you make must have a purpose and a form. Listeners like speeches with backbone. They dislike a "jellyfish" speech which is flabby, shapeless, begins nowhere, rambles on in all directions and ends up in the air.

Start your speech with a fire! Your speech is not well organized unless you are able to kindle a quick flame of spontaneous interest in the first sentence. You must introduce your subject in such a manner as to arrest the attention of your audience.

Don't forget that your listener lives on an island of his own interests. **You must build a bridge.** You must convince your listeners that your subject matters to them and is in their interest.

Then, get down to actual cases—give them some "for instances." **Illustrate your speech with enough concrete cases to carry conviction.** Listeners like to hear instances which involve famous people and history. They like examples in story form. Present them as "organized platoons in marching order." As Spurgeon says, "Never let your thoughts rush as a mob, but make them march as a troop of soldiers. Order, which is heaven's first law, must not be neglected by heaven's ambassadors."

In the conclusion of your speech, **do not forget to ask your audience for some specific action**—some action response which is in their power to give. What do you want them to do about all that you have said? When you feel tempted to end your speech without a request for action remember the Chinese proverb of the Middle Ages: "To talk much and arrive nowhere is the same as climbing a tree to catch a fish."

If your contact is to count, you must look at your listeners as individual people, not over their heads or as one composite blur. **Look at your listeners with friendly focused eyes**. Approach your speaking as you would to an individual friend in a conversation. You may have to speak more intensely and vigorously, but conversation makes a good model. To gain the natural responses of conversation in your speech, Richard Whatley gave this advice over one hundred and fifty years ago:

"The practical rule to be adopted... is not only to pay no studied attention to the voice, but studiously to withdraw the thoughts from it, and to **dwell as intently as possible on the Sense**; trusting to nature to suggest spontaneously the proper emphasis and tones." What is needed is the "full realization of the content of your words as you utter them."

If the speaker has a lack of understanding of what he is to say, the speaker will be lifeless, dull, and lacking in power. Only as a speaker grasps the deep significance of his ideas and their consequences if acted upon, will his desire to speak increase. He will then develop the kind of attitude toward himself, his idea, and his audience that will make him persuasive. His speech will carry conviction. His delivery will be direct. His speech will be filled with variety, vitality, and intensity, and a poise that comes through dedicating oneself to ideas.

Much of the speaker's success in concentrating on ideas and thereby increasing the effectiveness of his delivery can be developed through rehearsal. Never forget—practice makes perfect.

PRACTICE MAKES PERFECT

Every man or woman who wishes to acquire the art of speaking must practice it. Spurgeon writes, "It was by slow degrees that Charles Fox became the most brilliant and powerful debater that ever lived. He attributed his success to the resolution which he formed when very young, of speaking—well or ill—at least every night. "During five whole sessions," stated Fox, "I spoke every night but one, and I regret only that I did not speak on that night, too."

Practice makes perfect! Spurgeon suggested to his students, "At first, you may practice with only the chairs and books of your study, imitating the example of a gentleman, who, upon applying for admission to this college assured me that he had, for two years, practiced himself in extempore preaching in his own room. Students living together might be of great mutual assistance by alternatively acting as part of audience and speaker with a little friendly criticism at the close of each attempt."

"Conversation, too, may be edifying. Thought is to be linked with speech; that is the problem and it may assist a man in its solution, if he in his private musings thinks aloud. So has this become habitual to me that I find it very helpful to be able, in private devotion, to pray with my voice; reading aloud is more beneficial to me than the silent process; and when I am mentally working out a sermon, it is a relief to me to speak to myself as the thoughts flow forth.

"Of course, this only masters half the difficulty and you must practice in public, in order to overcome the intimidation occasioned by the sight of an audience. Good impromptu speech is just the utterance of a practiced thinker—a man of information, meditating on his legs and allowing his thought to march through his mouth into the air. Think aloud as much as you can when you are alone. The practice of calling upon one another to speak on a topic drawn at random from a bowl out of a wide selection has been introduced among you and must be more frequently resorted to."

Let us never forget that the man or woman who says, "I would do great things if only I had the time!" would do nothing if he or she had all the spare time in the world. There is always time—spare time—at the disposal of every person who has the energy to use it. As Longfellow aptly wrote, "Heights by great men gained and kept were not attained by sudden flight; but they while their companions slept, were toiling upward in the night."

CONCLUSION

Finally, for those men and women who would address the nation on God's behalf, there is one ingredient in public speaking that is essential—humility of spirit. God resists the proud, but gives grace unto the humble. When a child of God speaks, his goal must be to point the listener to the Lord Jesus Christ. God alone is the author of all that is good and true and right. We must be satisfied to be but verbal ambassadors.

34 *The Power of the Pen*

by Bob and Rose Weiner

Recognizing the power of the written word to move the hearts of men, Napoleon Bonaparte—in the height of his military career—stated: "There are only two powers in the world, the sword and the pen; and in the end the former is always conquered by the latter." We must never underestimate the power of the written word to influence the human race. Throughout history God has used writers to accomplish His purposes.

In Jeremiah, God spoke saying, "Take a scroll and write on it all the words which I have spoken to you" (Jer. 36:2). To Isaiah, the Lord said, "Take for yourself a large tablet and write on it… inscribe it on a scroll that it may serve in time to come as a witness forever" (Isa. 8:1). To Habakkuk, the prophet, God commanded: "Record the vision, and inscribe it on tablets (make it plain) that the one who reads it may run" (Hab. 2:2).

To John on the Isle of Patmos, He said, "Write, for these words are faithful and true" (Rev. 21:5). Throughout the Bible, God commanded His servants to not only preach His Word, but charged them to write down everything He told them. Why? God knew the importance of the written word to sway the hearts of men and women. He also recognized the value of writing to preserve truth for posterity and to insure the progress of the human race.

In civilizations where there has been a total lack of education and a failure on the part of its inhabitants to record happenings and discoveries, history records that its people progress very little, even after centuries have gone by. With no previous knowledge to build on, the people must rediscover and relearn what the earlier generations failed to record.

When the Pilgrims landed on our northeastern shores they found the American Indians in the same state as their fathers had been for centuries—because of the lack of a written language and body of literature.

God also understands the value of writing to develop the thinking and reasoning processes of men. The investigator, whether scientist, researcher, or student, who neglects to record his findings will find it difficult, if not impossible, to arrive at a conclusion. Think what would have happened to Thomas Edison if he had failed to record his experiments on the electric light bulb—which totaled to 10,000. How far would he have gotten in his investigations before he began to repeat himself and give up his research as hopeless?

In fact, it is in the writing of thoughts that many answers often occur. David found this to be true. As he was instructing Solomon on the plans that he had drawn up for building the temple of the Lord, he explained, "All this the Lord made me understand in writing by His hand upon me, all the details of this pattern" (1 Chron. 28:19). It was in the recording of the ideas that he had for the temple that the Lord caused David to understand every detail.

Nineteenth-century orator Henry Ward Beecher made this observation: "Thinking cannot be clear till it has had expression. We must write, or speak, or act our thoughts, or they will remain in a half torpid form. Our feelings must have expression, or they will be clouds, which till they descend as rain, will never bring up fruit or flower. So it is with the inward feelings; expression gives them development."

The classic *Pilgrim's Progress* is a prime example of this principle. John Bunyan wrote this famous book while he was in prison, having been incarcerated for preaching in the fields in his efforts to reform the

Church of England.

Bunyan explained that when he began his allegory, he did not intend to write a book, but rather was trying to divert his mind from despair while in prison. He stated that he never intended to show the writing to anyone, but was merely writing to gratify himself. The manner in which the allegory came to his mind is exemplary of the importance of writing to develop thoughts. Bunyan writes:

> When at the first I took my pen in hand,
> Thus for to write, I did not understand
> That I at all should make a little book
> In such a mode: nay, I had undertook
> To make another; which, when almost done,
> Before I was aware I this began.
>
> And thus it was: I writing of the way
> And race of saints, in this our gospel day,
> Fell suddenly into an allegory
> About their journey, and the way to glory,
> In more than twenty things which I set down:
> This done, I twenty more had in my crown;
>
> And they again began to multiply,
> Like sparks that from the coals of fire do fly.
> Nay, then, thought I, if that you breed so fast
> I'll put you by yourselves lest you at last
> Should prove ad infinitum, and eat out
> The book that I already am about.
>
> Well, so I did, but yet I did not think
> To show to all the world my pen and ink
> In such a mode; I only thought to make
> I knew not what: nor did I undertake
> Thereby to please my neighbor: no, not I;
> I did it mine own self to gratify.
>
> Neither did I but vacant seasons spend
> In this my scribble: nor did I intend
> But to divert myself in doing this,
> From worser thought which make me do amiss.
>
> Thus I set pen to paper with delight,
> And quickly had my thoughts in black and white.
> For having now my method by the end,

Still as I pulled, it came; and so I penned
It down: until it came at last to be,
For length and breadth, the bigness which you see.

Bunyan clearly states that as he wrote, a progression of thought occurred. It was in the writing that understanding came to him. What kind of influence did this book have in the providence of God? Over its three hundred years of existence the Pilgrim's tale has crossed the barriers of race and culture and penetrated deeply for three centuries into the Christian and non-Christian world alike.

Pilgrim's Progress has been translated into many languages, some of which were unknown to Europe when Bunyan lived. It has been read by Protestants, Catholics, Moslems, American Indians, and South Sea Islanders. It is the supreme classic of the English Puritan tradition and has carried the "heroic image of militant Puritanism" to world-wide audiences.

Bunyan's classic has not been limited to adult readers. It was a favorite among children in the colonial days of America. Its spiritual and moral outlook helped mold the children who, as men and women, gave us this great Republic in which we live. What a tragedy if Bunyan had not been one who took his thoughts seriously or had not been disciplined in the art of incorporating writing with his meditations.

RESHAPING THE WORLD

Christian economist, Gary North, exhorts in his book *Foundations of Christian Scholarship*: "Christianity is pre-eminently a religion of verbal written revelation. No other faith places more importance on the power of words to reshape the world. Man, made in the image of the Creator, is to think God's thoughts after him, subduing the earth to the glory of God, but only in terms of God's Word revealed to man.

"Christians should understand the power of the written word more than any other people: It is the foundation of their faith. But in the twentieth century, they have abandoned the world of scholarship to the secularists. They confine their writing to simple tracts, sentimental biographies, and pietistic devotional literature. Christians have made little impact on the world of ideas and scholarship.

"This failure has led to cultural irrelevance, pietistic retreat, and pessimism concerning the possibility of Christian reconstruction... The battle for the souls of men cannot be won apart from the battle for their minds."

Recognizing the importance of Christian books, Daniel Webster observed in the early beginnings of our Republic, "If truth be not diffused, error will be; if God and His word are not known and received, the devil and his works will gain the ascendance; if the evangelical volume does not reach every hamlet, the pages of a corrupt and licentious literature will; if the power of the gospel is not felt through the length and breadth of the land, anarchy and misrule, degradation and misery, corruption and darkness, will reign without mitigation or end."

If we follow Webster's logic through to its conclusion and compare it with North's observation, we will have to conclude that the one responsible for the deluge of pornography, gossip magazines, cheap novels and licentious literature is the Christian. We have failed to take dominion in the communicative arts and have become, in many respects, salt that has lost its savor. Not only have Christians been slothful about developing communicative skills, we have also been unaggressive in the publishing and marketing of the truth—which God has entrusted into our care. We have unfortunately lagged behind in the creativity, faith, and the hard work that it takes to take dominion in the publishing industry.

SOME PRACTICAL SUGGESTIONS

For those who have read thus far and have felt a stirring in their soul, accompanied with a desire to become more adept in the discipline of writing, the following suggestions are offered:

Practice putting your thoughts into writing. Many people think that unless they have an idea for writing a book, or have someone asking them to publish something, there is no reason to write. A person who entertains this thinking will most certainly never be asked to write anything. It is supply that creates a demand. Why should anyone be asked to write a book or article if their writing has never been seen or read by anyone?

Writing skills are developed though practice. It is in the doing that you learn to become a good writer. Hence, writing should always accompany your meditations and reading. You should always endeavor to write down exactly what God speaks to you through His word. Practice summarizing passages from the Bible and your insights about them. When reading a book, stop and close your book after each chapter and try to express on paper what the author has said.

BEN FRANKLIN'S ADVICE

Benjamin Franklin taught himself to write. He later wrote and published *Poor Richard's Almanac*, which was circulated throughout early America and Europe and was responsible for providing the practical common sense and moral wisdom that helped build the character of colonial America. Here are a few of Franklin's suggestions:

"Having chosen a book which was excellently written, I chose to imitate it. With this view, I took some of the papers, and making short hints of the sentiment in each sentence, laid them by a few days, and then, without looking at the book, tried to complete the papers again, by expressing each hinted sentiment at length, and as fully as it had been expressed before in any suitable words that should come to hand. Then I compared my writings with the original, discovered some of my faults and corrected them...

"I took some of the tales and turned them into verse, and after a time, when I had pretty well forgotten the prose, turned them back again. I also sometimes jumbled my collections of hints into confusion, and after some weeks endeavored to reduce them into the best order, before I began to form the full sentences and complete the paper. This was to teach me method in the arrangement of thoughts.

"By comparing my work afterwards with the original, I discovered many faults and amended them. But I sometimes had the pleasure of fancying that, in certain particulars of small import, I had been lucky enough to improve the method or the language, and this encouraged me to think I might possibly in time to come to be a tolerable English writer, of which I was extremely ambitious.

"My time for these exercises and for reading was at night, after work, or before it began in the morning... When my brother and the rest were going from the printing house to their meals, I remained there alone... eating no more than a slice of bread, a handful of raisins or a tart from the pastry-cook's and a glass of water. I had the rest of the time till their return for study, in which I made the greater progress, from the greater clearness of head and quicker apprehension which usually attend temperance in eating and drinking."

ADVICE FROM THE 19TH CENTURY

A textbook from the 1800s gives some other helpful suggestions:

"It will be beneficial to read aloud what you have written. If you have a literary friend, ask for his corrections and submit to his help. Make sure that you want advice and are not just looking for someone to admire your work. Keep a diary and describe scenes which you have seen or events you have witnessed.

"Good writing takes study and long practice. If you are never at a loss for words and your pen races across the page, take it as a fault to be avoided. Pause, reflect, and read what you have written and try to condense your thoughts and express them in fewer words.

"After having condensed your thoughts as much as possible, take your final copy and strike out without mercy every superfluous word, and substitute a vigorous or expressive word for a weak one. Sacrifice as many adjectives as possible without regret. When this has been done, rewrite the whole thing making the necessary corrections. To see what you have gained, be sure to compare the completed essay with the first draft.

"Simplicity is the charm of writing. Don't try to disguise what you have to say by beating around the bush. Be direct and to the point. Rambling sentences are most often the result of confused thought. As you purpose to write clearly, your thoughts will begin to become clear and definite. Your ability to express yourself in conversation and speaking will take on new skill and acuteness. Putting your thoughts on paper will reveal to you whether your thoughts are incomplete and shadowy."

SUGGESTIONS FROM 20TH-CENTURY ANALYST

Claude C. Cox, in a message entitled "Everyone is a Writer," gives these directives on writing: "Use nouns and verbs to communicate your meaning. Be careful not to blur the image by using unnecessary adjectives and adverbs or by using unfamiliar terms. Call a "spade" a "spade", not an "Implement of husbandry." The verb "hurl," for example, is stronger than "toss" or "throw." "Jesus wept" is stronger than, "Jesus sat down and produced a geyser of tears." Remember, the object of writing is to communicate. If communication has not taken place, then you are not writing.

"Don't chase rabbits in your writing. Be like a hunter with a rifle, not a shotgunner. Remember a shotgunner aims in the general direction of the target and then fires, hoping the buckshot will hit something. The rifleman aims at one single target and hits the most vulnerable spot." As you become more adept at writing, watch out for over-revision. If too much erasing is done in the drawing of an artist, it is possible to kill the drawing by overworking it. The same danger is possible in writing.

Claude Cox states, "Revising a script is a thing of tedious balance and must be done with care. One danger is over-revision. By going back to a script that was done spontaneously, when the creative juices were flowing, and giving it the high school English teacher's approach, you can rip the life out of a piece of writing.

"On the other hand, if you go back to your script with objectivity instead of subjectivity, and fine tune a word here and a phrase there, it can be improved. Most professional authors and screenwriters I know have one problem in common. There are times that they sit down to write and nothing leaves the brain and travels down to the fingers on the typewriter keys. It happens to us all.

"How do you cope with this malady? Some people wait until the last minute to write, and are forced to put something on paper whether it is good or not. This can work, but usually the script suffers. Many professionals will do additional reading and research into the topic, and most of the time an idea will emerge. Others may discuss the topic with anyone—either knowledgeable or ignorant of the subject—and be stimulated by something that is said in the conversation.

"Most writers conquer this problem by using discipline. Some people set aside a particular time each day for research and study, and allow nothing to interfere. Also, during that same day, these people set aside a certain block of time to write.

"My cure for the stagnant mind is to sit down well ahead of any deadline and put something—anything—on paper. The trick is getting off dead center. What I usually put on paper is something somewhat relative to the subject, but without any thought or form... For me writing comes easy, once I get almost anything on paper that can give me a springboard... From the point that the mental barrier has been broken, most any writer can wade into his task."

The only way to learn to write is to begin to do it. Christians, spend much time in secret with the Lord. Become acquainted with the still small voice of God until it becomes a burning fire within your spirit. Practice expressing your thoughts in writing. As you diligently practice the art of writing, and at the same time seek God to be used to affect your nation with the gospel, one day the world will hear the Spirit of God calling out through your pen, giving men and women a vision and a hope... and calling them into account for their transgressions.

The wise old patriarch, Job, was correct when he asserted "How forcible are right words!" Job 6:25a.

35 *Hasty and Unjust Judgment*

by Rev. John Todd

Scene: Two neighbors who live in a small farming community are talking to each other about their newest neighbor.

RADWAY. I have been informed that a stranger by the name of Goodman has settled near you. I hope you are finding him to be an agreeable neighbor.

DENVER. Far from it. I am sorry he has come here, for I fear he will spoil our neighborhood, which has always been so peaceful and harmonious.

RADWAY. I am sorry to hear that. But what are your objections to your new neighbor?

DENVER. There are very many, I assure you. In the first place, we do not agree in politics; and that, you know, is enough to prevent all intimacy.

RADWAY. I do not quite agree with you in that. I do not think an honest difference of opinion in political matters ought to prevent friendship between neighbors.

DENVER. Also he is so distant and reserved. And I have heard that he is very cheap and stingy.

RADWAY. In what way does he show it?

DENVER. His plain, no, frugal style of living is not equal to his fortune; and he seems to manifest a miserly spirit in everything he does.

RADWAY. Perhaps he spends his money in charity, and wishes to set an example of frugal economy.

DENVER. His economy is evidently nothing but stinginess; and as to charity, he seems to be the last man one could expect to do an act of that kind. Why, only last week, a poor man whose house and barn had been burned, and who

	had lost all he possessed, called on him with a donation paper, in which were the names of most of the gentlemen in the neighborhood, and the only answer he gave was, he would consider it.
RADWAY.	Do you know whether he did consider it or not?
DENVER.	I do not. I suppose it was only an excuse to get rid of doing anything for the poor man. As for myself, I have reason to think he bears no good-will toward me.
RADWAY.	Then he is greatly in the wrong; for I presume you entertain no ill-will toward him. But in what way does he show ill feeling toward you?
DENVER.	In various ways. He had a valuable cow which he wished to sell. I took a liking to her, and offered him more than she was worth; but as soon as he found I wanted her, he sent her away and sold her to the butcher. My wife, you know, is very fond of cultivating flowers, and, seeing a beautiful plant growing in Mr. Goodman's garden, she requested the gardener to ask his employer to sell her a small root or cutting of it; but, instead of obliging her, he charged the gardener not to meddle with the plant on any account.
RADWAY.	That was very strange conduct, indeed; but perhaps he had some good reason for refusing to comply with these requests. Have you any other complaints to make against him?
DENVER.	Yes. About three weeks ago, I discharged my hired hand for being careless and impudent; but as he had lived with me many years, and had been generally a very trusty and useful servant, I meant to take him back again, upon his submission, which I was sure would soon happen. Instead of that he offers himself to my obliging neighbor who, without contacting me for a statement of his character, provides him with a job. Evidently, he has not the least consideration for my feelings; and glad indeed would I be, if he would leave the neighborhood forever.

RADWAY.	It must surely be a very great misfortune to have so disagreeable a neighbor, especially in the country. But who is that man coming up the lane?
DENVER.	Ah! he is the poor fellow who was burned out last week. [*Enter Nathan.*] Well, Nathan, how do you succeed with your charity drive?
NATHAN.	Admirably! thanks to Providence and my kind friends, my losses are nearly all made up.
DENVER.	I am very glad to hear that. When I saw you last, you had not obtained one-half the amount.
NATHAN.	True; but you remember asking me what Mr. Goodman had subscribed, and I told you he wished to consider the subject. Well, the next day I learned he had made very particular inquiries among my neighbors, about me and my losses; and when I called on him, a few days after, he told me he was very glad to find that I bore so good a character, and that the neighbors had so kindly and generously come to my relief. He then subscribed three hundred dollars, and gave me a check on the bank for that amount.
DENVER.	Three hundred dollars! You astonish me! A noble gift indeed! I never could have thought it. I rejoice at your good fortune. I am sure you are greatly obliged to Mr. Goodman.
NATHAN.	Indeed I am sir, and to all my good friends who have so generously contributed to my necessity. [*Exit.*]
RADWAY.	Well, Mr. Denver, that does not look much like the act of a stingy or hard-hearted man. I think you will be obliged to entertain a more favorable opinion of Mr. Goodman.
DENVER.	Indeed, I do already! I find I was mistaken in that respect at least, and I am willing to confess that my suspicion was unjust. But what a pity it is that men of such noble generosity should not be amiable in their manners, and as ready to oblige in trifles as in matters of

greater importance!

RADWAY. Yes; it is a pity, when that is really the case.

DENVER. It certainly would not have required a very great sacrifice to have shown a little civility about a flower-root!

RADWAY. No, indeed; but what do you think about your gardener coming down the road, with a large flower in his hands? [*Enter gardener.*]

DENVER. Why, Richard, where did you get that beautiful flower?

GARDENER. It came from Mr. Goodman's garden. He has sent it as a present to Mrs. Denver.

DENVER. Sent it? I hope you did not go and ask for the flower?

GARDENER. His gardener, sir, sent me word to come for it; and Mr. Goodman said he would have sent it before, but he thought it could not be safely removed.

DENVER. I hope he did not rob himself by sending it.

GARDENER. He had only a small plant left, sir; but, hearing that madam took a fancy to it, he was resolved to send it to her, and a choice plant it is!

DENVER. Well, take it home, and set it in a good place. [*Exit Gardener.*]

RADWAY. This certainly shows that Mr. Goodman is not lacking in civility.

DENVER. It really does. It shows that he is thoughtful and polite in small matters, and I am obliged to him for the favor. Perhaps he wishes to make amends for past incivility. But here comes his hired man [*Enter Thomas.*] Well, Thomas, how much more did you get for Mr. Goodman's cow than I offered him?

THOMAS. Ah! Mr. Denver, you would never have been pleased with that animal, she was so unruly and vicious; and Mr. Goodman well knew it. She was a fine creature to look at, but too unsafe to keep. So he sold her to the butcher for less than you offered him.

DENVER. And was that the reason why Mr. Goodman refused to sell the cow to me?

THOMAS. It was, indeed, sir.

DENVER. Then I am greatly obliged to him. That was really a neighborly act!
[*Exit Thomas.*]

RADWAY. Yes; I think his conduct shows something more than politeness; it displays real goodness of heart.

DENVER. It does indeed. I find I must change my opinion of him, and I do it with pleasure. But, after all, his conduct respecting my hired man is somewhat unaccountable.

RADWAY. His conduct in relation to other matters has been so noble, that I am inclined to think he will show himself equally honorable in that also.

DENVER. Why, here comes Andrew now. I wonder what apology he has to make for his conduct.
[*Andrew approaches, taking off his hat.*]

ANDREW. Sir, I wish to say to your honor that—

DENVER. What have you to say to me now, Andrew?

ANDREW. I came to ask pardon for my misconduct, and beg that you will take me into your employment again.

DENVER. Why have you so soon parted with your new master?

ANDREW. Mr. Goodman never was my master, sir. He only kept me till you could be reconciled to take me into your service again; for, he said, he was sure you were too honorable to turn off an old servant without good reason, and he hoped you would accept my excuses, and receive me again.

DENVER. Did Mr. Goodman say all that?

ANDREW. He did, sir; and he advised me not to delay any longer asking your forgiveness.

DENVER.   Well, you may go to my house, and I will talk with you
              on the subject when I return.
              [*Andrew exits.*]

RADWAY.   Now, friend Denver, what do you think of your new
              neighbor, after all this?

DENVER.   I think more than I can well express. It will be a lesson to
              me never again to make such hasty judgment. I ac-
              knowledge my error. But it is the misfortune of these re-
              served characters, that they are so long in making
              themselves known; but when they are known they are
              often the most sincere and valuable of friends.

❦ Comprehension Questions

1.   There is an old saying, "You can't judge a book by its cover." How does
     this saying apply to the story you just read?

2.   Denver was ultimately forced to acknowledge his error in judgment
     when it came to his neighbor. However, did this man ever truly repent
     from his sins? If not, do you think that Mr. Denver is likely to do the same
     thing in the future?

3.   Do you think that it is dangerous and destructive to listen to gossip?
     Why?

36 *The Crucible*

by Ruth E. McDaniel

Ruth McDaniel is a mother, home school teacher, homemaker, and gifted free-lance writer. She resides with her family in Missouri where she writes for the glory of God and the good of her family.

This short story illustrates the truth that without Christ, a person's life remains vain and selfish. Only Christ can enable us to practice charity towards others without regard to our personal benefit, but for His sake alone.

Sam Levine was just walking past the alcove where one of the telephones was located when it rang. He waved the maid away with a flick of his well-manicured hand and answered it, himself.

"This is the Levine residence," he announced impatiently, expecting to hear the slightly nasal voice of his new vice president on the other end. He could feel his blood pressure going up. Couldn't he even take one day off without receiving a panic call?

"Dad? Hello! I wasn't expecting you to answer the phone. This is Brad!"

Sam's flushed face returned to its normal shade, and he felt a sudden surge of pride as the image of his strong, handsome son came to mind. Brad had inherited the thick curly hair, broad shoulders, and enviable height of five generations of Levine men, and he had his mother's warm complexion and deep blue eyes. He was a son any father could be proud of! When he graduated from the military academy, he was so striking in his uniform that all eyes were focused on him. Everyone who was anyone knew that Brad Levine would go far… whether it was through the military ranks, or following his father's footsteps in banking.

"Where are you, son?"

"I'm in Maryland, at the moment."

"I didn't know you were back in the States! Are you on leave?"

"In a manner of speaking…"

That's wonderful news! If I know your mother, she'll have a large 'Welcome Home!' party planned at the club within hours."

"I'd rather she didn't…" Brad began, then he took a deep breath and started over. "I might be coming home in the next two weeks, and I'd like to bring a friend with me, if that's all right with you and Mom."

"Of course, son! We have plenty of room! You know your friends are always welcome… especially, bright, young officers. Does he play tennis or golf? We could set up a foursome. I'll call Upjohn and ask him to reserve some time…"

"Wait, Dad! I think I should explain… my friend was severely injured during our last tour of duty."

Sam's eyebrows came together in a sudden frown. "You want to bring someone home with you who has medical problems?"

There was a moment of silence on the other end of the line, then Brad said, quietly, "Yes, sir."

"Well… what exactly do you mean when you say that your friend was 'severely injured'?"

With barely a pause, Brad replied, "He stepped on a land mine. Now, he's blind, badly burned… and both of his legs have been amputated."

"Are you out of your mind?" Sam exploded. "Why… he would need round-the-clock care! We'd have to hire a nurse! How would you entertain him? He'd have to stay in the house… and, what about your mother's bridge club? How would people react to him? Why, he would make them… all of us… extremely uncomfortable!

"No…I'm sorry, Brad, but it's impossible! You just haven't thought this thing through. Your friend should stay in the hospital where he belongs! After all, he's the military's responsibility, not ours."

After another long silence, Brad said, "I'm sorry you feel that way, Dad." Without another word, he hung up.

Sam shook his head in disbelief and replaced the receiver. How could an intelligent person like Brad even think of such an idea? They rarely heard from their only son, and then, he calls with this outlandish plan! Well, once he thought it over, he'd see that his father was right!

"Disfigured, you say?" Brad's mother's eyes widened in shock, after hearing about her son's request. "How ghastly! I agree with you, of course… the boy needs to remain at the hospital. I can't imagine Brad wanting to bring home a… 'deformed' person! I feel sorry for him, of course, but what on earth would we 'do' with him? Brad certainly couldn't introduce him to his friends… or, take him anywhere!"

As the weeks and months passed and Brad didn't write, call, or come home, his parents shrugged off their concern, saying, "He's just being unreasonable. One day, he'll understand!"

Then, they received another phone call.

This time, the caller was Brad's commanding officer. He was calling to inform them that their son had died.

"Died! How? What happened?" Stunned, Sam clutched the telephone to his ear as the voice droned on about 'heart failure' and 'complications.' The one message he comprehended was that his son's body was being shipped home by plane. It would arrive the next afternoon.

The dazed, grief-stricken parents accompanied their son's coffin from the airport to the funeral home.

"We'd like a private showing, before the service begins," they told the funeral director, once the arrangements had been made. They wanted to see their son's strong, handsome face, one more time, before his interment.

The lid was slowly raised. The funeral director stood before the open coffin for a long time, then, he finally stepped back and nodded to the Levines.

Hand-in-hand, Brad's parents approached the coffin and looked down upon their son, who was... blind, badly burned, and a double amputee!

—Ruth McDaniel, © 1993

◖ *Comprehension Questions*

1. Read Galatians 6:1-10 and Matthew 25. Did Mr. and Mrs. Levine fail to understand their obligation to show mercy unto the least of God's creatures? If so, how?

2. How would these parents have possibly viewed this situation differently had they lived by the command to "love thy neighbor as thyself"?

3. What conditions did Mr. and Mrs. Levine place on Brad's "friend" before they would be willing to show love to him?

4. How do you think Brad's parents felt when they looked in the coffin?

5. What techniques did the author use to help the reader take a personal interest in the story?

37   *The Value of a Dollar*

by Ruth E. McDaniel

"I'm sorry, Jake," Father said, "but there's no extra money in the budget for guitar lessons, right now. Have you thought about saving part of your allowance?"

"I only get $10 a week. How can I save from that small sum?"

"When I was your age ..."

Sixteen-year-old Jake groaned and rolled his eyes. "I know, you had to sell newspapers... and, you didn't receive an allowance ... I remember those stories. But, you don't know how expensive it is, being a teenager these days. The cost of living was much lower when you were my age!"

"Don't forget, the average income was lower, too," Father added. "I'm sorry, but, I can't raise your allowance, either."

"I could find a job, but, you said you didn't want me to work after school," Jake reminded his father.

"I don't think it's a good idea for you to work part-time," Father agreed. "Between studies and football, when would you find time to work? You could give up football, I suppose. You're certainly not giving up study time."

Jake rubbed his short, red hair in frustration. "Maybe there would be extra money available if you budgeted more economically. That's what we're studying in my accounting class. I might be able to make some suggestions... that is, if you'll let me see the family budget."

Jake's father sat back in his easy chair and considered his son's request. "Yes," he replied thoughtfully, "perhaps it's time for you to learn the value of a dollar."

Suddenly, Father slapped his knee and stood up. "You're right, son! Go into the dining room and clear off the table so we'll have lots of room to spread out. I'll collect the ledger, paper, pencils, and calculator."

Five minutes later, Jake and his father were leaning over the ledger and other items arranged on the dining room table.

"You're familiar with income and expenses... debits and credits, aren't you?" Father asked.

"Of course." Jake responded with confidence.

"All right, this column represents my income, and the next column represents the family expenses. Each expense is identified in the left-hand column." Father sat back and let Jake review the ledger.

When Jake saw the amount of his father's monthly income, his eyes widened. He had no idea his father earned so much money. He could hear guitar strings strumming in his head, already. This should be a cinch, he thought. Then, he looked at the expenses. The first item was 'Church—10%.'

"Could you reduce your donation to church, a little?" Jake asked, hopefully, pencil poised above his paper.

"I'm surprised at you, Jake! Don't even consider touching the Lord's money," Father admonished.

Jake's face flamed, momentarily, and he nodded in embarrassment. Then, he proceeded to the next set of expenses. Income tax, social security, disability, personal property tax... no trimming costs there. House payment, food, and household needs; all necessary expenditures. Utilities, car payment, license fees, medical, dental, pharmacy, retirement annuity... hmmmm.

"What about lowering your retirement contribution?" One look into his father's eyes answered that question. Besides, retirement savings was even larger on the school budget.

Savings account, college fund, emergency fund... this was a possibility. "What's the 'emergency fund'?"

"Do you remember when Doug kicked his football through the front window? And, when you needed a new bike helmet? Or, last week, when you had to turn in your school yearbook money?"

Jake disappointedly turned back to the ledger. His and Sandy's allowances were next. He almost asked if his little sister's allowance could be reduced but he caught himself, just in time. She received half as much as Jake received; if his parents cut hers, they would lower his, too. They were very fair-minded!

The list continued. Trash, sewer, water, car maintenance and repair, gas, house maintenance, haircuts, carpet cleaning, and dry cleaning. Miscellaneous expenditures was the last entry.

"What does miscellaneous expenditures include?"

Jake's father smiled and said, "That's the family entertainment expenses: movies, football games, dining out, etc. You probably wouldn't want to delete that one."

Jake shook his head. Then, one by one, he reviewed each expense, again. Then, a third time. After the third examination, Jake realized that something was missing.

"There are no weekly allowances for you and Mother."

"No," Father agreed.

Somehow, that didn't seem fair. Finally, Jake sat back and put his paper and pencil on the table. There wasn't a single expense that could be eliminated.

Jake glanced at his father and felt a little ashamed of himself. His and Sandy's allowances, and a few family entertainment expenses were the only frivolous items on the budget.

"Dad, you don't need any help from me," Jake, finally, admitted. "But, would you help me set up a small budget of my own... for my weekly allowance?"

Jake's father grinned and shook his son's hand in agreement.

—Ruth McDaniel, © 1993

🔥 Comprehension Questions

1. Write a paragraph that describes what items belong in a family budget.

2. How do you think Jake felt after he talked with his dad about the family budget?

3. Why did Jake's father refuse to lower his giving to the Lord? Why do you think Jake's dad put God first in his expenses ledger?

4. What does it mean to give a *tithe* of your goods to the Lord? Read Malachi 3:6–12.

38 *Home*

by Edgar A. Guest

It takes a heap of living in a house to make it home,
A heap of sun and shadow, and ye sometimes have to roam
Before ye really appreciate the things ye left behind,
And hunger for them somehow, with them always on your mind.
It doesn't make any difference how rich ye get to be,
How much your chairs and tables cost, how great your luxury,
It ain't home to you, though it be the palace of a king,
Until somehow your soul is sort o' wrapped around everything.
Home is not a place that gold can buy or get up in minute;
Before it's home there's got to be a heap of livin' in it;
Within the walls there's got to be some babies born, and then
Right there you have to bring them up as good women and good men;
And gradually, as time goes on, ye find ye wouldn't part
With anything they ever used—they've grown into your heart:
The old high chairs, the playthings, to the little shoes they wore
Ye hoard; and if you could you'd even keep the thumbmarks on the
         door.
Ye've got to weep to make it home, you've got to sit and sigh
And watch beside a loves one's bed, and know that Death is nigh;
And in the stillness of the night to see Death's angel come,
An' close the eyes of her that smiled, and leave her sweet voice dumb.
For these are scenes that grip the heart, and when your tears are dried,
Ye find the home is dearer than it was, and sanctified;
And tugging at ye always are the pleasant memories
Of her that was and is no more—ye can't escape from these.
Even the roses around the porch still blossom year by year,
Reminding you of someone dear who trained them just to run
Who used to love them long ago, so's they would get the early morning
         sun;
Ye've got to sing and dance for years, ye've got to romp and play,
And learn to love the things ye have by using them each day.
Ye've got to love each brick and stone from cellar up to dome:
It takes a heap of living in a house to make it home.

🌿 Comprehension Questions

1. What did the poet mean when he stated that a home can not be made up in a minute?

2. List three things that the author considered to be necessary for a house to be a home.

3. Why do you think that God established the people of earth in families?

4. Write a paragraph explaining the importance of family relationships in light of this poem.

39 The Fool's Prayer

Edward R. Sill

Edward R. Sill was born in Connecticut on April 29, 1841, and died February 27, 1887.

The royal feast was done; the King
  Sought some new sport to banish care,
And to his jester cried: "Sir Fool,
  Kneel now, and make for us a prayer!"

The jester doffed his cap and bells,
  And stood the mocking court before;
They could not see the bitter smile
  Behind the painted grin he wore.

He bowed his head, and bent his knee
  Upon the monarch's silken stool;
His pleading voice arose: "O Lord,
  Be merciful to me, a fool!

"No pity, Lord, could change the heart
  From red with wrong to white as wool;
The rod must heal the sin: but, Lord,
  Be merciful to me, a fool!

" 'Tis not by guilt the onward sweep
  Of truth and right, O Lord, we stay;
'Tis by our follies that so long
  We hold the earth from heaven away.

"These clumsy feet, still in the mire,
  Go crushing blossoms without end;
These hard, well-meaning hands we thrust
  Among the heart-strings of a friend.

"The ill-timed truth we might have kept—
  Who knows how sharp it pierced and stung?
The word we had not sense to say—
  Who knows how grandly it had rung?

"Our faults no tenderness should ask,
  The chastening stripes must cleanse them all;
But for our blunders—oh, in shame

Before the eyes of heaven we fall.

"Earth bears no balsam for mistakes;
    Men crown the knave, and scourge the fool
That did his will; but Thou, O Lord,
    Be merciful to me, a fool!"

The room was hushed; in silence rose
    The King, and sought his gardens cool,
And walked apart, and murmured low,
    "Be merciful to me, a fool!"

❧ Comprehension Questions

1. This poem derives much of its impact from the contrast of a fool offering up such a wisdom-laden prayer. What are some of the expressions of the folly for which he asks the Lord's mercy?

2. How can you avoid living a foolish life?

40 The Search for the City of Satisfaction

by Ruth E. McDaniel

This allegorical story depicts three young people who desire to be on their own. Through hard experience, their immaturity gives way to the realization that "the grass is *not* always greener on the other side."

Once upon a time, three brothers lived in a charming two-story cottage. Their names were Content, Restless, and Curious.

They were very different from each other, although Restless and Curious were more alike than not. Content was the oldest of the three. He spent many happy years with his parents, the Cobblers, in the cottage located on the outskirts of the small town of Ordinary. Even as a toddler, he was content to play with the bits of leather on the floor at his father's feet. And so, they called him Content.

When Curious was born, the whole family had to be more alert, for the new baby had an insatiable curiosity and was constantly investigating inside and out, upstairs and down, over and under every nook and cranny.

Then, finally Restless came along, and the family knew no peace from that day forth. Restless whined and cried and was never happy.

As the children grew, Mother and Father Cobbler became old and feeble. Content willingly took over his father's duties and supported the family by making and repairing shoes. Curious relieved their mother of her food-finding and cooking chores; his curiosity made him well-suited to the task, and he created some original and very strange meals. Restless was in charge of housekeeping, repairs, and wood-chopping. This allowed him to move constantly, which his restless nature demanded.

By the time Mother and Father Cobbler died, the three brothers were old enough to take care of themselves and they worked well together... for awhile. But, the day came when Restless wanted more. He'd been talking to the Unreliable brothers, and they told him about a beautiful city they'd heard of, filled with never-ending excitement and riches for all. They said it was called "The City of Satisfaction."

"How do you get to the City of Satisfaction?" asked Curious.

"According to Most Unreliable, you climb to the top of Hard Luck

Mountain where you earn the right to enter the Valley of Maturity. The City of Satisfaction is located at the farthest end of the Valley."

"You can't trust those Unreliable boys," warned Content. "They're too undependable!"

"I knew you would say that," growled Restless, "so, I went to Judge Know-It-All! He said there was definitely a mountain of hard luck out there, usually followed by a valley of maturity. He had never seen the City of Satisfaction, but he was certain that most people found satisfaction at the end of their journey from hard luck to maturity!"

"Are you going?" asked Curious.

"Of course!" Restless responded.

Content shook his head, sadly. He knew that no amount of reasoning would change his brother's mind, so he said nothing.

"Well, if you're going, so am I!" Curious said, giving Content a defiant look. But, once again, Content said nothing.

Although he couldn't understand it, Content had always known that, sooner or later, Restless and Curious would leave their happy home. He sensed that Restless' restlessness and Curious' curiosity would overcome them, one day. It appeared that day had arrived.

Within a week, Restless and Curious began their journey. Content made a special pair of strong, sturdy shoes for each of them. He had no way of knowing when he would see his younger brothers again. At least he would know they were well-shod for the difficult climb up Hard Luck Mountain. He watched them until they disappeared from sight and felt heavy-hearted. Only the sweet smiles of Happy, the grocer's daughter, kept Content from becoming depressed. As the days passed, he made special daily trips to the grocery store just to see and talk to her. The stronger their relationship grew, the more optimistic Content became. Somehow, he knew it would all turn out right.

Meanwhile, Restless and Curious were busy climbing Hard Luck Mountain. They ran into numerous difficulties on the way. For example, curiosity caused Curious to explore every cave they passed, and he just barely escaped being mauled by mountain lions, twice, and a large, angry bear, once. Restless, eager to reach the top of the mountain, was impatient with his brother's constant forays into the caves they came across. They argued continuously, which made their journey even more difficult.

Weeks, then months, then years passed and still they failed to reach the top of the mountain. The two brothers experienced every hardship known to man: hunger, thirst, sickness, poverty, despair. Their clothing became ragged and their hair long and unkept. Only the shoes that Content made with such love and care were still in good condition. Every night, when they sat beside their small campfire before trying to sleep on the cold, hard ground, they would hang their heads and stare morosely at their feet. Quite often, they would focus on their sturdy shoes and think of their older brother, Content, and the family cottage they had left behind. After a time, the reasons they left home became harder to remember. The City of Satisfaction became a vague dream.

Then, finally, the moment came when they lost all desire to continue on their journey.

"What is it we're seeking?" asked Curious, one night.

"When we started out, we sought the City that offered unending excitement and riches for all." Restless shook his head wearily. "But, now, I'm too old and tired to want endless excitement, and the only riches I desire can be found in the happy home of our youth."

"It seems you're no longer filled with restlessness," Curious observed, "and curiosity doesn't compel me as it once did."

"Since I am now No Longer Restless, and you are Formerly Curious, don't you think it's time for us to go home?"

The brothers looked at each other and smiled for the first time in many years. They agreed to start for home at daybreak.

When morning arrived, the two weary men made a surprising discovery. They were standing on top of Hard Luck Mountain!

"I wonder which direction would take us to the Valley of Maturity?" Formerly Curious mused. "Not that I'm interested!" he quickly added.

No Longer Restless shrugged. "Does it really matter?"

The brothers took one last look at the panoramic view, and then they started descending the mountain, using the same path that had caused them so many difficulties on the way up. But, this time, the journey was very different. Formerly Curious ignored the many caves he had originally explored so thoroughly. And, No Longer Restless plodded happily along at an even pace; although he was looking forward to getting home, he wasn't filled with anxiety as he had been in previous years.

The trip down the mountain took only a fraction of the time the earlier trip had taken and wasn't nearly as hard. The travelers had learned, over the years, how to handle hardships, hunger, and poverty. Without realizing it, they had earned the right to enter the Valley of Maturity which now stretched out before them, wide and green and level. They found themselves walking more quickly as they approached their home town. Somehow, they didn't find the town of Ordinary so boring anymore! They greeted old friends and neighbors with a wave and a smile but didn't stop; they were eager to see their older brother and their beloved home!

Just as the setting sun touched the distant horizon and everything was bathed in gold, they caught sight of the cottage. Then, as if by magic, the door opened, and Happy and Content stood arm-in-arm on the threshold, while their children, Serene and Cheerful played happily in the background.

A glorious reunion followed with much laughing and crying, hugging and kissing, and numerous questions. Happy and Content had married many years before, and they had expanded the cottage to accommodate their growing family. But, all through the years, they had kept the two missing brothers' room ready. Content always knew they would learn, some day, and their happiness would then be complete!

As the moon rose over the joy-filled cottage, No Longer Restless and Formerly Curious made one last discovery: after all the years of hardship and travel, they found that the City of Satisfaction really did exist: It was always right there… in their own backyard.

—Ruth McDaniel, © 1993

41 *At Home in Heaven*

by Thomas A. Morris

This poem was first printed in 1849 along with a large collection of hymns published by the Methodist Church.

Forever with the Lord!
  Amen, so let it be!
Life from the dead is in that word,
  'Tis immortality.

Here in the body pent
  Absent from Him I roam;
Yet mightily pitch my moving tent
  A day's march nearer home.

Forever with the Lord!
  Father, it is thy will,
The promise of that faithful word,
  E'en here to me fulfill.

So when my latest breath
  Shall rend the veil in twain,
By death I shall escape from death,
  And life eternal gain.

Apostles, martyrs, prophets there,
  Around my Saviour stand;
And soon my friends in Christ below
  Will join the glorious band.

O when, thou city of my God,
  Shall I thy courts ascend,
Where congregations ne'er break up,
  And Sabbaths have no end?

Knowing as I am known,
  How shall I love that word,
And oft repeat before the throne,
  Forever with the Lord!

42 *The Book of Jonah*

by the Prophet Jonah

Now the word of the Lord came unto Jonah the son of Amittai, saying, Arise, to go Nineveh, that great city, and cry against it; for their wickedness is come up before me. But Jonah rose up to flee unto Tarshish from the presence of the Lord, and went down to Joppa; and he found a ship going to Tarshish: so he paid the fare thereof, and went down into it, to go with them unto Tarshish from the presence of the Lord.

But the Lord sent out a great wind into the sea, and there was a mighty tempest in the sea, so that the ship was like to be broken. Then the mariners were afraid, and cried every man unto his god, and cast forth the wares that were in the ship into the sea, to lighten it of them. But Jonah was gone down into the sides of the ship; and he lay, and was fast asleep. So the shipmaster came to him, and said unto him, What meanest thou, O sleeper? arise, call upon thy God, if so be that God will think upon us, that we perish not.

And they said every one to his fellow, Come, and let us cast lots, that we may know for whose cause this evil is upon us. So they cast lots, and the lot fell upon Jonah. Then said they unto him, Tell us, we pray thee, for whose cause this evil is upon us; What is thine occupation? and whence comest thou? what is thy country? and of what people art thou? And he said unto them, I am a Hebrew; and I fear the Lord, the God of heaven which hath made the sea and the dry land. Then were the men exceedingly afraid, and said unto him, Why hast thou done this? For the men knew that he fled from the presence of the Lord, because he had told them. Then said they unto him, What shall we do unto thee, that the sea may be calm unto us? For the sea wrought, and was tempestuous. And he said unto them, Take me up, and cast me forth into the sea; so shall the sea be calm unto you: for I know that for my sake this great tempest is upon you. Nevertheless the men rowed hard to bring it to the land; but they could not: for the sea wrought, and was tempestuous against them. Wherefore they cried unto the Lord, and said, We beseech thee, O Lord, we beseech thee, let us not perish for this man's life, and lay not upon us innocent blood: for thou, O Lord, hast done as it pleased thee. So they took up Jonah, and cast him forth into the sea: and the sea ceased from her raging. Then the men feared the Lord exceedingly, and offered a sacrifice unto the Lord, and made vows.

Now the Lord had prepared a great fish to swallow up Jonah. And Jonah was in the belly of the fish three days and three nights. Then Jonah prayed unto the Lord his God out of the fish's belly, and said, "I cried by reason of mine affliction unto the Lord, and he heard me; out of the belly of hell cried I, and thou heardest my voice. For thou hadst cast me into the deep, in the midst of the seas; and the floods compassed me about: all thy billows and thy waves passed over me. Then I said, I am cast out of thy sight; yet I will look again toward thy holy temple. The waters compassed me about, even to the soul: the depth closed me round about, the weeds were wrapped about my head. I went down to the bottoms of the mountains; the earth with her bars was about me for ever: yet hast thou brought up my life from corruption, O Lord my God. When my soul fainted within me I remembered the Lord: and my prayer came in unto thee, into thine holy temple. They that observe lying vanities forsake their own mercy. But I will sacrifice unto thee with the voice of thanksgiving; I will pay *that* that I have vowed. Salvation is of the Lord." And the Lord spake unto the fish, and it vomited out Jonah upon the dry land.

And the word of the Lord came unto Jonah the second time, saying,

Arise, go unto Nineveh, that great city, and preach unto it the preaching that I bid thee. So Jonah arose, and went unto Nineveh, according to the word of the Lord. Now Nineveh was an exceeding great city of three days' journey. And Jonah began to enter into the city a day's journey, and he cried, and said, Yet forty days, and Nineveh shall be overthrown.

So the people of Nineveh believed God, and proclaimed a fast, and put on sackcloth, from the greatest of them even to the least of them. For word came unto the king of Nineveh, and he arose from his throne, and he laid his robe from him, and covered him with sackcloth, and sat in ashes. And he caused it to be proclaimed and published through Nineveh by the decree of the king and his nobles, saying, Let neither man nor beast, herd nor flock, taste any thing: let them not feed, nor drink water: But let man and beast be covered with sackcloth, and cry mightily unto God: yea, let them turn every one from his evil way, and from the violence that is in their hands. Who can tell if God will turn and repent, and turn away from his fierce anger, that we perish not?

And God saw their works, that they turned from their evil ways; and God repented of the evil, that he had said that he would do unto them; and he did it not. But it displeased Jonah exceedingly, and he was very angry. And he prayed unto the Lord, and said, I pray thee, O Lord, was not this my saying, when I was yet in my country? Therefore, I fled before unto Tarshish: for I knew that thou art a gracious God, and merciful, slow to anger, and of great kindness, and repentest thee of the evil. Therefore now, O Lord, take, I beseech thee, my life from me; for it is better for me to die than to live.

Then the Lord said, Doest thou well to be angry? So Jonah went out of the city, and sat on the east side of the city, and there made him a booth, and sat under it in the shadow, till he might see what would become of the city. And the Lord God prepared a gourd, and made it to come up over Jonah, that it might be a shadow over his head, to deliver him from his grief. So Jonah was exceeding glad of the gourd. But God prepared a worm when the morning rose the next day, and it smote the gourd that it withered.

And it came to pass, when the sun did arise, that God prepared a vehement east wind; and the sun beat upon the head of Jonah, that he fainted, and wished in himself to die, and said, It is better for me to die than to live. And God said to Jonah, Doest thou well to be angry for the gourd? And he said, I do well to be angry, even unto death. Then said the Lord, Thou hast had pity on the gourd, for the which thou hast not labored, neither madest it grow; which came up in a night, and perished in a night: And should not I spare Nineveh, that great city, wherein are more than sixscore thousand persons that cannot discern between their right hand and their left hand; and also much cattle?

—From the Authorized King James Version of the Holy Bible, 1611

🌿 *Comprehension Questions*

1. Do you think that Jonah had a hard time setting priorities? If so, why?

2. The story of Jonah helps us understand how God accomplishes His perfect will in spite of the fact that He uses very imperfect people to serve Him. Explain how this principle is revealed in the story of Jonah.

3. Write a paragraph or two that describes how Jonah could have improved his attitude about his ministry to those in Nineveh.

4. Jesus in the New Testament said, "An evil and adulterous generation seeketh after a sign; and there shall no sign be given to it, but the sign of the prophet Jonah: For as Jonah was three days and three nights in the whale's belly, so shall the Son of man be three days and three nights in the heart of the earth. The men of Nineveh shall rise in judgment with this generation, and shall condemn it; because they repented at the preaching of Jonah; and behold, a greater than Jonah is here" (Matt. 12:39–41). How do you think that Jonah's life was a type of Christ and His work?

43

All Glory to the Triune God

by Edward S. Jones

This selection was written by Pastor Edward S. Jones for inclusion in a Methodist Hymnal printed in 1849. It reflects upon the glory of God as three Persons in one being, the only source of salvation and creation. We must not as His creatures claim any glory for ourselves. This is why we are called to worship Him alone, since He alone is to be glorified by us as our chief end in life.

> To Father, Son, and Holy Ghost,
>   Who sweetly all agreed
> To save a world of sinners lost,
>   Eternal glory be.
>
> The God of mercy be adored,
>   Who calls our souls from death,
> Who saves by his redeeming word,
>   And all excelling Grace.
>
> Praise the God of our salvation;
>   Praise the father's boundless love;
> Praise the Lamb, our expiation;
>   Praise the Spirit from above,—
>
> Author of the new creation,—
>   Him by whom our spirits live;
> Undivided adoration
>   To the one Jehovah give.
>
> To Father, Son and Spirit,
>   Ascribe we equal glory;
> One Deity, in Persons Three
>   Let all thy works adore thee:
>
> As was from the beginning,
>   Glory to God be given,
> By all who know thy Name below,
>   And all thy hosts in heaven.

To thee be praise forever,
   Thou glorious King of kings:
Thy wondrous love and favor
   Each ransom'd spirit sings:

We'll celebrate thy glory,
   With all thy saints above,
And shout the joyful story
   Of thy redeeming love.

44

Sinners in the Hands of an Angry God

by Jonathan Edwards

A little over two hundred and fifty years ago, one of the most famous sermons in American history was delivered. "Sinners in the Hands of an Angry God," was preached by Jonathan Edwards (1703–1758) at a church in Enfield, Connecticut, on July 8, 1741. Edwards was a visiting pastor from a congregational church in Northampton, Massachusetts. He was asked to preach to the Enfield congregation by their local minister because the people at Enfield were particularly stubborn to the gospel message.

Professor John D. Currid from Grove City College writes the following concerning the significance of the now-famous sermon that Edwards delivered to the congregation at Enfield:

> The response of the Enfield congregation to the sermon was absolutely amazing. Before the sermon was finished, people were moaning, groaning, and crying out such things as 'What shall I do to be saved?' An eyewitness account by another minister reported that 'there was such a breathing of distress, and weeping, that the preacher (i.e., Edwards) was obliged to speak to the people and desire silence that he might be heard.

Through the years, Edwards has been unfairly criticized for this sermon because many think that its predominant teaching is the punishment of the ungodly in the fires of hell. While that image is certainly present in the sermon, it is not its prevailing image. On the contrary, as E.H. Cady points out, "The focus of the sermon is on the predicament of the sinner, how dreadfully he dangles just before he plunges to eternal agony, and how he has time to repent and be saved." Consequently, the purpose of the sermon was chiefly evangelistic—an attempt to present the true condition of fallen men, their precarious position in the world, and their need for the salvific work of Christ. Edwards's concept of hell fire was a tool to persuade men of their uncertain circumstance. As he said elsewhere, "the fears of hell tend to convince men of the hardness of their hearts."

Although "Sinners in the Hands of an Angry God" was delivered by Edwards over 250 years ago, its message is desperately required in our day of great ungodliness. We need revival. But, as in Edward's day, men must be made to feel the real nature and danger of sin. Their eyes must be opened to their perilous state as they stand uncovered before the Creator. If revival is to come in our beloved land, people will need to experience genuine Holy Spirit conviction regarding their true estate as guilty sinners.

Jonathan Edwards was a well-respected pastor and evangelist who was used by God to win thousands to Christ. Many historians credit Edwards as the primary leader of the great Spiritual Revival that swept the American Colonies during the 1730s and 1740s. History books often refer to this period as the first Great Awakening.

DEUTERONOMY 32:35
THEIR FOOT SHALL SLIDE IN DUE TIME

In this verse is threatened the vengeance of God on the wicked unbelieving Israelites, who were God's visible people, and who lived under the means of grace; but who, notwithstanding all God's wonderful works towards them, remained (as vs. 28) void of counsel, having no understanding in them. Under all the cultivations of heaven, they brought forth bitter and poisonous fruit; as in the two verses next preceding the text. The expression I have chosen for my text, *Their* foot shall slide *in due time*, seems to imply the following things, relating to the punishment and destruction to which these wicked Israelites were exposed.

1. That they were always exposed to *destruction*; as one that stands or walks in slippery places is always exposed to fall. This is implied in the manner of their destruction coming upon them, being represented by their foot sliding. The same is expressed in Psalm 73:18: "Surely thou didst set them in slippery places; thou castedst them down into destruction."

2. It implies that they were always exposed to sudden unexpected destruction. As he that walks in slippery places is every moment liable to fall, he cannot foresee one moment whether he shall stand or fall the next; and when he does fall, he falls at once without warning: Which is also expressed in Psalm 73:18–19, "Surely thou didst set them in slippery places; thou castedst them down into destruction: How are they brought into desolation as in a moment!"

3. Another thing implied is that they are liable to fall *of themselves*, without being thrown down by the hand of another; as he that stands or walks on slippery ground needs nothing but his own weight to throw him down.

4. That the reason why they are not fallen already, and do not fall now is only that God's appointed time is not come. For it is said, that

when that due time, or appointed time comes, *their* foot shall slide. Then they shall be left to fall, as they are inclined by their own weight. God will not hold them up in these slippery places any longer, but will let them go; and then, at that very instant, they shall fall into destruction; as he that stands on such slippery declining ground, on the edge of a pit, he cannot stand alone, when he is let go he immediately falls and is lost.

The observation from the words that I would now insist upon is this—"There is nothing that keeps wicked men at any one moment out of hell, but the mere pleasure of God." By the *mere* pleasure of God, I mean his *sovereign* pleasure, his arbitrary will, restrained by no obligation, hindered by no manner of difficulty, any more than if nothing else but God's mere will had in the least degree, or in any respect whatsoever, any hand in the preservation of wicked men one moment. The truth of this observation may appear by the following considerations.

1.   There is no lack of *power* in God to cast wicked men into hell at any moment. Men's hands cannot be strong when God rises up. The strongest have no power to resist him, nor can any deliver out of his hands. He is not only able to cast wicked men into hell, but he can most easily do it. Sometimes an earthly prince meets with a great deal of difficulty to subdue a rebel, who has found means to fortify himself, and has made himself strong by the numbers of his followers. But it is not so with God. There is no fortress that is any defense from the power of God. Though hand join in hand, and vast multitudes of God's enemies combine and associate themselves, they are easily broken in pieces. They are as great heaps of light chaff before the whirlwind; or large quantities of dry stubble before devouring flames. We find it easy to tread on and crush a worm that we see crawling on the earth; so it is easy for us to cut or singe a slender thread that any thing hangs by: thus easy is it for God, when he pleases, to cast his enemies down to hell. What are we, that we should think to stand before him, at whose rebuke the earth trembles, and before whom the rocks are thrown down?

2.   They *deserve* to be cast into hell; so that divine justice never stands in the way, it makes no objection against God's using his power at any moment to destroy them. Yea, on the contrary, justice calls aloud for an infinite punishment of their sins. Divine justice says of the tree that brings forth such grapes of Sodom, "Cut it down, why cumbereth it the ground?" (Luke 13:7). The sword of divine justice is every moment brandished over their heads, and it is nothing but the hand of arbitrary mercy, and God's mere will, that holds it back.

3.   They are already under a sentence of *condemnation* to hell. They do not only justly deserve to be cast down thither, but the sentence of the law of God, that eternal and immutable rule of righteousness that God has fixed between him and mankind, is gone out against them, and stands against them; so that they are bound over already to hell (John 3:18). "He that believeth not is condemned already." So that every unconverted man properly belongs to hell; that is his place; from thence he is (John 8:23). "Ye are from beneath." And thither he is bound; it is the place that justice, and God's word, and the sentence of his unchangeable law assign to him.

4.   They are now the objects of that very same anger and wrath of God, that is expressed in the torments of hell. And the reason why they do not go down to hell at each moment, is not because God, in whose power they are, is not then very angry with them; as he is with many miserable creatures now tormented in hell, who there feel and bear the fierceness of his wrath. Yea, God is a great deal more angry with great numbers that are now on earth: yea, doubtless, with many that are now in this congregation, who it may be are at ease, than he is with many of those who are now in the flames of hell.

So that it is not because God is unmindful of their wickedness, and does not resent it, that he does not let loose his hand and cut them off. God is not altogether such an one as themselves, though they may imagine him to be so. The wrath of God burns against them, their damnation does not slumber; the pit is prepared, the fire is made ready, the furnace is now hot, ready to receive them; the flames do now rage and glow. The glittering sword is whet, and held over them, and the pit hath opened its mouth under them.

5.   The *devil* stands ready to fall upon them, and seize them as his own, at what moment God shall permit him. They belong to him; he has their souls in his possession, and under his dominion. The scripture represents them as his goods (Luke 11:12). The devils watch them; they are ever by them at their right hand; they stand waiting for them, like greedy hungry lions that see their prey, and expect to have it, but are for the present kept back. If God should withdraw his hand, by which they are restrained, they would in one moment fly upon their poor souls. The old serpent is gaping for them; hell opens its mouth wide to receive them; and if God should permit it, they would be hastily swallowed up and lost.

6.   There are in the souls of wicked men those hellish *principles* reigning, that would presently kindle and flame out into hell fire, if it

were not for God's restraints. There is laid in the very nature of carnal men, a foundation for the torments of hell. There are those corrupt principles, in reigning power in them, and in full possession of them, that are the seeds of hell fire. These principles are active and powerful, exceeding violent in their nature, and if it were not for the restraining hand of God upon them, they would soon break out into numerous flaming corruptions. The same enmity against God rests in the hearts of souls that are already tormented in hell as it does in damned souls. The souls of the wicked are in scripture compared to the troubled sea (Isa. 57:20). For the present, God restrains their wickedness by his mighty power, as he does the raging waves of the troubled sea, saying, "Hitherto shalt thou come, but no further" but if God should withdraw that restraining power, it would soon carry all before it. Sin is the ruin and misery of the soul; it is destructive in its nature; and if God should leave it without restraint, there would need nothing else to make the soul perfectly miserable. The corruption of the heart of man is immoderate and boundless in its fury; and while wicked men live here, it is like fire pent up by God's restraints, whereas if it were let loose, it would set on fire the course of nature; and as the heart is now a sink of sin, so if sin was not restrained, it would immediately turn the soul into a fiery oven, or a furnace of fire and brimstone.

7. It is no security to wicked men for one moment, that there are no visible means of death at hand. It is no security to a natural man, that he is now in health, and that he does not see which way he should now immediately go out of the world by any accident, and that there is no visible danger in any respect in his circumstances. The manifold and continual experience of the world in all ages, shows this is no evidence that a man is not on the very brink of eternity, and that the next step will not be into another world. The unseen, unthought-of ways and means of persons going suddenly out of the world are innumerable and inconceivable. Unconverted men walk over the pit of hell on a rotten covering, and there are innumerable places in this covering so weak that they will not bear their weight, and these places are not seen. The arrows of death fly unseen at noon-day; the sharpest sight cannot discern them. God has so many different unsearchable ways of taking wicked men out of the world and sending them to hell, that there is nothing to make it appear that God needs to work a miracle, or go out of the ordinary course of his providence, to destroy any wicked man at any moment. All the means that there are of sinners going out of the world are so in God's hands, and so universally and absolutely subject

to his power and determination, that it does not depend on anything more than the mere will of God, whether sinners shall at any moment go to hell.

Albrecht Durer, The Four Horsemen of the Apocalypse, 1498.

8.   Natural men's prudence and care to preserve their own lives, or the care of others to preserve them, do not secure them a moment. To this, divine providence and universal experience do also bear testimony. There is this clear evidence that men's own wisdom is no security to them from death; that if it were otherwise we should see some difference between the wise and politic men of the world, and others, with

regard to their liableness to early and unexpected death: but how is it in fact? (Eccles. 2:16). "How dieth the wise man? even as the fool."

9. All wicked men's pains and *contrivance* which they use to escape hell, while they continue to reject Christ, and so remain wicked men, do not secure them from hell one moment. Almost every natural man that hears of hell, flatters himself that he shall escape it; he depends upon himself for his own security; he flatters himself in what he has done, in what he is now doing, or what he intends to do. Every one lays out matters in his own mind how he shall avoid damnation, and flatters himself that he contrives well for himself, and that his schemes will not fail. They hear indeed that there are but few saved, and that the greater part of men that have died heretofore are gone to hell; but each one imagines that he lays out matters better for his own escape than others have done. He does not intend to come to that place of torment; he says within himself, that he intends to take effectual care, and to order matters so for himself as not to fail.

But the foolish children of men miserably delude themselves in their own schemes, and in confidence in their own strength and wisdom; they trust in nothing but a shadow. The greater part of those who heretofore have lived under the same means of grace, and are now dead, are undoubtedly gone to hell; and it was not because they were not as wise as those who are now alive: it was not because they did not lay out matters as well for themselves to secure their own escape. If we could speak with them, and inquire of them, one by one, whether they expected, when alive, and when they used to hear about hell, ever to be the subjects of misery: we doubtless, should hear one and another reply, "No, I never intended to come here: I had laid out matters otherwise in my mind; I thought I would find a way out by a good scheme. I intended to take effectual care; but it came upon me unexpected; I did not look for it at that time, and in that manner; it came as a thief: Death outwitted me: God's wrath was too quick for me. Oh, my cursed foolishness! I was flattering myself, and pleasing myself with vain dreams of what I would do hereafter; and when I was saying, Peace and safety, then sudden destruction came upon me."

10. God has laid himself under *no obligation*, by any promise to keep any natural man out of hell one moment. God certainly has made no promises either of eternal life, or of any deliverance or preservation from eternal death, but what are contained in the covenant of grace, the promises that are given in Christ, in whom all the promises are yea and amen. But surely they have no interest in the promises of the covenant

of grace who are not the children of the covenant, who do not believe in any of the promises, and have no interest in the Mediator of the covenant.

So that, whatever some have imagined and pretended about promises made to natural men's earnest seeking and knocking, it is plain and manifest, that whatever pains a natural man takes in religion, whatever prayers he makes, till he believes in Christ, God is under no manner of obligation to keep him a moment from eternal destruction.

So that, thus it is that natural men are held in the hand of God, over the pit of hell; they have deserved the fiery pit, and are already sentenced to it; and God is dreadfully provoked, his anger is as great towards them as to those that are actually suffering the executions of the fierceness of his wrath in hell, and they have done nothing in the least to appease or abate that anger, neither is God in the least bound by any promise to hold them up one moment. The devil is waiting for them, hell is gaping for them, the flames gather and flash about them, and would fain lay hold on them, and swallow them up; the fire pent up in their own hearts is struggling to break out: and they have no interest in any Mediator. There are no means within reach that can be any security to them. In short, they have no refuge, nothing to take hold of; all that preserves them every moment is the mere arbitrary will, and uncovenanted, unobliged forbearance of an incensed God.

APPLICATION

The use of this awful subject may be for awakening unconverted persons in this congregation. This that you have heard is the case of every one of you that are out of Christ. That world of misery, that lake of burning brimstone, is extended abroad under you. There is the dreadful pit of the glowing flames of the wrath of God; there is hell's wide gaping mouth open; and you have nothing to stand upon, nor any thing to take hold of; there is nothing between you and hell but the air; it is only the power and mere pleasure of God that holds you up.

You probably are not sensible of this; you find you are kept out of hell, but do not see the hand of God in it; but look at other things, as the good state of your bodily constitution, your care of your own life, and the means you use for your own preservation. But indeed these things are nothing; if God should withdraw his hand, they would avail no more to keep you from falling, than the thin air to hold up a person that is suspended in it.

Your wickedness makes you as it were heavy as lead, and to tend downwards with great weight and pressure towards hell; and if God should let you go, you would immediately sink and swiftly plunge into the bottomless gulf, and your healthy constitution, and your own care and prudence, and best contrivance, and all your righteousness, would have no more influence to uphold you and keep you out of hell than a spider's web would have to stop a falling rock. Were it not for the sovereign pleasure of God, the earth would not bear you one moment; for you are a burden to it; the creation groans with you; the creature is made subject to the bondage of your corruption, not willingly; the sun does not willingly shine upon you to give you light to serve sin and Satan; the earth does not willingly yield her increase to satisfy your lusts; nor is it willingly a stage for your wickedness to be acted upon; the air does not willingly serve you for breath to maintain the flame of life in your vitals, while you spend your life in the service of God's enemies. God's creatures are good, and were made for men to serve God with, and do not willingly subserve to any other purpose, and groan when they are abused to purposes so directly contrary to their nature and end. And the world would spew you out, were it not for the sovereign hand of him who hath subjected it in hope. There are the black clouds of God's wrath now hanging directly over your heads, full of the dreadful storm, and big with thunder; and were it not for the restraining hand of God, it would immediately burst forth upon you. The sovereign pleasure of God, for the present, stays his rough wind; otherwise it would come with fury, and your destruction would come like a whirlwind, and you would be like the chaff of the summer threshing floor.

The wrath of God is like great waters that are dammed for the present; they increase more and more, and rise higher and higher, till an outlet is given; and the longer the stream is stopped, the more rapid and mighty is its course, when once it is let loose. It is true, that judgment against your evil works has not been executed hitherto; the floods of God's vengeance have been withheld; but your guilt in the mean time is constantly increasing, and you are every day treasuring up more wrath; the waters are constantly rising, and waxing more and more mighty; and there is nothing but the mere pleasure of God, that holds the waters back, that are unwilling to be stopped, and press hard to go forward. If God should only withdraw his hand from the floodgate, it would immediately fly open, and the fiery floods of the fierceness and wrath of God, would rush forth with inconceivable fury, and would come upon you with omnipotent power; and if your strength were ten thousand times greater than it is, yea, ten thousand times greater than the strength of the stoutest, sturdiest devil in hell, it would be nothing to withstand or endure it.

The bow of God's wrath is bent, and the arrow made ready on the string, and justice bends the arrow at your heart, and strains the bow, and it is nothing but the mere pleasure of God, and that of an angry God, without any promise or obligation at all, that keeps the arrow one moment from being made drunk with your blood. Thus all you that never passed under a great change of heart, by the mighty power of the Spirit of God upon your souls; all you that were never born again, and made new creatures, and raised from being dead in sin to a state of new, and before altogether unexperienced light and life, are in the hands of an angry God. However you may have reformed your life in many things, and may have had religious affections, and may keep up a form of religion in your families and closets, and in the house of God, it is nothing but his mere pleasure that keeps you from being this moment swallowed up in everlasting destruction. However unconvinced you may now be of the truth of what you hear, by and by you will be fully convinced of it. Those that are gone from being in the like circumstances with you, see that it was so with them; for destruction came suddenly upon most of them; when they expected nothing of it, and while they were saying, Peace and safety: now they see, that those things on which they depended for peace and safety, were nothing but thin air and empty shadows.

The God that holds you over the pit of hell, much as one holds a spider, or some loathsome insect over the fire, abhors you, and is dreadfully provoked: his wrath towards you burns like fire; he looks upon you as worthy of nothing else, but to be cast into the fire; he is of purer eyes than to bear to have you in his sight; you are ten thousand times more abominable in his eyes, than the most hateful venomous serpent is in ours. You have offended him infinitely more than ever a stubborn rebel did his prince; and yet it is nothing but his hand that holds you from falling into the fire every moment. It is to be ascribed to nothing else, that you did not go to hell last night; that you were permitted to awake again in this world, after you closed your eyes to sleep. And there is no other reason to be given, why you have not dropped into hell since you arose in the morning, but that God's hand has held you up. There is no other reason to be given why you have not gone to hell, since you have sat here in the house of God, provoking his pure eyes by your sinful wicked manner of attending his solemn worship. Yea, there is nothing else that is to be given as a reason why you do not this very moment drop down into hell.

O sinner! Consider the fearful danger you are in: it is a great furnace of wrath, a wide and bottomless pit, full of the fire of wrath, that you are held over in the hand of that God, whose wrath is provoked and incensed as much against you as against many of the damned in hell. You hang by a slender thread, with the flames of divine wrath flashing about it, and ready every moment to singe it, and burn it asunder; and you have no interest in any Mediator, and nothing to lay hold of to save yourself, nothing to keep off the flames of wrath, nothing of your own, nothing that you ever have done, nothing that you can do, to induce God to spare you one moment. And consider here more particularly,

1. Whose wrath it is: it is the wrath of the infinite God. If it were only the wrath of man, though it were of the most potent prince, it would be comparatively little to be regarded. The wrath of kings is very much dreaded, especially of absolute monarchs, who have the possessions and lives of their subjects wholly in their power, to be disposed of at their mere will (Prov. 20:2). "The fear of a king is as the roaring of a lion: Whoso provoketh him to anger, sinneth against his own soul." The subject that very much enrages an arbitrary prince is liable to suffer the most extreme torments that human art can invent, or human power can inflict. But the greatest earthly potentates in their greatest majesty and strength, and when clothed in their greatest terrors, are but feeble, despicable worms of the dust, in comparison of the great and almighty Creator and King of heaven and earth. It is but little that they can do, when most enraged, and when they have exerted the utmost of their fury. All the kings of the earth, before God, are as grasshoppers; they are nothing, and less than nothing: both their love and their hatred is to be despised. The wrath of the great King of kings, is much more terrible than theirs, as his majesty is greater. Luke 12:4– 5: "And I say unto you, My friends, Be not afraid of them that kill the body, and after that, have no more that they can do. But I will forewarn you whom you shall fear: fear him, which after he hath killed, hath power to cast into hell: yea, I say unto you, Fear him."

2. It is the fierceness of his wrath that you are exposed to. We often read of the fury of God, as in Isa. 59:18, "According to their deeds, accordingly he will repay fury to his adversaries." So Isa. 66:15: "For behold, the Lord will come with fire, and with his chariots like a whirlwind, to render his anger with fury, and his rebuke with flames of fire." And in many other places. So, in Rev. 19:15 we read of "the

wine press of the fierceness and wrath of Almighty God." The words are exceeding terrible. If it had only been said, "the wrath of God," the words would have implied that which is infinitely dreadful: but it is "the fierceness and wrath of God." The fury of God! The fierceness of Jehovah! Oh, how dreadful must that be! Who can utter or conceive what such expressions carry in them! But it is also "the fierceness and wrath of *Almighty* God." As though there would be a very great manifestation of his almighty power in what the fierceness of his wrath should inflict, as though omnipotence should be as it were enraged, and exerted, as men are wont to exert their strength in the fierceness of their wrath. Oh! then, what will be the consequence! What will become of the poor worms that shall suffer it! Whose hands can be strong? And whose heart can endure? To what a dreadful, inexpressible, inconceivable depth of misery must the poor creature be sunk who shall be the subject of this!

Consider this, you that are here present, that yet remain in an unregenerate state. That God will execute the fierceness of his anger implies that he will inflict wrath without any pity. When God beholds the ineffable extremity of your case, and sees your torment to be so vastly disproportioned to your strength, and sees how your poor soul is crushed, and sinks down, as it were, into an infinite gloom; he will have no compassion upon you, he will not forbear the executions of his wrath, or in the least lighten his hand; there shall be no moderation or mercy, nor will God then at all stay his rough wind; he will have no regard to your welfare, nor be at all careful lest you should suffer too much in any other sense, than only that you shall not *suffer beyond what strict justice requires*. Nothing shall be withheld, because it is so hard for you to bear. Ezek. 8:18: "Therefore will I also deal in fury: mine eye shall not spare, neither will I have pity; and though they cry in mine ears with a loud voice, yet I will not hear them." Now God stands ready to pity you; this is a day of mercy; you may cry now with some encouragement of obtaining mercy. But when once the day of mercy is past, your most lamentable and dolorous cries and shrieks will be in vain; you will be wholly lost and thrown away of God, as to any regard to your welfare. God will have no other use to put you to, but to suffer misery; you shall be continued in being to no other end; for you will be a vessel of wrath fitted to destruction; and there will be no other use of this vessel, but to be filled full of wrath. God will be so far from pitying you when you cry to him, that it is said he will only "laugh and mock" (Prov. 1:25–26,etc.).

How awful are those words, Isa. 63:3, which are the words of the great God. "I will tread them in mine anger, and will trample them in my fury, and their blood shall be sprinkled upon my garments, and I will stain all my raiment." It is perhaps impossible to conceive of words that carry in them greater manifestations of these three things, *viz.* contempt, and hatred, and fierceness of indignation. If you cry to God to pity you, he will be so far from pitying you in your doleful case, or showing you the least regard or favour, that instead of that, he will only tread you under foot. He will not only hate sin, he will hold each sinner in the utmost contempt: no place shall be thought fit for you, but under his feet to be trodden down as the mire of the streets. His hatred of rebellious sinners is both perfect and holy.

3.   The *misery* you are exposed to is that which God will inflict to that end, that he might show what that wrath of Jehovah is. God hath had it on his heart to show to angels and men, both how excellent his love is, and also how terrible his wrath is. Sometimes earthly kings have a mind to show how terrible their wrath is by the extreme punishments they would execute on those that would provoke them. Nebuchadnezzar, that mighty and haughty monarch of the Chaldean empire, was willing to show his wrath when enraged with Shadrach, Meshach, and Abednego; and accordingly gave orders that the burning fiery furnace should be heated seven times hotter than it was before; doubtless, it was raised to the utmost degree of fierceness that human art could raise it. But the great God is also willing to show his wrath, and magnify his awful majesty and mighty power in the extreme sufferings of his enemies. Rom. 9:22: "What if God, willing to show his wrath, and to make his power known, endured with much long-suffering the vessels of wrath fitted to destruction?" And seeing this is his design, and what he has determined, even to show how terrible the unrestrained wrath, the fury and fierceness of Jehovah is, he will do it to effect. There will be something accomplished and brought to pass that will be dreadful with a witness. When the great and angry God hath risen up and executed his awful vengeance on the poor sinner, and the wretch is actually suffering the infinite weight and power of his indignation, then will God call upon the whole universe to behold that awful majesty and mighty power that is to be seen in it. Isa. 33:12-14: "And the people shall be as the burnings of lime, as thorns cut up shall they be burnt in the fire. Hear ye that are far off, what I have done; and ye that are near, acknowledge my might. The sinners in Zion are afraid; fearfulness hath surprised the hypocrites ..."

Thus it will be with you that are in an unconverted state, if you continue in it; the infinite might, and majesty, and terribleness of the omnipotent God shall be magnified upon you, in the ineffable strength of your torments. You shall be tormented in the presence of the holy angels, and in the presence of the Lamb; and when you shall be in this state of suffering, the glorious inhabitants of heaven shall go forth and look on the awful spectacle, that they may see what the wrath and fierceness of the Almighty is; and when they have seen it, they will fall down and adore that great power and majesty. Isa. 66:23–24: "And it shall come to pass, that from one new moon to another, and from one Sabbath to another, shall all flesh come to worship before me, saith the Lord. And they shall go forth and look upon the carcasses of the men that have transgressed against me; for their worm shall not die, neither shall their fire be quenched, and they shall be an abhorring unto all flesh."

4. It is *everlasting* wrath. It would be dreadful to suffer this fierceness and wrath of Almighty God one moment; but you must suffer it for all eternity. There will be no end to this exquisite horrible misery. When you look forward, you shall see forever a boundless duration before you, which will swallow up your thoughts and amaze your soul; and you will absolutely despair of ever having any deliverance, any end, any mitigation, any rest at all. You will know certainly that you must wear out long ages, millions of millions of ages, in wrestling and conflicting with this almighty merciless vengeance; and then when you have so done, when so many ages have actually been spent by you in this manner, you will know that your misery will never end. So that your punishment will indeed be infinite. Oh, who can express what the state of a soul in such circumstances is! All that we can possibly say about it gives but a very feeble, faint representation of it; it is inexpressible and inconceivable: For "who knows the power of God's anger?"

How dreadful is the state of those that are daily and hourly in the danger of this great wrath and infinite misery! But this is the dismal case of every soul in this congregation that has not been born again, however moral and strict, sober and religious, they may otherwise be. Oh that you would consider it, whether you be young or old! There is reason to think that there are many in this congregation now hearing this discourse that will actually be the subjects of this very misery to all eternity. We know not who they are, or in what seats they sit, or what thoughts they now have. It may be they are now at ease, and hear all these things without much disturbance, and are now flattering themselves that they are not the persons, promising themselves that they shall escape. If we knew that there was one person, and but one, in the whole congregation, that was to be the subject of this misery, what an awful thing would it be to think of! If we knew who it was, what an awful sight would it be to see such a person! How might all the rest of the congregation lift up a lamentable and bitter cry over him! But, alas! instead of one, how many is it likely will remember this discourse in hell? And it would be a wonder if some that are now present should not be in hell in a very short time, even before this year is out. And it would be no wonder if some persons that now sit here in some seats of this meeting-house, in health, quiet and secure, should be there before tomorrow morning. Those of you that finally continue in a natural condition, that shall keep out of hell longest will be there in a little time!

Your damnation does not slumber; it will come swiftly, and, in all probability, very suddenly upon many of you. You have reason to wonder why you are not already in hell. It is doubtless the case that some whom you have seen and known, that never deserved hell more than you, have already been condemned before the judgment seat of Christ. Their case is past all hope; they are crying in extreme misery and perfect despair; but here you are in the land of the living and in the house of God, and have an opportunity to obtain salvation. What would not those poor damned hopeless souls give for one day's opportunity such as you now enjoy! A free and full pardon now exists. You must ask Jesus Christ to give you a new heart, a heart of faith!

And now you have an extraordinary opportunity, a day wherein Christ has thrown the door of mercy wide open, and stands in calling and crying with a loud voice to poor sinners; a day wherein many are flocking to him, and pressing into the kingdom of God. Many are daily coming from the east, west, north, and south; many that were very lately in the same miserable condition that you are in, are now in a happy state, with their hearts filled with love to him who has loved them, and washed them from their sins in his own blood, and rejoicing in hope of the glory of God. How awful is it to be left behind at such a day! To see so many others feasting, while you are pining and perishing! To see so many rejoicing and singing for joy of heart, while you have cause to mourn for sorrow of heart, and howl for vexation of spirit! How can you rest one moment in such a condition? Are not your souls as precious as the souls of the people at Suffield, where they are flocking from day to day to Christ?

Are there not many here who have lived long in the world, and are not to this day born again? and so are aliens from the commonwealth of Israel, and have done nothing ever since they have lived but treasure up wrath against the day of wrath? Oh, sirs, your case, in an especial manner, is extremely dangerous. Your guilt and hardness of heart is extremely great. Do you not see how generally persons of your years are passed over and left, in the present remarkable and wonderful dispensation of God's mercy? You had need to consider yourselves and awake thoroughly out of sleep. You cannot bear the fierceness and wrath of the infinite God. And you, young men, and young women, will you neglect this precious season which you now enjoy, when so many others of your age are renouncing all youthful vanities, and flocking to Christ? You especially have now an extraordinary opportunity; but if you neglect it, it will soon be with you as with those persons who spent all the precious days of youth in sin, and are now come to such a dreadful pass in blindness and hardness. And you, children, who are unconverted, do not you know that you are going down to hell, to bear the dreadful wrath of that God, who is now angry with you every day and every night? Will you be content to be the children of the devil, when so many other children in the land are converted, and are become the holy and happy children of the King of kings? Do you want to be adopted by a loving Saviour?

And let every one that is yet out of Christ, and hanging over the pit of hell, whether they be old men and women, or middle aged, or young people, or little children, now harken to the loud calls of God's word and providence. This acceptable year of the Lord, a day of such great favour to some, will doubtless be a day of as remarkable vengeance to others. Men's hearts harden, and their guilt increases apace at such a day as this, if they neglect their souls; and never was there so great danger of such persons being given up to hardness of heart and blindness of mind. God seems now to be hastily gathering in his elect in all parts of the land; and probably the greater part of adult persons that ever shall be saved, will be brought in now in a little time, and that it will be as it was on the great out-pouring of the Spirit upon the Jews in the apostles' days; the election will obtain, and the rest will be blinded. If this should be the case with you, you will eternally curse this day, and will curse the day that ever you was born, to see such a season of the pouring out of God's Spirit, and will wish that you had died and gone to hell before you had seen it. Now undoubtedly it is, as it was in the days of John the Baptist, the axe is in an extraordinary manner laid at the root of the trees, that every tree which brings not forth good fruit, may be hewn down and cast into the fire.

Therefore, let every one that is out of Christ now awake and fly from the wrath to come. The wrath of Almighty God is now undoubtedly hanging over a great part of this congregation. Let every one fly out of Sodom: "Haste and escape for your lives, look not behind you, escape to the mountain, lest you be consumed."

❦ Comprehension Questions

1. It is often said that "the truth is hard to bear." How does this comment apply to the sermon you just read?

2. Do you think that Jonathan Edwards would consider the sin of pride to be a major hindrance to the work of the gospel in the lives of people? If so, why?

3. Has your view of hell changed after reading this sermon?

4. It was not uncommon for Puritan preachers of early America to preach for two to three hours each Sabbath day. Do you think that modern American Christians would have the patience or commitment to accept this style of preaching today? Please explain your answer.

45 The Sinking of the Titanic

by John J. Floherty

The ship that cannot sink—such was the bold advertisement for the luxury steamship *Titanic* before it sailed on its maiden voyage across the Atlantic in April 1912. The largest, the fastest, the safest passenger vessel ever built by man! And truly she was a wonder of the sea: the queen of ships. Yet the name Titanic has become a symbol of tragedy.

A dozen men sat around an expansive teakwood table on which there was a confusion of papers, blueprints, and drawings. On panelled walls hung paintings of ships old and new and portraits of stern-faced men who had been personages in the world of shipping.

The wall at one end of the room was occupied by a large map of the North Atlantic. It was interlaced with red lines on which were mounted here and there tiny flags bearing numbers. Beneath the map stood a corpulent and shiny terrestrial globe.

The chairman of the board was speaking: "…and furthermore, gentlemen, the prestige of the company will be greatly enhanced by the operation of such a ship—the largest, the fastest, and the safest passenger vessel ever built by man. We must keep step with the times. The traveling public demands better and pleasanter facilities, and greater safety, than they have enjoyed heretofore. True, she will cost a large sum—seven million dollars, to be exact—but if we are fortunate enough to be blessed with fine weather on her maiden crossing, I have every reason to believe she will hang up a record that will be worth a million, yes, several million dollars, in publicity—that will make her the most popular ship afloat. That, gentlemen, means dividends!"

One of the directors, a small elderly man near the end of the table, interrupted. "May I ask, Mr. Chairman," he said quietly, "how many persons will this vessel accommodate?"

"Passengers and crew, approximately three thousand," the chairman replied.

"And may I ask further," continued the director, "if she will have lifeboats to accommodate that number?"

The chairman was silent a moment, then he frowned and answered sharply, "She is a lifeboat, my dear sir, a gigantic unsinkable lifeboat that will conquer any gale, and in case of collision in which one or several of her compartments are flooded, she will still float and land her passengers safely. Her fire-detection and alarm system and her fire-fighting equipment are the most complete that ever have been installed in a vessel. In fact, if I were aboard and disaster overtook her, I would stick to the ship rather than take to a boat." The chairman beamed with pride and the directors nodded their approval, all but the little man who had asked questions. He just raised an eyebrow.

The keel of the great ship was laid. It had a length of four city blocks and, like a forest of steel, her giant frame grew tall and strong. Her decks and superstructure mounted tier on tier until they were as high as a six-story building. Riveting hammers buzzed day and night like cicadas in late summer. The snorting of donkey engines, the clang of steel, the thud of sledge hammers, the shouts of sweat-stained men sent up a mighty chorus glorifying the advent of a new creation. Cranes swung their long necks hither and yon, bearing plates of steel that soon enveloped the ship's gaunt skeleton. Little by little, chaos gave way to order, confusion bowed to beauty, until one day a shipwright with pride in the fruit of his labor exclaimed, "Ain't she a sweetheart!"

Launching day! The birth of a queen was announced in headlines throughout two continents. The bursting of a champagne bottle on the bow of the ship was a signal that was to open a new era in transatlantic shipping. The dreams of daring men had taken concrete form that would beget more dreams of greater ships to come. To the blare of bands and the cheers of a great throng, the flag-bedecked vessel moved majestically down the ways and curtsied to the water as she entered. Then and there the *Titanic* was proclaimed queen of merchant ships!

A few months at the fitting-out dock where she received an extensive beauty treatment in preparation for her wedding with the sea. Then to Southampton for the great day—the sailing day of her maiden voyage.

The gathering at the dock of friends and well-wishers is a custom as old as shipping itself. It is a relic of the period when a transatlantic voyage was a great and often perilous adventure. In the days of the packet ships, and indeed in the early days of steam, the dock was lined with weeping relatives and friends as a ship moved out into the stream. In those days, there was no radio or other means of communication with the shore save the entries in the logs of arriving ships that might have sighted certain vessels. Once beyond the horizon, the departing ship was hidden behind the dark curtain of uncertainty sometimes for weeks at a time. Too often, the weeks dragged into weary months until all hope had vanished. The roster of noble ships that disappeared without trace was appalling. News-gathering facilities were sparse; ship-owners were uncommunicative; newspapers carried meager items, usually statements that such and such a vessel, long overdue, had been listed as "lost." Although it was normally certain that many of the vessels that failed to make port during the spring and early summer were victims of ice, mention of that fact was carefully avoided.

Ever since man first put out to sea, it has been customary to give a new vessel a rousing send-off on the occasion of her maiden voyage, even though the music and merrymaking were mingled with tears and foreboding.

As the *Titanic* with 2,218 souls on board pulled away from her Southampton dock, a cheer went up from the crowd that had come to bid her passengers and crew Godspeed. The cheer was soon punctuated with shouts of alarm. The turning propellers of the *Titanic* created an irresistible suction that wrenched the nearby steamship *New York* away from her berth. Her breast lines and spring lines snapped with gunshot reports. Soon adrift and without power, the smaller liner swung almost under the bow of the *Titanic*. Quick action on both vessels averted disaster, with but a few inches to spare. The sailors on the dockside shook their heads. One of them growled, "It's an omen, sure as you live!"

Bellowing three blasts from her whistle, when the crisis had passed, the great ship squared away for the English Channel and the Atlantic.

The first day at sea filled the passengers with nervous activity. They roamed all over the ship like tourists in a strange city. The chief steward was stormed with requests for seats at such and such a table in the dining saloon. The deck steward was harried by those who wanted deck chairs on the portside which on a western passage gets the afternoon sun. Deck quoits, shuffleboard, and incessant promenading were all in full swing.

Then gradually in all parts of the ship—saloon, second class, and steerage—men, women, and children took on a holiday mood that reminded the British passengers of Margate and the Americans of Coney Island. The great size and easy motion of the ship caused many to exclaim, "It is hard to realize you are not in a fine hotel." In fact, there was not a passenger aboard who gave a thought to the treachery of the sea.

That evening, the sun went down under a canopy of crimson and gold. A mile to starboard, a British ship, bowing to the gentle swell, slipped off into the gathering darkness. By ones and twos, and then by whole platoons, lights flashed through the hurrying liner. From an orchestra in the main saloon, the swaying rhythms of the "Blue Danube" filtered through to the deck. From the steerage an accordion huffed and puffed a lively polka.

Men and women in evening clothes lounged in little groups. Tweedy travelers continued their incessant promenades. Dowagers and debutantes, the prominent and the unknown, all contributed to the babbling din of conversation, music, and laughter. The pattern of life on a luxury liner was established before her first day at sea was ended.

The third day out was Sunday. From horizon to horizon there was not a cloud in the sky. Save for a gentle swell from the south, the sea was calm and unruffled. The soft breath of spring raised the spirits of passengers and crew. Winter with its ice and snow and chilly winds seemed to have departed.

Shortly before noon in the wireless shack close to the bridge, one of the ship's wireless operators was busily engaged in doing certain paperwork that had to be completed by the end of his watch. Through the phones clamped to his ears came the signal of the nearby *Californian*; she was calling *Titanic*. Her operator tapped out in Morse code a message referring to ice. So deeply was the *Titanic* operator engrossed in his work, he paid little attention to it. At that time of the year such messages were by no means rare. Besides, the weather was clear and lookouts were posted. On the stroke of eight bells he gathered up his papers and was relieved by another operator.

At 1:45 p.m. the steamship *Baltic* radioed, "Heavy ice in steamer tracks." A copy of the message was sent to the captain at once. Captain Smith, making his usual tour of the ship, was on the promenade deck when the message was handed to him. He read it carefully, then looking around, he saw the chairman and managing director of the line chatting with a small group of passengers. Handing the official the message, the captain continued his tour. The director read the message and amiably told his listeners that they might have an opportunity to see one or more majestic icebergs during the evening. The passengers were delighted at the prospect of such an unusual spectacle.

That evening, the palatial dining room was a scene of gaiety and gracious living. Out-of-season delicacies, wines of rare vintage, epicurean specialties of a ten-thousand-dollar-a-year chef were faultlessly served by an army of highly trained stewards. Soft music complemented conversation.

At the captain's table, the high altar on shipboard, the managing director held forth on the superlative features of the ship, her tremendous horsepower capable of driving her at a speed unheard of in passenger vessels. Even with two boilers cold, she was logging off the knots at a rate that promised a record run.

Captain Smith, a sailor of long and wide experience with the treacheries of the North Atlantic, pulled his beard, frowned and remained silent. Even a captain may not cross a managing director; captains must live. With one ear on the table talk and the other on the propeller's revolutions, the dinner was to him an ordeal. Occasionally, he glanced through a nearby porthole and was heartened by a cold but clear sky and the shimmering of several stars that during many a night's vigil had become old friends of his. Fog, fortunately, was not one of his worries!

After dinner few of the cabin passengers went on deck; the night was unpleasantly cold. In the second-class quarters, stateroom lights flickered out here and there. The steerage was almost in darkness; its occupants, even at sea, lived up to their everyday maxim, "early to bed and early to rise."

At ten o'clock, the first officer took over the bridge. He found entries—in the rough log—of several warnings against ice from other ships. He placed extra lookouts with instruction to be more alert than usual. Stepping out on the starboard wing, he noticed that a slight haze was gathering and that the less brilliant stars had disappeared. A glance over the side revealed the rollicking bow wave all flecked with phosphorescence. "Hm-m," he muttered, "twenty knots or I'm a Dutchman!" For the first time he doubted the captain's wisdom in maintaining such speed under the circumstances, but then he remembered the managing director and the publicity satellites hankering for a record or for at least an unusually fast passage.

Shortly after ten o'clock a call came in from the *Californian* stating she was hemmed in by heavy ice. It was handed to the captain and later was sent to the bridge. Still the great ship tore along at express speed. The officer's first impulse on receiving the message was to ring for low speed; then he remembered that in the cabin immediately abaft the bridge a small group, in which were two company officials, was enjoying the captain's hospitality. He recalled also that Captain Smith was never unmindful of the safety of his ship. He decided to wait and hope. He looked at the ship's clock on the bulkhead: it was 11:40.

The phone rang, "Iceberg dead ahead!" There was horror in the voice of the lookout in the crow's-nest. The officer sprang to the engine telegraph and signalled Full Astern, shouting to the quartermaster at the wheel, "Starboard Hard!" Then he released the master control of the automatic doors that divided the ship into sixteen water-tight compartments.

At the first quiver of the reversed propellers, Captain Smith rushed to the bridge. Even as he entered he could see the ghostly gray mass of ice bearing down on the swinging bow of the vessel with scarcely a boat's length between them. Floating ice was already drumming on the stern and bow of the ship. In spite of the restraining effect of the engines, the liner retained considerable momentum; it takes time to stop fifty thousand tons, once it gets in motion. The captain and all hands on the bridge braced themselves for the shock. The vessel did not strike the berg full on; she rather jostled it with a shouldering blow that made her lurch a little. The impact was scarcely felt throughout the ship but it was followed by a prolonged crunching that seemed to travel aft for nearly half her length. Ice chips, sheared from the berg, avalanched on the foredeck. There was no panic; rather an uneasy curiosity. Bedroom stewards were showered with questions—"What is the matter?" "Why have we stopped?" "Has something gone wrong?" "Is there any danger?" The answer was always the same, "Don't know, sir—or madam—but we'll be under way presently."

Only below decks in the engine room and fireroom was it known that the ship had received a mortal wound. Through a ragged gash three hundred feet long, torn open by an underwater spur projecting from the iceberg, the water rushed into the doomed vessel in a devastating flood. The bridge was notified of conditions below. Captain Smith, although shocked by the tragic turn of events, upheld the traditions of the sea. Cool and deliberate, he gave his orders in a voice devoid of alarm but bursting with authority. His first order was to send out a wireless call for assistance, the dreaded CQD. Simultaneously he ordered rockets fired from the foredeck.

It was then fate played its most tragic trick. Beyond the horizon, almost in sight, steamed the *Californian*, a little more than a half-hour run from where the *Titanic* was already sinking. Her single wireless operator had shut down his key and turned in. While he slept, the frantic calls from the *Titanic* filled the airwaves, "CQD!—CQD!—TITANIC—WE ARE SINKING!—LAT 41.26 N—LON 50.14 W—CQD!—SOS!" The message pleaded over and over. The *Californian*, oblivious of the tragedy, sailed on. However, several ships, some of them hundreds of miles away heard the call, changed their courses and headed at top speed for the scene of the disaster.

At twelve midnight, the passengers now aware of the ship's plight, crowded corridors and decks. There was no panic. Through the murmur of subdued voices came now and then the wailing of children snatched from sleep and hurriedly dressed. The orchestra played lively tunes with scarcely a pause between them. An unruffled passenger spoke words of encouragement to various bewildered people, "Nothing to worry about. She *can't* sink, you know!"

On the bridge Captain Smith, still in mess jacket and gold braid, gave orders and listened to reports. His voice was as steady, his manner as unruffled as though he were waiting with his officers at noon to "shoot the sun." The third officer entered. "Making water fast, sir. I'm afraid she's done for," he said quietly.

"We'll hope for the best, Mister," replied the captain. "Bear in hand with the boats and remember there are many green men in the crew."

At 12:20, the passengers got their first inkling of danger. From the boat deck above slowly descended the gaunt form of a lifeboat silhouetted against the hazy sky; it was a forbidding omen. It was followed by another and another until several were lined outside the rail of the promenade deck. Passengers watched in silent horror. It was as if they were witnessing a weird stage drama as spectators rather than actors.

Rockets! From somewhere topside the fiery missiles snaked skyward to be lost in the overhanging mist. The first officer shouldered through the crowd. Several passengers attempted to question him. "Not now, not now!" was his only reply. He halted abreast number one boat and climbed the rail, holding onto a stanchion for support. Looking down on the terrified assembly, he spoke calmly and with firm voice. "As a precaution, passengers will enter the boats. There is nothing to fear. The sea is calm and help is already on the way. Women and children first!"

Wives clung appealingly to husbands. Puzzled children gripped more tightly the hands of parents. No one moved. The boats, hanging on slender falls thirty feet above the black water, were symbols of doom.

The deck underfoot was as stable as it had been in Southampton Harbor. The lights were bright. The ship rode high. The lively tunes played by the orchestra had the usual rhythm and spirit. Officers and crew went about their duties as if the tragic affair were an everyday occurrence. No one could believe that, even then, the huge ship was actually sinking under them.

During great crises human beings often act like sheep; many follow where one leads.

A sailor in number one boat broke the spell of fear that gripped the crowd. "Step lively, girls!" he shouted heartily. "All Aboar-r-rd!" with a rising inflection in the best manner of a train conductor. In spite of the tension, an underlying touch of hysteria rippled the throng. A woman with a twelve-year-old daughter said, "Well, here goes!" and stepped to the opening in the rail. Mother and daughter were helped aboard the lifeboat. Others followed. An elderly woman, wife of one of America's great merchants, decided to stay with her husband. Another woman refused to leave the ship without her dog, then confined to the ship's kennels. A silver-haired old lady coaxed and pleaded with the women, "Do as the officer says, dearies!" Some refused, others tearfully stepped into the boat. For the length of the deck the same scene was being enacted in a dozen places. A few men tried to board some of the boats but were held back by the ship's people.

Number one boat was lowered while it had only half its registered complement; another was dangerously overloaded. A boat near the stern got out of control; it fell and dangled on the forward falls like a dead fish.

At sea, while there is life there is discipline. Two bells—one o'clock.

The time was struck on the ship's bell as it had been each half-hour since the vessel was put in commission. Now, an hour and forty minutes after she struck the ice, the ship was perceptibly down by the head; she had also a list to starboard. Even a landsman could tell that her life was ebbing. Her slight but easy roll to the swell was now uncertain and labored as thousands of tons of water slowly washed from side to side in her damaged compartments.

Boat after boat, loaded to the gunwales, was lowered, the huddled passengers frantic with fright. Some with green men at the oars were having difficulty amid floating ice. Others rowed away aimlessly from the sinking vessel. At 1:30, the passengers left on board were showing signs of panic. On several occasions men, brushing women aside, fought to get in the boats; they were repulsed. A group of a dozen or more fear-crazed passengers rushed one of the boats and were prevented from taking possession of it by an officer who fired several shots over their heads. Everywhere was poignant drama; husbands picked up their frenzied wives bodily and placed them in the boats. An elderly couple stood with arms clasped around each other and refused to enter a boat. "Let the younger people live!" they said. "We've lived our lives." A bewildered child, clutching a doll, got separated from its parents. Someone picked it up and placed it in a boat. In the confusion the doll fell overboard. A crew member rescued it later.

The head of one of New York's proudest families, a man of great wealth and prestige, stood alone and calmly watched the frenzy of the crowd struggling for places in the few remaining boats. His keen mind told him too plainly that many were to die. There were still hundreds of people on the deck for whom there would be no room in the boats. Crew members passed out ill-fitting cork life jackets that were snatched away by madly eager hands. He made no move to secure one. He had placed his young wife in a lifeboat and with a farewell kiss stepped back and waited for whatever might come.

Social distinctions had vanished. First class, second class, and steerage were now whipped together like ingredients in a pudding. Jewelled fingers clasped the leathery hand of a Yarmouth fisherman; a beshawled woman sobbed on the shirt front of a railroad vice-president.

In a corner of the library, a leading dramatist, an artist of world fame, one of Britain's foremost publishers, and an American millionaire book collector sat around a table. Bracing themselves to keep from sliding about, they discussed the situation calmly. From the deck outside came a babel of anguished voices. Screams from terrified women, hoarse shouts of crazed men, the cries of children rose and fell like gusts in a storm.

"Poor fools!" said the dramatist, rising, "They do not seem to understand that this is the moment of their deliverance." As he spoke, the lights dimmed and the ship's head seemed to snuggle more deeply like a tired sleeper into a pillow. He made his way with difficulty to the door that led out on deck. In the dim twilight of the flickering bulbs, the milling passengers, wearing cumbersome life jackets, looked like bloated inhabitants from another planet. The instincts of the dramatist prevailed. "What a scene for a second act!" he exclaimed.

In the wireless shack high on the hurricane deck, the two wireless operators took turns at the key. For time on end they had pounded out the same appeal for help. The ship was now at a crazy angle. Her forecastle deck was awash; her giant propellers were high above the water, powerless as the wings of a dead gull.

From out of the darkness came pandemonium—shrieks and wails and shouts, the splashing of oars, the thud of floating ice against the boats, commands and curses, prayers and piteous calls for help mingled with the rhythmic beat of the orchestra. Along the vessel's rail crowded hundreds of the doomed. Below them the dimly lit water was dotted with the heads of struggling men and women who had leaped or fallen overboard. Here and there floated lifeless forms supported by grotesque cork jackets.

Panic had spent itself: the storm of voices had died to a whisper. Tears had dried; on every face was the dull look of resignation. The orchestra, now a bit tremulous, abandoned the livelier harmonies for hymns: "Rock of Ages," "Onward, Christian Soldiers" seemed to act as a sedative on the distracted throng. Many sought solitude; others left the deck for the seclusion of their cabins. If death must come, it was better in peace than in the turmoil of drowning hundreds.

At 2:15, the shudder of a collapsing bulkhead passed through the ship. Her foredeck sank deep under the surface. Ice drummed against the forward superstructure. The stern of the vessel was now high out of water. A foothold on the decks was no longer possible without a hand grip on some stationary object. The masts leaned forward like slender poplars before a gale. One of the stacks as large as a railroad tunnel, weakened by the shock of impact with the berg, toppled with a terrifying crash. Strange rumblings ran through the bowels of the vessel as thousands of tons of water tumbled into newly opened cavities.

The fires, long since drawn from under the boilers, lay in glowing pyramids on the steel deckplates of the stokehold. The inrushing water converted the red hot heaps of coals into seething volcanoes of steam and noxious gases, and sent an overwhelming stench throughout the vessel.

Heroes are born of crises. During the awful period of hopeless waiting there were many acts of heroism and self-sacrifice. A tall middle-aged man, clad only in shirt and trousers, saw a woman standing dejectedly at the rail. Her blouse hung in tatters from naked shoulders, having been torn in one of the mad rushes for a boat. "I say!" he exclaimed in a broad British accent, "Where is your life jacket?" The woman gave him a dazed look and shook her head. Without another word he threw off the life preserver he was wearing and fastened it securely around her. "There!" he said, "that's better!" and walked away.

A young woman, daughter of a diplomat, wearing a Russian sable coat, spied a sweet-faced old lady sitting huddled on the deck, her back against the superstructure. The frail figure shuddered as the bitter cold breeze of early morning chilled the marrow of her ancient bones. "Can I help you?" the younger woman asked. "No, my dear!" replied the old lady in a quavering but spirited voice. "Only God can help me now." In a jiffy the rich fur of which a queen might be proud was tenderly wrapped around the protesting old lady. "I won't be needing it," said the girl cheerfully as she replaced her life jacket. "Good luck!"

A sailor, spying a battered Bible being trampled under panicky feet, rescued it and reverently placed it on a deck chair.

With each passing minute, now, the ship assumed a more critical angle. Forward the rail stanchions were already submerged; deck chairs were afloat and drifting away from the ship; boat falls and their heavy block hanging from the davits smashed against the sides of the vessel like so many giant black-jacks. The weary orchestra went into the simple air of "Nearer My God to Thee." There was no attempt at harmonizing; the instruments played in soft unison. Presently in tremulous voice a woman picked up the refrain. A disheveled man joined in and soon a dozen derelicts who knew well how prophetic were the words, sang quaveringly.

> Nearer my God to Thee
> Nearer to Thee
> E'en though it be a cross...

The stern of the ship lurched upward, a swell rolled in on the deck and curled, seething, along the superstructure to where the remaining passengers were huddled. Around the ship the water was boiling white, as air under heavy pressure escaped from a thousand vents. The inclination of the deck was now as steep as the roof of a house. Passengers in groups lay flat and clutched each other to keep from sliding. Scores leaped over the side only to be knocked unconscious as their clumsy life jackets struck the water.

At 2:20, the part of the ship still above water suddenly assumed an almost vertical position. The helpless victims slid downward as if through a chute. There were a few last cries and prayers as the cold Atlantic closed over the great vessel.

For nearly five hours after the first frenzied SOS, Captain Rostrom paced the bridge of the passenger ship *Carpathia*. On receiving word of the *Titanic's* plight he laid a course for the sinking ship, then about a hundred miles away, and called on the engine department for the last ounce of speed. Again and again, he went to the speaking tube that led to the engine room. "Can't you do better?" he pleaded. "Just a few more revolutions! Lives are in danger!" More speed meant more steam. In the insufferable heat of the stokehold, sweat-stained men, naked to the waist and black as Hottentots from coal dust, strained at shovels and slicing bars, feeding and trimming the fires. Plunging through the darkness into the ice-infested area was an ordeal that tired the souls of officers and crew. Captain Rostrom at an open window on the bridge peered ahead into the gloom, thanking God for every minute that passed safely. From the crow's-nest high on the foremast came the voice of the lookout, "Floating ice ahead!" Without taking his eyes from the path of the ship, the captain ordered half speed.

Eight bells—four o'clock—had just struck. The voice of the lookout was heard again, "Boats two points off starboard bow!" The engine telegraph rang for slow.

Aboard ship, as ashore, there is a grapevine through which information seeps, no matter how carefully guarded, and spreads into every cranny of the vessel. Although no announcement had been made, passengers on the *Carpathia* were soon aware that they were about to witness the final act of one of the sea's great tragedies. Many had made a night of it; lights were bright throughout the ship; there was indeed a cheerful air of expectancy.

As the vessel nosed cautiously through broken ice to where the drifting boats were scattered, faint cries were heard. Boats were lowered from the *Carpathia* and the search for those who were still afloat was begun. At 4:10 A.M., the first castaway was taken aboard. The *Titanic's* boats, some of them crowded far beyond capacity, others almost empty, were towed to the side of the *Carpathia*.

For several hours, rescue boats combed the sea, selecting the quick from the dead. Some of the rescued were unconscious when lifted from the water; others babbled vaguely. A woman, still clutching the photograph of a child, was reciting nursery rhymes; like many others, consciousness did not leave her until she was safely in the ship.

Before the gruesome task was completed, the pink of dawn was broadcast over the eastern sky. Its radiance crowded the darkness from the ocean, revealing the killer. It was a small berg, as bergs go, but it was firm and hard as granite. It was crystalline blue-white with none of the spongy pallor of the older bergs that sometimes traipse the northern seas for years after leaving the mother glaciers. From a thousand facets on its crags it flung back insolently the sun's rays. Deep under water it carried its concealed weapon, the giant dagger of flint-hard ice that gave the *Titanic* her death wound.

Passengers and refugees on the *Carpathia* stared, awed by its treacherous beauty. A man who had lost his wife shook his fist at the berg. "Murderer!" he shouted hoarsely.

A careful tally was made of the survivors. They totaled 711; 103 were women and 53 were children. One thousand, five hundred and seven lives had been sacrificed on an altar of ice!

❦ *Comprehension Questions*

1. How many passengers travelled on the *Titanic*?

2. In what manner did the ship's orchestra attempt to calm and minister to the panic stricken passengers as the ship was sinking? Did this effort help?

3. How did the captain of the *Titanic* react when he knew that his ship was mortally wounded?

4. One of the most interesting and ironic aspects of this true story is that the news media, as well as the ship owners, stated that the *Titanic* was built so strongly that "even God could not sink the *Titanic*." Do you think that the owners of the *Titanic* learned a profound lesson regarding the folly of questioning the Lord's power? Please explain your answer.

5. How do you think that you would have reacted to the news of the ship's peril if you were a passenger? If you had children on board, what would you tell them as the ship began to sink?

46 *Letter to His Children*

by John Rodgers

Mr. John Rodgers, minister of the gospel in London, was the first martyr in Queen Mary's reign, and was burnt at Smithfield, February 14, 1554. His wife with nine small children and one at her breast, followed him to the stake; with which sorrowful fight he was not in the least daunted, but with wonderful patience died courageously for the gospel of Jesus Christ. Some few days before his death, he wrote the following advice to his children.

Give ear my children to my words
    Whom God hath dearly bought,
Lay up his laws within your heart,
    and print them in your thoughts.

I leave you here a little book
    for you to look upon,
That you may see your father's face
    when he is dead and gone:

Who for the hope of heavenly things,
    While he did here remain,
Gave over all his golden year,
    to prison and to pain.

Where I, among my iron bands,
    inclosed in the dark,
Not many days before my death,
    I did compose this work:

And for example to your youth,
    to whom I wish all good,
I send you here God's perfect truth,
    and seal it with my blood.

To you my heirs of earthly things:
    which I do leave behind,
That you may read and understand
    and keep it in your mind.

That as you have been heirs of that
    that once shall wear away,
You also may possess that part,
    which never shall decay.

Keep always God before your eyes,
　　with all your whole intent,
Commit no sin in any wise,
　　keep his commandment.

Abhor that errant whore of Rome,
　　and all her blasphemies,
And drink not of her cursed cup,
　　obey not her decrees.

Give honor to your mother dear,
　　remember well her pain,
And recompense her in her age,
　　with the like love again.

Be always ready for her help,
　　and let her not decay,
Remember well your father all,
　　who would have been your stay.

Give of your portion to the poor,
　　as riches do arise,
And from the needy naked soul,
　　turn not away your eyes:

For he that doth not hear the cry
　　of those that stand in need,
Shall cry himself and not be heard,
　　when he does hope to speed.

If GOD hath given you increase,
　　and blessed well your store,
Remember you are put in trust,
　　and should relieve the poor.

Beware of foul and filthy lust,
　　let such things have no place,
Keep clean your vessels in the LORD,
　　that he may you embrace.

Ye are the temples of the LORD,
　　for you are dearly bought,
And they that do defile the same,
　　shall surely come to nought.

Be never proud by any means,
   build not your house too high,
But always have before your eyes,
   that you are born to die.

Defraud not him that hired is,
   your labor to sustain,
But pay him still without delay,
   his wages for his pain.

And as you would that other men
   against you should proceed,
Do you the same to them again,
   when they do stand in need.

Impart your portion to the poor,
   in money and in meat
And send the feeble fainting soul,
   of that which you do eat.

Ask counsel always of the wise,
   give ear unto the end,
And ne'er refuse the sweet rebuke
   of him that is thy friend.

Be always thankful to the LORD,
   with prayer and with praise,
Begging of him to bless your work,
   and to direct your ways.

Seek first, I say, the living GOD,
   and always him adore,
And then be sure that he will bless,
   your basket and your store.

And I beseech Almighty GOD,
   replenish you with grace,
That I may meet you in the heavens,
   and see you face to face.

And though the fire my body burns,
   contrary to my kind,
That I cannot enjoy your love
   according to my mind:

Yet I do hope that when the heavens
   shall vanish like a scroll,

I shall see you in perfect shape,
   in body and in soul.

And that I may enjoy your love,
   and you enjoy the land,
I do beseech the living LORD,
   to hold you in his hand.

Though here my body be adjudg'd
   in flaming fire to fry,
My soul I trust, will straight ascend
   to live with GOD on high.

What though this carcass smart awhile
   what though this life decay,
My soul I hope will be with GOD,
   and live with him for aye.

I know I am a sinner born,
   from the original,
And that I do deserve to die
   by my fore-father's fall:

But by our SAVIOR'S precious blood,
   which on the cross was spilt,
Who freely offer'd up his life,
   to save our souls from guilt.

I hope redemption I shall have,
   and all who in him trust,
When I shall see him face to face,
   and live among the just.

Why then should I fear death's grim look
   since CHRIST for me did die,
For King and Caesar, rich and poor,
   the force of death must try.

When I am chained to the stake,
   and fagots girt me round,
Then pray the LORD my soul in heaven
   may be with glory crown'd.

Come welcome death the end of fears,
   I am prepar'd to die:
Those earthly flames will send my soul
   up to the Lord on high.

Farewell my children to the world,
    where you must yet remain;
The LORD of hosts be your defense,
    'till we do meet again.

Farewell my true and loving wife,
    my children and my friends,
I hope in heaven to see you all,
    when all things have their end.

If you go on to serve the LORD,
    as you have now begun,
You shall walk safely all your days,
    until your life be done.

GOD grant you so to end your days,
    as he shall think it best,
That I may meet you in the heavens,
    where I do hope to rest.

—From *The New England Primer*, Boston: Edward Draper, 1777

47

Psalm CXXXVI

By John Milton

John Milton (1608–1674) was one of the greatest English poets of the seventeenth century. Born in London, Milton became a follower of the Reformation and Puritanism. Because of this his work reflects much of a Christian worldview. The following piece was written in 1624.

> Let us with a gladsome mind
>   Praise the Lord for he is kind;
> For his mercies aye endure,
>   *Ever faithful, ever sure.*
>
> Let us blaze his Name abroad,
>   For of gods he is the God;
> For his mercies aye endure,
>   *Ever faithful, ever sure.*
>
> O let us his praises tell,
>   That doth the wrathful tyrants quell;
> For his mercies aye endure,
>   *Ever faithful, ever sure.*
>
> That with his miracles doth make
>   Amazed Heaven and Earth to shake;
> For his mercies aye endure,
>   *Ever faithful, ever sure.*
>
> That by his wisdom did create
>   The painted heavens so full of state;
> For his mercies aye endure,
>   *Ever faithful, ever sure.*
>
> That did the solid Earth ordain
>   To rise above the watery plain;
> For his mercies aye endure,
>   *Ever faithful, ever sure.*
>
> That by his all-commanding might,
>   Did fill the new-made world with light;
> For his mercies aye endure,
>   *Ever faithful, ever sure.*

And caused the golden-tressed Sun
  All the day long his course to run;
For his mercies aye endure,
  Ever faithful, ever sure.

The horned Moon to shine by night
  Amongst her spangled sisters bright;
For his mercies aye endure,
  Ever faithful, ever sure.

He, with his thunder-clasping hand,
  Smote the first-born of Egypt land;
For his mercies aye endure,
  Ever faithful, ever sure.

And, in despite of Pharao fell,
  He brought from thence his Israel;
For his mercies aye endure,
  Ever faithful, ever sure.

The ruddy waves he cleft in twain
  Of the Erythraean main;
For his mercies aye endure,
  Ever faithful, ever sure.

The floods stood still, like walls of glass,
  While the Hebrew bands did pass;
For his mercies aye endure,
  Ever faithful, ever sure.

But full soon they did devour
  The tawny King with all his power;
For his mercies aye endure,
  Ever faithful, ever sure.

His chosen people he did bless
  In the wasteful Wilderness;
For his mercies aye endure,
  Ever faithful, ever sure.

In bloody battail he brought down
  Kings of prowess and renown;
For his mercies aye endure,
  Ever faithful, ever sure.

He foiled bold Seon and his host,
  That ruled the Amorrean coast;
For his mercies aye endure,
  Ever faithful, ever sure.

And large-limbed Og he did subdue,
  With all his over-hardy crew;
For his mercies aye endure,
  Ever faithful, ever sure.

And to his servant Israel
  He gave their land, therein to dwell;
For his mercies aye endure,
  Ever faithful, ever sure.

He hath, with a piteous eye,
  Beheld us in our misery;
For his mercies aye endure,
  Ever faithful, ever sure.

And freed us from the slavery
  Of the invading enemy;
For his mercies aye endure,
  Ever faithful, ever sure.

All living creatures he doth feed,
  And with full hand supplies their need;
For his mercies aye endure,
  Ever faithful, ever sure.

Let us, therefore, warble forth
  His mighty majesty and worth;
For his mercies aye endure,
  Ever faithful, ever sure.

That his mansion hath on high,
  Above the reach of mortal eye;
For his mercies aye endure,
  Ever faithful, ever sure.

48

To Thee, Jehovah Come I Singing

by Bartholomæus Crasselius and Johann Sebastian Bach

J. S. Bach (1685–1750), born in Eisenach, Germany, where Luther once attended school, was one of the greatest composers of history. He sought to reform church music in the same way the Protestant Reformation sought to reform the church. His work represented not only in music but in words the great truths of Scripture and the Reformation. Here we have the words written by Bartholomæus Crasselius (1667–1724), a German pastor who wrote hymns full of force and beauty, which Bach set to music. It expresses the dedication of our music to Christ.

To Thee, Jehovah, come I singing.
Where is another God like unto Thee?
To Thee my music come I bringing.
Make Thou my melodies sturdy and free.
In Jesus' Name do I tender them here,
so may they sound delightful to Thine ear.

Lead me to Thy dear Son, O Father,
that He may lead me back to Thee again.
Grant that Thy Holy Spirit guide me,
deep in my heart supreme to rule and reign;
So may I feel the peace Thy Spirit brings.
wherefore my heart with joy Thy glory sings.

Give to my song, O Lord, Thy blessing.
Make Thou my cadences sweet, true and strong:
That with my music I may please Thee,
praise Thee in spirit and truth by my song.
So in Thy worship my voice will I raise,
join with Thine Angels singing in Thy praise.

Jesus will plead for me in Heaven,
pleading in tones to which God will give heed,
Jesus will teach me how to worship,
show me to be the child of God indeed;
Child and joint Heir with Jesus Christ am I,
wherefore with Him I Abba, Father cry.

When from my heart my song is pouring,
  fired by Thy Holy Spirit from above,
Then will the Father's heart, relenting,
  turn to me glowing with Heavenly love.
    Nor can the Father then refuse the plea,
    which His Beloved Son has made for me.

All that Thy Holy Spirit teaches,
  all will according to Thy will be done.
Even to Heav'n our prayer reaches,
  when in the name of Thy Beloved Son.
    Thru Him am I Thine own child and Thine heir,
    receiving from Thee grace beyond compare.

Happy am I with this assurance,
  my heart with joy and hope is all 'aglow.
Well do I know that ev'ry blessing,
  all I may ask of Thee wilt Thou bestow.
    Thru Thee abundance great do I acquire,
    more than I might ask of Thee or desire.

Happy am I that Jesus loves me,
  pleads for me there at His Father's Right Hand.
He is my Alpha, my Omega,
  under His banner do I take my stand.
    Happy am I to whom such joy Thou send,
    so will I praise Thee ever without end.

—BWV 299 (Bartholomæus Crasselius, 1695)

🔥 Comprehension Questions

1. One of the great truths of the Bible is that everything in life can and should be done to the glory of God. Read 1 Corinthians 10:31 and explain why it is foolish for any Christian, young or old, to view any activity of life as "secular," or non-spiritual.

2. Do you think that Christians have the duty to influence the world in areas such as the arts, sciences, and philosophy? If so, why?

49

They Sing the Song of Moses

by Robert Murray M'Cheyne

Born in 1813, the author of this poem was a pastor in the Free Presbyterian Church of Scotland. Though he died in 1843 at thirty years of age, he became a great influence in his own and succeeding generations. The following poem, written in 1835, reflects upon the fact that God's care for His people in the Old Testament is the same care He extends to His people today.

Dark was the night, the wind was high,
    The way by mortals never trod;
For God had made the channel dry,
    When faithful Moses stretched the rod.

The raging waves on either hand
    Stood like a massy tott'ring wall,
And on the heaven-defended band
    Refused to let the waters fall.

With anxious footsteps Israel trod
    The depths of that mysterious way;
Cheered by the pillar of their God.
    That shone for them with favoring ray.

But when they reached the opposing shore,
    As morning streaked the eastern sky,
They saw the billows hurry o'er
    The flower of Pharaoh's chivalry,

Then awful gladness filled the mind
    Of Israel's mighty ransomed throng,
And while they gazed on all behind,
    Their wonder burst into a song.

Thus, thy redeemed ones, Lord, on earth,
    While passing through this vale of weeping.
Mix holy trembling with their mirth,
    And anxious watching with their sleeping.

The night is dark, the storm is loud,
    The path no human strength can tread;
Jesus, be Thou the pillar-cloud,

Heaven's light upon our path to shed.

And oh! when, life's dark journey o'er,
   And death's enshrouding valley past,
We plant our foot on yonder shore,
   And tread yon golden strand at last.

Shall we not see with deep amaze,
   How grace hath led us safe along;
And whilst behind-before, we gaze,
   Triumphant burst into a song!

And even on earth, though sore bested,
   Fightings without, and fears within;
Sprinkled to-day from slavish dread,
   To-morrow captive led by sin:

Yet would I lift my downcast eyes
   On Thee, Thou brilliant tower of fire—
Thou dark cloud to mine enemies—
   That hope may all my breast inspire.

And thus the Lord, my strength, I'll praise,
   Though Satan and his legions rage;
And the sweet song of faith I'll raise,
   To cheer me on my pilgrimage.

50

The Sea of Galilee

by Robert Murray M'Cheyne

Written by the Sea of Galilee, July 16, 1839

How pleasant to me thy deep blue wave,
  O sea of Galilee!
For the glorious One who came to save
  Hath often stood by thee.

Fair are the lakes in the land I love,
  Where pine and heather grow;
But thou hast loveliness far above
  What Nature can bestow.

It is not that the wild gazelle
  Comes down to drink thy tide,
But He that was pierced to save from hell
  Oft wandered by thy side.

It is not that the fig-tree grows,
  And palms, in thy soft air,
But that Sharon's fair and bleeding Rose
  Once spread its fragrance there.

Graceful around thee the mountains meet,
  Thou calm reposing sea;
But ah! far more, the beautiful feet
  Of Jesus walked o'er thee.

These days are past—Bethsaida, where?
  Chorazin, where art thou?
His tent the wild Arab pitches there,
  The wild reeds shade thy brow.

Tell me, ye mouldering fragments, tell,
  Was the Saviour's city here?
Lifted to heaven, has it sunk to hell,
  With none to shed a tear ?

Ah! would my flock from thee might learn
  How days of grace will flee;
How all an offered Christ who spurn,
  Shall mourn at last, like thee.

And was it beside this very sea,
  The new-risen Saviour said
Three times to Simon, "Lovest thou me
  My lambs and sheep, then, feed."

O Saviour! gone to God's right hand!
  Yet the same Saviour still,
Graved on Thy heart is this lovely strand
  And every fragrant hill.

Oh! give me, Lord, by this sacred wave,
  Threefold Thy love divine,
That I may feed, till I find my grave,
  Thy flock—both Thine and mine.

51 Trial by Jury

by Ruth E. McDaniel

PART ONE

A noise roused Toby Berger from a deep sleep. He lifted his head from the pillow and listened. The faint sound of a siren wailed in the distance. It seemed to be coming closer.

Fully awake, now, Toby jumped out of bed and raced to his window, pulling the drapes aside. The moon was full and his back yard was an unfamiliar landscape of light and shadows. A bright light flickering against the leaves drew his attention. SOMETHING WAS ON FIRE! It must be in the front of the house, he thought. Just as he was turning to go to the front windows, Toby thought he saw a shadow move. He stopped and stared.

A hooded figure slipped from behind a tree and ran toward the back fence. As he left the shadows, he turned to glance in the direction of the flickering light. For a second, his face was illuminated. Toby strained his eyes, trying to identify the trespasser, but he was too far away. There's something familiar about him, Toby thought as he watched the figure vault over the fence and disappear. Throwing on his shirt and jeans, Toby made a mental note of everything he saw. Then he ran to the front door.

"Dad! What's going on?" Toby asked as he joined his parents. They were standing on the front lawn watching the activity. Two police cars and a firetruck had just pulled up to the end of the block. The flickering light had developed into a full-blown fire, partially hidden by the firetruck.

"It looks like Mrs. Parker's old shed is burning down," his father said.

"Not our clubhouse!" Toby cried. He ran down the sidewalk to the end of the block to join the spectators who were beginning to gather. Being small for his twelve years, Toby had a difficult time getting a clear view of the burning shack through the crowd. He moved to the farthest edge and saw, with a sinking heart, his clubhouse going up in flames.

The police were setting up a barricade to keep everyone back. Flames escaped through the roof of the old wooden building and sparks flew everywhere as the firemen quickly unrolled their hoses and moved into position.

Toby caught sight of Mrs. Parker, the old woman who owned the shack. Her husband has used it as a garage until he died, three years earlier. After she sold his car, Toby's club (known as the Eastchesters) approached her about using the wooden garage as their clubhouse. Since she knew most of the boys and their parents, she readily agreed. "Just keep the noise down to a minimum and maintain the building," she had said, "and you can use it as long as you want."

"Hi, Mrs. Parker," Toby said as he walked to her side.

"Toby, isn't this, terrible? How do you suppose it happened?" The old woman was clutching her robe about her and shaking her head, sadly.

Just as Toby opened his mouth to speak, a policeman asked Mrs. Parker to give him some information. Toby watched the two of them walk away, then turned back to the fire.

"Hey, Toby! What's up?"

Toby looked around at the sound of his name and saw Jason McQueen walking toward him. "See for yourself," Toby said, gesturing at the burning shack.

"Oh, no!" Jason ran both hands through his short blond hair and stared in fascination at the scene before him. "How did it start?"

"I don't know," Toby said. He looked up at his neighbor and fellow-member of the Eastchester Club and confided, "But, I think I might have seen who started it. I saw someone running through my back yard when the siren woke me up."

Jason's eyes widened in shock. At fourteen, Jason was quite a bit taller than Toby. So, he bent down to ask, confidentially, "Do you know who it is?"

"No. At least, I don't think so." Toby turned to Jason. "He seemed to be about your height. But, he was wearing a dark hooded sweat shirt, so I couldn't see his hair. I saw his face, but he was too far away for me to make out any details. He was ducking in and out of the shadows, and he jumped over the fence before I got a good look at him."

Jason rubbed his hands over his bare arms. He had on a thin white tee-shirt and Levi's, and the night air was chilly. "That's too bad," he murmured. "I'd really like to catch the person who did this."

"Me, too," Toby agreed, turning back to watch the fireman bring the blaze under control. "Who would want to burn down our clubhouse?"

"That's easy," Jason said, "Matt Donohue."

"Matt?" Toby stared at Jason in confusion. Matt was a member of a rival club, The Westchesters. But, Toby had never had a problem with Matt. He seemed like a nice enough guy. "Why do you think it's Matt?"

Jason shrugged and said, "Remember the blowup we had during the basketball game, the other night? Matt was really mad at me for accusing him of committing a foul. In fact," Jason looked around to make sure no one was listening, "Matt told me he was going to 'get even' with me."

"Maybe we'd better tell the police about this," Toby said.

"No, wait!" Jason grabbed Toby's arm to stop him. "The Eastchesters should handle this, themselves. After all, it's just hearsay. Nobody else heard Matt's threat." Jason leaned down to Toby, again. "Besides, Matt's thirteen—the police would only turn him over to his parents. He's a juvenile, remember? And, nobody's interested in that old shack, except us ... and maybe Mrs. Parker. Now, think hard ... could Matt be the person who cut through your back yard?"

In his mind's eye, Toby reviewed the earlier scene. "Well, Matt is as tall as you. And, he has dark brown hair—it would blend in if the hood slipped back." The more Toby thought about the athletic movements of the trespasser, the more convinced he became that it was Matt Donohue. "I've seen Matt jump hurdles at gym. This guy hopped the fence exactly the way Matt jumps hurdles!" Toby's eyes widened in recognition. "I think you're right!"

Jason looked around, once more. "Okay, we're in agreement. Here's what we'll do ... tomorrow morning, I'll call the group together and we'll meet at Steve's house. As president of the Eastchesters, he should decide where we go from here." "Come on, son," Toby's father said, placing a hand on his shoulder. "The excitement's over for the night."

Toby turned back to the soggy, burned-out rubble where his clubhouse once stood. The firemen had extinguished the flames, but there was little left of the original building. In a few hours, it would be Saturday. The Eastchesters could rummage through the ashes to see if anything was salvageable.

Jason and Toby nodded good night to each other and headed back to their houses. Tomorrow would be an interesting day.

Part Two

Saturday morning dawned bright and clear. For a minute, as Toby got out of bed and dressed, he thought he might have dreamed the whole thing. But, when he stepped out the front door, he smelled charred wood. A quick glance down the street showed in stark detail the drama of the previous night.

Toby picked his way through the mud, ashes, and wet debris, being careful not to step on nails protruding from blackened boards. He thought about what the inside of the shed looked like, before the fire.

As you entered the 9'x 12' one-room clubhouse there was a square table and four folding chairs to the right (donated by Steve's mother when she bought a new set). A stuffed, faded brown corduroy sofa and matching chair were pushed against the left wall; the group had purchased them from a second-hand store, along with the small wooden desk and chair that sat in the far, right-hand corner. Normally, the president occupied those when a meeting was in session. A kerosene lamp always sat on the corner of the desk, in case it was overcast or raining outside. On sunny days, the windows on both walls provided enough light for them to read by. An assortment of plastic crates and cardboard boxes were scattered about the room and held magazines, soda cans, and trash.

As the youngest in the group, it was Toby's job to empty the trash every Saturday…he guessed he could skip it, this time.

With one last look, Toby sighed and headed for Steve Winger's house.

"Steve and Jason are in the recreation room," Mrs. Winger told Toby when she opened the front door. "I'm so sorry to hear about your clubhouse."

"Thank you, Mrs. Winger," Toby said as he headed downstairs.

The doorbell rang, again. It was the twins, John and Joey Carver, and their next-door neighbor, Alex Robbins. All three of them were thirteen years old, and they went everywhere together.

Soon, the six boys were seated, facing each other in a rough circle. The twins had claimed both ends of the sofa and each had one leg draped over the padded arms.

Alex occupied the center cushion. He was laying back with his left ankle resting on his right knee and both hands clasped behind his head. His eyes were closed, but he was listening closely to the discussion that was going on around him.

Toby sat in a wooden rocking chair, his body hunched forward with both elbows on his knees.

Jason turned a desk chair around and sat straddling it.

Steve leaned forward in the recliner, grabbed the arms of the chair, and said, "Toby, why don't you fill everyone in on what happened, last night."

Toby slowly repeated the incident from the night before, beginning with the siren that had awakened him and ending with his visit to the site of the burned-out clubhouse, this morning.

There was a long silence following Toby's recitation. Everyone was experiencing the shock that Toby and Jason had felt when they witnessed the event. Suddenly, they all began talking at once.

"Are you sure it was Matt?" Alex asked.

"What are we going to do about it?" Joey wanted to know.

"I say we report him to the police," John said, angrily.

Steve held up both hands to bring the group under control. When everyone had quieted down, he turned to Toby. "First, let's get the facts straight, Toby, are you certain Matt set the fire?"

Toby glanced at Jason who nodded. "Well, why else would he have been cutting through my back yard at that hour? Why was he wearing a dark hooded sweat shirt and running away from the fire? Everyone else was going to see what happened."

"But, you said you didn't see his face clearly," Steve reminded him.

"No, he was too far away," Toby admitted.

"Don't forget that Toby recognized him by the way he moved and vaulted over the back fence," Jason added.

"At school, when someone is running track or jumping hurdles, you don't have to see his face to know who it is," Toby said.

"That's true," Steve agreed. He rubbed his chin thoughtfully.

Suddenly, John stood up. "Let's go see Matt!"

"Yeah!" "Right!" Alex and Joey stood up, too.

"Wait a minute," Steve said. "We can't barge in on him at his house and accuse him of arson. His mother will panic and call the police."

"Why don't you call Joe Hampton, the Westchesters' president, and have Matt meet us at his house? Matt's a member of his group—Joe will want to become involved," Alex suggested.

"That's a good idea," Steve said. "I can talk to Joe as one president to another. And, Matt won't feel as if he's being mobbed."

When Steve went upstairs to use the telephone, Alex, John, Joey and Toby excitedly reviewed the incident, once again. Jason just sat quietly, watching and listening.

PART THREE

The Eastchesters gathered on the spacious front porch of the Hampton home, later that morning, waiting for Matt to join them.

"There's no way you can convince me that Matt set the fire," Joe Hampton told the rival group. "He wouldn't do something like that."

"Well, let's see what Matt has to say for himself," Steve said. "Here he comes, now."

Seven pairs of eyes swung around to watch Matt Donohue ride toward them on his bicycle. As he approached, Matt's eyebrows drew together in a puzzled frown. It wasn't every day that the two rival groups met.

"What's up?" Matt asked as he came to a stop at the bottom of the steps.

"You're an arsonist—that's what's up!" Joey shouted, jumping to his feet. The other members stood up, too.

"Hold it!" Steve quickly joined Joe who was standing on the steps separating Matt from the others. "Wait a minute! Let me handle this," he said, motioning for everyone to sit back down.

Matt had hopped off of his bike and was standing at the bottom of the steps, facing the group. "What are you talking about?" he asked, his voice quivering with surprise and anger.

Joe looked at Matt and nodded toward the others. "The Eastchesters' clubhouse burned down, last night. Toby says he saw you running away from the fire."

"What time was it?"

"Around 2:00 am," Toby said.

"That's crazy! I was in bed asleep at 2:00 am!" Matt brushed his dark curly hair off of his forehead in a gesture of impatience.

"Prove it!" Jason said.

"I don't have to prove anything," Matt responded taking one step forward.

"Wait!" Joe put his hand on Matt's chest to hold him back. Then, he turned to Steve. "This is getting out of hand. I think it's time to call in a mediator."

"Who?" Steve asked, eyeing his friends nervously.

"My next-door neighbor, Justin Powell."

"What does Justin have to do with this?" Jason angrily asked the group in general. "He doesn't belong to either one of our clubs. He doesn't even go to our school—he attends a Christian school!"

"Exactly. He's impartial. And, everyone knows he plans to become a judge, someday. Who could settle this better than Justin?"

Steve thought this over and nodded his agreement. "You're right.

We need someone who isn't involved, one way or the other ... someone we can all trust."

"I'll go get him," Joe said. "Now, everyone just cool down!"

With Steve's assurance that he'd keep tempers under control, Joe ran next door to ask Justin to come to their rescue.

Part Four

Justin Powell was not like other teenagers in his neighborhood. For one thing, he had never attended a public school. He and his younger sister and brother had been going to their small church school since kindergarten. Secondly, Justin knew from the time he first learned how to read that he wanted to become a judge. The law fascinated him. And, now that he was fifteen, he was even more determined.

In addition to knowing exactly what direction he wanted his life to take, Justin had developed a great deal of wisdom in his fifteen years. No doubt, this was due in part to his constant study of the Bible and of his hero, King Solomon, son of David. It never failed to thrill him when he read Solomon's words. "O Lord God ... I am very young and don't know how to rule ... So, give me the wisdom I need to rule your people with justice and to know the difference between good and evil" (1 Kings 3:7-9). It was a prayer that he prayed daily.

Some of his friends had even given him the nickname, 'Judge' Justin, because of his ability to settle disputes among his peers.

For that reason, Joe Hampton now stood at Justin's front door ringing the doorbell to summon his friend, neighbor, and, hopefully, peacemaker.

The door opened and a young girl said, "Hi, Joe."

"Hi, Shelly," Joe responded automatically. He glanced over at the group on his front porch. "Is Justin home?"

"I think he's downstairs using the computer."

"Would you ask him if he can come over to my house, for a minute? Tell him it's urgent."

Shelly gave Joe a puzzled look, then she closed the door to take the strange message to her older brother.

A moment later, the door was opened by Justin, himself. His friendly blue eyes held a hint of concern as Justin asked, "What's wrong, Joe?"

"There's some bad feelings brewing on my front porch," Joe said, "I was wondering if you would help resolve them."

"Sure, I'll be happy to do what I can."

Together, Joe and Justin approached the uneasy group. Justin studied each of them and tried to seek out the source of their anger. His eyes finally settled on Jason who was slouched against a wall, scowling at Matt Donohue.

"Here's the situation," Steve said, grabbing Justin's attention. "Toby," Steve pointed to the young man on the porch, "saw Matt cut through his back yard at 2:00 this morning, running away from a fire that, we think, was deliberately set to burn down our clubhouse."

"That's a lie!" Matt shouted. He turned to Justin and said, "I was sound asleep at 2:00 am. Besides, why would I want to burn down that old shack they call a clubhouse?"

"So you could get even with me for pointing out your foul, the other night at the basketball game," Jason said, pushing away from the wall to walk to the edge of the porch.

"What are you talking about?"

"Don't play dumb," Jason snapped, "you said you'd 'get even'."

"I didn't say that. And, there was no foul."

"Oh, yeah?" Jason's hands formed into fists.

"Why don't you both calm down and let me ask some questions," Justin said in a soothing voice. He stepped in front of Matt to break off the angry look which passed between Matt and Jason.

Toby patted Jason on the shoulder and mumbled something to him. Then, Jason shrugged and returned to lean against the wall.

Justin looked at Toby. "Are you absolutely sure it was Matt you saw in your back yard?"

Toby glanced at Jason who glared back at him. "Yes."

Justin turned to Matt. "And, you're saying you were home asleep at the time of the fire."

Matt nodded, too angry to speak.

Justin thoughtfully examined each person's face and came back to rest on Joe's. "There's only one thing to do—give Matt a 'mock' trial by jury."

"What?" "Are you crazy?" "How?" Several voices joined in a shocked response.

Justin calmly faced the dubious group and said, "Amendment fourteen of the Constitution states that 'no person shall be deprived of (liberty) without due process of law'. I recommend that we assemble a jury of twelve peers, assign a defense attorney," he pointed to Joe, "and a prosecuting attorney," he pointed to Steve, "and give Matt his due process of law. I can act as presiding judge, if you want."

Steve appeared to be mulling over Justin's recommendation.

Joe grinned at his neighbor and nodded his agreement and understanding. Justin had instantly diffused their bottled up anger by giving them something else to think about. The 'Judge' had scored, again.

"I accept," Joe said, placing his arm around Matt's shoulders. "Don't worry, Matt. I'll see that your name is cleared—and you won't even have to pay me."

"I accept, too," Steve said. "But, where are we going to get the twelve jurors? There are only six members in each club, and four of us are serving in other capacities: eyewitness, accused, defense and prosecuting attorneys."

"You're not going along with this, are you?" Jason interrupted in disbelief.

"Yes, I think it's a great idea," Steve acknowledged. "It's the only fair way to handle it." Steve turned back to Justin for a reply to his question.

"We'll ask the kids in the neighborhood if they'd be willing to serve," Justin said. "It would be a good idea to have some outsiders— including girls—on the jury, as well as an even number of Eastchesters and Westchesters. And, we can use my basement as the courtroom— I'm sure Mom won't mind."

"Why can't they just take my word for it?" Matt asked indignantly.

"Because, there will always be doubt in peoples' minds," Joe said. "This way, the majority will be in agreement."

"I still say it's stupid!" Jason muttered. He jumped off the side of the porch and headed for home, his hands jammed into his back pockets.

"Now," Justin said to Steve and Joe, "you're both going to have to study to find out what you're supposed to do. Why don't you come with me and we'll go over some of my notes. We can, also, go to the library to get some information. Then, there's the encyclopedia..."

"Well, let's not get carried away," Steve said, grinning.

As the group broke up, Justin pulled Matt aside and told him, "Don't worry, Matt. I promise that the truth will come out during this trial."

"I hope you're right," Matt said. Slowly, he climbed onto his bike and pedaled away.

PART FIVE

"Mom, I'm home," Justin called as the three boys entered the Powell residence.

"Go on down to the basement and make yourselves comfortable," he told Joe and Steve. "I'll be down in a minute—I just want to make sure that having the 'court' here is all right with Mom."

The two rival club presidents went downstairs, and Justin ran up to the second floor in search of his mother. "Shelly, have you seen Mom?" Justin asked as his sister stuck her head out of her bedroom.

"I think she's in the back yard," Shelly answered. "What's going on?"

"I'll tell you all about it, later," Justin said, retracing his steps to the first floor. He looked out the back door and saw his mother bent over her tomato plants.

"Hi, Mom, do you need help with that?" Justin asked as he joined her.

"No, thanks, dear. I can manage." Mrs. Powell straightened up and shaded her eyes to look at her son. "Is everything all right? It sounded like there were some angry people, next door."

"Yes, everything's fine, now." Justin stepped closer to his mother, stopping at the short wire fence which separated the tomatoes from the zoysia grass. "Joe came over to ask me to help calm down some guys he goes to school with. You know that Joe is president of a club called The Westchesters?"

Justin's mother nodded. "I'd heard that," she said.

"Well, there's a rival club called The Eastchesters—they all live east of Manchester Road. That's how the names of the two clubs originated."

Mrs. Powell pulled off her gloves, picked up her basket of tomatoes and stepped onto the grass. They slowly walked back to the house as Justin continued.

"Last night, or, rather, early this morning at 2:00 am, the Eastchesters' clubhouse caught fire and burned down. One of their members said he saw a member of the rival group running away from the fire."

"Ah," his mother said, knowingly. "And the angry voices I heard belonged to the Eastchesters?"

"Yes—and the boy they accused of setting the fire." Mrs. Powell looked at her son in concern. "Did he?"

"I don't think so, but that's what we're hoping to find out. I wanted to know—is it all right with you if we hold a 'mock' trial in the basement?"

"When? And, how many people would be there?"

Justin thought for a moment, then said, "I think I'd have it next Saturday afternoon. That would give us all time to prepare. We're planning to pick a jury of twelve, plus, the two attorneys, the witness...."

Justin's mother smiled at her son, fondly. "I wonder whose idea that was?"

Grinning back at her, Justin opened the door and let his mother enter the house first. "What do you think?"

"I think that would be just fine. If you need anything, let me know."

"Thanks, Mom. But, Shelly, Joe, and the others can help me set up the jury box and the rest of the courtroom. And, we won't need snacks, or anything. 'No eating or drinking in the courtroom', remember?"

Mrs. Powell touched her son's cheek affectionately and smiled. "Okay, dear, I trust your judgment."

Justin joined Steve and Joe in the basement and motioned them to the table standing in the middle of the room. "Have a seat," he said, carefully moving Shelly's partly-assembled puzzle to a safer place. Then, he gathered pencils, paper, and sat down at the table, too.

Justin distributed sheets of lined paper and pencils. "Now, at the top of your page, write, 'The Case of Eastchesters Versus Matt Donohue'." When all three of them had written down this title, Justin continued, "Next, Joe, as Defense Attorney, you'll need to make a list of evidence or witnesses who can convince the jury your client is innocent. If Matt has no alibi, you might want to put a 'character witness' on the stand to testify to his good character. Actually, your job is the easiest because you only have to establish a 'reasonable doubt' as to his guilt—but, we'll get into that later.

"Steve," Justin turned to the second boy, "as the Prosecuting Attorney, your job is to present evidence and witnesses to prove that Matt committed the crime. Both you and Joe must present a list of witnesses to 'the bench'—that's the judge—and he'll give a copy to each of you. You're not supposed to bring in 'surprise witnesses' at the last minute, unless you're Perry Mason."

They all laughed and sat back in their seats.

Steve looked admiringly at Justin. "You really know about this stuff, don't you?"

"Not everything, but I'm learning," Justin said. "It's pretty basic. For our purposes, it should only take one afternoon. First, the jury is chosen. Second, the evidence is presented to the jury. Third, the counsel for the defense sums up, or, addresses the jury and reviews evidence, makes final comments, etc.. Fourth, the counsel for the prosecution sums up. Fifth, the judge charges the jury to retire from the courtroom to 'deliberate'; they must agree 100% on a verdict of 'guilty' or 'not-guilty'. Finally, the verdict is read.

"Now, you'll have to decide on the judge and the court date. I recommend next Saturday at 1:00 pm. Three hours should do it."

"I vote for Justin as judge," Joe said, looking at Steve.

"I second that," Steve agreed.

"I accept," Justin said, nodding. "And, is Saturday all right?"

Steve and Joe both nodded their agreement.

"Okay, now we should decide on how we want to set up the courtroom." Justin and the other two looked around the basement. Justin placed his hand on the table they were seated at. "This is good enough for 'the bench'. And, we have two free-standing TV trays that would work as defense and prosecution tables. I can bring the kitchen chairs down here—there's six of them—and we have six folding chairs for a total of twelve. But, the three of us will need chairs, too. Plus, we'll need one for the witness stand, and one for Matt … that leaves only seven chairs for the jury."

"I can bring over four folding chairs," Joe offered. "And, I'll bring four," Steve added.

"Great! That's fifteen—twelve for the jury and three extra for spectators. If anyone else comes, they can sit on the sofa or the floor."

Justin glanced down at his notes. "Well, I think that takes care of the preliminaries. What else do you want to know?"

"How did you become interested in the law?" Steve asked.

PART SIX

"Hey, Matt, wait up!"

Matt Donohue stopped his bike and looked around. To his left, he saw Marc Nicholson emerging from his house. "Hi, Marc," he said in a distracted way.

"Where are you going?" Marc asked as he walked alongside Matt.

"I don't know. Home, I guess. Have you heard the news?"

"What news?"

"The Eastchesters' clubhouse burned down, last night—and they think I did it!" Matt's cheeks burned with indignation.

"You're kidding! who said?"

"The whole club—they called me over to Joe's house, this morning, and accused me of torching their shack. I told them I was sound asleep, but Toby Berger said he saw me cutting across his back yard."

"That little twerp! He must need glasses."

"The discussion was getting heated, so Joe went next door to ask Justin Powell to straighten everything out—you know Justin, don't you?"

"Yeah, we go to the same church. So, what did Justin do?"

"We were all getting pretty angry—especially Jason McQueen—so, Justin said we ought to have a trial. He called it 'a trial by jury'."

"That's 'Judge' Justin, all right," Marc said grinning.

"Afterwards, Justin came up to me and said, 'Don't worry, the truth will come out.' It sounded like he believed me."

"Of course he did! You didn't do it!"

"Why would Toby say he saw me?" Matt frowned as he thought it over.

"And, why would Jason be so angry?" Marc asked. "Something doesn't sound right. Maybe I'll do some investigative work—I'll dig around, a little, and see what I can come up with. When's the trial?"

"Joe just told me it's going to be next Saturday at 1:00 pm. Justin thought we should give both 'attorneys' time to prepare for their case."

Marc laughed and nodded, "They don't call him 'Judge' for nothing. Okay, I'll try to find out what's going on. I can even be your character witness! This sounds like it's going to be fun."

Matt glanced at Marc. "I'm glad somebody's enjoying himself!"

"Don't worry, Matt. We know you're innocent, and we're going to prove it. Stay away from Jason and his club for the next few days; I'll get back to you, later."

Matt shrugged and waved as Marc ran off in the direction of Joe Hampton's house.

PART SEVEN

The school cafeteria seemed particularly noisy to Toby as he sat down to eat at his usual table, near the back wall.

"Do you mind if we sit here?"

Toby looked up and saw three members of the Westchester Club standing in front of him. Marc Nicholson and Kevin Moore were both twelve, and Tim Donley was thirteen. Teenagers rarely hung out with the twelve-year-olds at Parkway Middle School. Toby felt uneasy. He looked around for moral support, but Alex and the twins were sitting all the way across the cafeteria. "What do you want?"

"We just want to talk," Marc said as he set his tray down on the table and sat down. Tim and Kevin did the same.

"I don't think this is a good idea," Toby said.

Marc ignored him and took a bite out of his sandwich. After he chewed and swallowed, he said, "You have a pretty big back yard, don't you?"

Toby shrugged.

"How far would you say your back fence is from your bedroom?"

Toby frowned. "Why do you want to know?"

"Just curious," Marc replied, taking another bite out of his sandwich.

"I think our back yards are about the same size," Tim Donley said. He took a drink of milk, wiped his mouth and added, "It's a good seventy-five feet from my bedroom window to the back fence in my yard."

"Where does Jason McQueen live?" Kevin Moore asked the group in general.

"I think he lives on the next block, behind you, doesn't he?" Marc asked Toby.

Toby looked from one to the other. "Yeah, why?"

"No special reason. You know, I'm sort of looking forward to the trial, this Saturday, aren't you?" Marc put the last of his sandwich in his mouth.

Toby shrugged, again. He took a big bite of spaghetti and watched his plate as he chewed. Normally, Toby got along well with everyone—but, the upcoming trial was making him nervous.

"Hi! Can we sit here?"

The boys looked up and saw Andrea Hampton, Joe's twelve-year-old sister, and Katy Anderson, one of their classmates, approach their table.

"Sure!" Marc waved them forward.

"I was telling Katy about the trial this Saturday, and she wants to try out for the jury, too," Andrea said, her brown eyes shining with excitement.

"I don't know why everyone's making such a big deal out of it," Toby mumbled.

"Because it is a big deal when someone's accused of a crime he didn't commit," Marc said, quietly.

Toby glanced up at Marc and their eyes held for a moment. Then, Andrea started talking, again. Toby took advantage of the distraction to finish eating. Then, he picked up his books and his tray and left.

"Do you think you'll be on the jury, Marc?"

Marc watched Toby leave the cafeteria, then he turned to Katy.

"No, I'm going to testify for Matt—you know, like a character witness."

"This is going to be so neat," Katy said. "The whole school is talking about it. I hope Justin Powell has a big basement; he may have 'standing room, only', by the time Saturday rolls around."

Andrea agreed. Then, she added, "But, I can't imagine anyone thinking Matt would set fire to that garage."

They all turned to look at the suspected arsonist who was sitting with his friends at the far end of the cafeteria. At that moment, Matt glanced up at them. Marc held up two fingers in the 'V-for victory' sign.

PART EIGHT

Saturday rolled around faster than he would have imagined, and Matt found himself back at Joe Hampton's house. Joe's sister, Andrea, answered the doorbell.

"Matt's here," Andrea called over her shoulder. Then, she turned to Matt and smiled. "I'm going to try out for the jury," she said pointing to the sign taped to the front of Justin's house. It read: 'jurors wanted—1 to 5 pm, today—ages 11 through 16, only'.

Matt blushed and mumbled, "Well—um—I'll see you there, then."

"Don't worry—it will work out," Andrea said. She moved aside to let her older brother join Matt.

"Well, I think I'm ready," Joe announced as he stepped onto the front porch. He carried a folder filled with notes and copies.

"What's that?" Matt asked, eyeing the folder curiously.

"This is your defense," Joe said, flipping through the numerous pages. "Justin, Steve, and I studied the legal system, together—we, even, went to watch a real trial, last week, so we'd know what to do. It was pretty interesting and gave us a lot to think about." They walked around the side of Justin's house to the basement entry.

Justin's basement door was propped open and a sign was taped to it with an arrow pointing inside. It read: Courtroom. A small crowd was gathered at the entrance.

"Follow me," Joe said to Matt, bypassing the group.

"Good luck, Matt," a girl said as they walked by.

Matt turned around and saw Stacie Evan standing with the others. She was in Matt's Art class at school. He nodded then hurried to catch up with Joe.

As they entered the basement, Matt looked around with interest. Against the far wall, Justin Powell sat at a wooden table. He was talking to Sara Marlow, one of Steve's neighbors. A solitary chair in front of

Justin's desk would be used for witnesses. The "jury box" was split—six chairs were lined up along the left wall and six chairs lined the right wall. Some of the jury seats were already filled. On the left, Jason McQueen sat in the center with Tim Donley and Kevin Moore on either end. 'Justin must be seating them', Matt thought in amusement. Jason didn't look very happy setting between two members of a rival club.

On the right, the inseparable threesome, Alex and the twins, occupied the first, third, and sixth chairs.

Matt and Joe walked over to a small table on the left, facing Justin and the split jury. "Have a seat," Joe told Matt. "I have to see 'the judge'."

Matt sat down and glanced to his right. Steve Winger and Toby Berger were seated at another small table facing the bench. They were in a deep discussion and didn't seem to notice that the room was slowly filling up.

'Judge' Justin directed Sara to the vacant jury seat between Jason and Tim. Then, he beckoned to the small group at the back of the room. Andrea, Katy, and Shelly Powell came forward with Mike Hampton, Joe's eleven-year-old brother and the youngest member of the Westchesters.

Joe acknowledged the passing group as he rejoined Matt. "It won't be long, now. Justin is almost finished seating the jury. The trial will start in a few minutes." He looked up as more people entered the basement. "I'd better take down those signs, or they'll keep coming in."

As Joe left to remove the signs and inform the newcomers that the jury was filled, Marc Nicholson sat down behind Matt.

"Hi, Matt!" Marc looked around the basement. "Wow! This is even beginning to look like a courtroom."

As Justin directed the rest of the jury to their seats, Marc leaned close to Matt and whispered, "Toby's going to feel like hamburger when Joe is finished cross-examining him." He grinned knowingly at Matt, but Joe returned before he could say more.

"Here we go!" Joe said.

Marc sat back in his chair.

Matt and Joe turned to face the judge and the jury.

Toby ran back to close the basement door and asked the spectators to take a seat.

It was time for the trial to begin!

PART NINE

"May I have your attention?" RAP! RAP! RAP! Justin banged his gavel on the desk, calling for order in the court.

The room became silent and everyone faced Justin Powell. He set his gavel aside, stood up, and picked up his Bible.

"Since this is just a 'mock' trial, we won't follow every step required in a real court. I'm asking both attorneys to accept the jury—as is."

Joe and Steve nodded in agreement.

"Now, please bow your heads and pray that justice will be served, this afternoon." Justin closed his eyes and said, "Lord, I lift up this trial to You and ask for Your divine guidance. Let the truth be known…"

Some foot shuffling to the right of the room made Matt and Joe look sideways. Toby's face was pink and he hunkered down lower in his seat.

"And, Father," Justin continued, "let me remember Your instructions in Leviticus 19:15, to 'Be honest and just when (I) make decisions in legal cases… Amen! "

Everyone said, "Amen!", and chairs screeched on the tile floor as they all settled more comfortably in their seats. The latest newcomers sat in the remaining chairs and sofas, or sat cross-legged on the floor. The basement was filled was friends, neighbors and classmates.

"First, I'll introduce the jury. Starting on your left: Tim Donley, Andrea Hampton, Sara Marlow, Jason McQueen, Katy Anderson, and Kevin Moore. On your right: John Carver, Stacie Evan, Alex Robbins, Shelly Powell, Mike Hampton, and Joe Carver." Justin looked at the split panel and said, "Jury, do you swear to hear the testimony, fairly and objectively, and try to reach an impartial decision, so help you God?" The jury answered, "We do." Then, Justin turned back to the courtroom.

"Copies of the jury lineup have been given to both attorneys.

Justin looked at Joe and Steve and they nodded.

"Next, the Prosecuting Attorney, Steve Winger, will make his opening statement to the jury." Justin sat down and turned the floor over to Steve.

Picking up his folder of notes, Steve stepped in front of his table and faced Justin and the jury. "Ladies and gentlemen of the jury," Steve began … then stopped when everyone laughed. "Well, you know what I mean," he said, pausing to allow the mood to become more serious. Then, he began, again. "One week ago, today, the Eastchester's clubhouse burned down. An eyewitness saw the defendant, Matt Donohue,

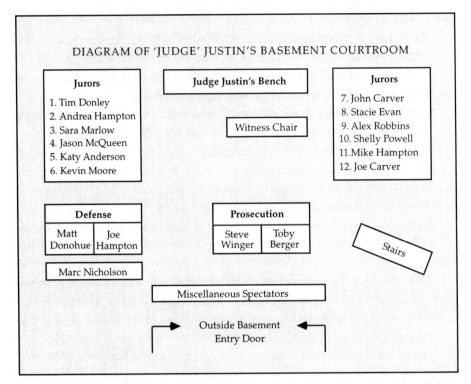

DIAGRAM OF 'JUDGE' JUSTIN'S BASEMENT COURTROOM

Jurors
1. Tim Donley
2. Andrea Hampton
3. Sara Marlow
4. Jason McQueen
5. Katy Anderson
6. Kevin Moore

Judge Justin's Bench

Witness Chair

Jurors
7. John Carver
8. Stacie Evan
9. Alex Robbins
10. Shelly Powell
11. Mike Hampton
12. Joe Carver

Defense	
Matt Donohue	Joe Hampton

Marc Nicholson

Prosecution	
Steve Winger	Toby Berger

Stairs

Miscellaneous Spectators

Outside Basement Entry Door

running away from the scene of the crime. We contend that the defendant set the fire."

"That's not true!" Matt cried out in frustration.

RAP! RAP! "You'll have your turn, Matt," Justin gently admonished.

"That's all, Your Honor," Steve said, taking his seat.

"At this time, Defense Attorney Joe Hampton will make his opening statement."

Joe stood up and spoke from his place at the table. "My client, Matt Donohue, was asleep in his bed when the fire started. He is innocent of this crime." With that, Joe sat back down.

Justin looked at Steve and said, "Mr. Winger, you may present your witness."

Steve got up. "I call Toby Berger to the witness stand."

Toby walked self-consciously to the empty chair in front of Justin's desk.

Justin stood up and held out the Bible, saying, "Place your left hand on the Bible and raise your right hand." When Toby had complied, Justin continued, "Do you swear to tell the truth, the whole truth, and nothing but the truth, so help you God?"

"I do," Toby mumbled.

"Be seated," Justin instructed, taking his seat, as well.

"Now, Mr. Berger," Steve began, noting with satisfaction that the spectators in the courtroom no longer giggled at intervals, "will you tell the court what took place on the morning of the fire?"

Toby cleared his throat and said, "Around two o'clock last Saturday morning, the sound of sirens woke me up. I ran to my bedroom window to see what was happening. Everything seemed all right in the back yard, so I was turning to go to the front of the house when I saw Matt Donohue, wearing a dark hooded sweat shirt with the hood up, run across my yard and hop over the fence."

The screeching of a chair being pushed back stopped Toby's testimony for a moment. Joe whispered something to Matt, and he settled back, glaring at Toby.

Jason McQueen leaned forward, resting his elbows on his knees, and looked intently at the witness.

"When I got dressed and ran out to the front of the house, I saw that our clubhouse was on fire," Toby continued.

"How do you know it was Matt Donohue in your back yard?" Steve asked.

"There was a full moon, that night, and I could see him when he left the shadows. He turned around, once, and looked toward the house. Then, he jumped the fence."

"And, why would Matt Donohue want to set fire to our clubhouse?" Steve asked.

"He told Jason he was going to get even with him for reporting a foul during a basketball game, two nights before," Toby responded.

"Objection!" Joe interrupted. "That's hearsay, Your Honor."

"Sustained." Toby turned around in confusion, and Justin told him, "You can only repeat what you heard directly."

"No more questions, Your Honor," Steve said as he took his seat.

"Mr. Hampton, do you want to examine this witness?" Justin asked.

"Yes, Your Honor, I certainly do!" Joe glanced at his notes. Then, he stood up and walked forward. "Mr. Berger, I'm told your back fence is at least 75 feet away from your window. So, even with a full moon, how could you see my client's face clearly on the night of the fire?"

"Well ... I didn't exactly see his features, but, I recognized him, anyway."

"If you didn't see his face, how could you recognize him?" Joe asked, stopping two feet in front of Toby.

Toby looked over at Jason, but Joe stepped between them and repeated his question.

"Well … uh … I could tell by his height and the way he moved. It was Matt, all right. And, he had dark hair…"

"Didn't you say the trespasser wore a hooded sweat shirt?"

"Yes, but, you know, they don't cover your hair completely. He had to have dark hair—light or blonde hair would have showed."

"Not if the hood was tied tightly around his face to keep his hair hidden," Joe added. "How tall would you say Matt is?"

"Oh … about 5'9", or 5'10"." Toby's face was pink, again.

"Well, I'm 5'10", and I have dark hair, too," Joe pointed out. "Why didn't you think it was me?"

"Because, I recognized the way Matt vaulted over the fence. I've seen him jump hurdles at school dozens of times—that, plus his height and build … well, I just recognized him, that's all!"

Joe leaned toward Toby and said, "I think you saw a trespasser but didn't know who it was, until someone later convinced you it was Matt. Isn't that true?"

"I object!" Jason McQueen yelled.

RAP! RAP! RAP! 'Judge' Justin turned to Jason and said, "Members of the jury are not allowed to speak during a trial."

"But, Matt said…"

"McQueen, please sit back and be quiet!"

"I don't want to be a member of the jury," Jason said, angrily. "I want to testify!"

Justin asked Steve and Joe to approach the bench. When they did, Justin said, "This would never be allowed in a real courtroom, but—if you're both in agreement, I can assign Marc Nicholson to replace Jason. Then, Jason can testify." Steve agreed.

Joe looked from Jason to Marc. "Well, I was going to use Marc as a character witness, but … okay." Joe turned and motioned for Marc to come forward.

Justin informed everyone of the change, then asked, "Mr. Hampton, have you finished questioning Toby Berger?"

"As soon as he answers my last question, Your Honor." Joe asked Toby, once more, "Isn't it true that you didn't see the trespasser's face clearly and didn't connect him with my client until someone convinced you it was Matt—and, remember, you're still under oath!"

Toby looked over at Steve, then shrugged. "Yes, I guess so."

"I have no further questions, Your Honor."

Toby hurried to the back of the room to sit next to the door, and Steve said, "I call Jason McQueen to the witness stand."

Murmurs accompanied Jason's short walk to the witness chair. Justin held out the Bible and swore Jason in, but he barely heard Jason mumble, "I do!"

"Would you tell us, in your own words, what took place on, and just prior to, the morning of the fire?" Steve asked.

Jason sat rigid with hostility. He stared at Matt as he spoke, "Two nights before the fire, Matt shoved me during the basketball game. I went to the referee and reported the foul, and Matt got mad. Later, he said, 'I'll get even with you.' So, when I saw the clubhouse burning and heard the description of the guy who jumped Toby's fence—I put two-and-two together."

"No more questions." Steve looked troubled when he sat down.

Joe approached the witness. "Did anyone else hear this so-called 'threat'?"

"I don't know," Jason shrugged and slumped down in his chair.

"Judge, can I ask the spectators a question?" Joe asked.

Justin's eyebrows drew together. "Well, not during a real trial—but, I guess it's okay, here."

Joe turned around and asked, "Were any of you present at the basketball game, that night?"

Two boys raised their hands and said, "We played on Jason's team."

"Did either one of you see that 'foul', or hear a 'threat'?

They looked at each other, then back at Joe, and shook their heads.

Joe turned to Jason. "But one more thing—where were you when the fire started?"

"What's that supposed to mean?" Jason sat up and glared at Joe as the courtroom erupted in conversation.

RAP! RAP! RAP! RAP! Justin banged his gavel several times before everyone quieted down. Then, he told the witness, "Answer the question."

Jason slouched down, again, and said, "I was asleep!"

"You live on the block behind Toby Berger, and yet, you were at the scene of the fire, fully dressed, shortly after Toby arrived. Isn't that true?"

Jason refused to meet Joe's eyes. "I don't know when Toby got there."

"And can you kindly explain to the court why you appeared at the scene of the fire on a chilly night without a coat or sweat shirt?"

Jason turned to the Judge and complained that he was not the one on trial and therefore should not be required to answer such a question. "Very well", said the judge, "I will require the question to be stricken from the record."

"Your Honor, I'm finished with the witness." Joe turned to his chair.

Steve stared thoughtfully at Jason.

"The witness can step down," the judge told Jason. Then, he asked Steve, "Does the prosecution have any more witnesses?"

"No, Your Honor."

"Does the defense have any witnesses?"

"No, Your Honor," Joe responded. He whispered to his client, "No need for you to testify, Matt."

Everyone watched as Jason walked to the back of the basement, went outside, and slammed the door behind him. Toby stood staring at the floor.

"Then, it's time for summation," Justin announced.

PART TEN

"Mr. Hampton will address the jury, first," 'Judge' Justin informed the court.

Joe stood between the twelve jurors and made eye-contact with each one of them. Finally, he said, "Members of the jury, you've heard the testimony of a witness who didn't actually see the trespasser's face, and an accuser, who tells of a confrontation on a crowded basketball court that no one else saw or heard." He paused. "The prosecution failed to prove his case. Therefore, you must find my client 'not guilty' of setting fire to the Eastchester's clubhouse." Joe nodded to Justin, then returned to his seat.

"Is the prosecution ready to address the jury?" Justin asked.

Steve looked up from his notes, glanced at Matt, then looked at the jury. "I have nothing more to say, Your Honor."

Justin spoke directly to the panel, "Normally, the judge would tell the jury to retire from the courtroom so you can deliberate. However, I think it's all right for you to group together, at this end of the basement, while we all step down to the other end.

"First, you must choose a 'foreman'—someone who will speak for you and turn in your verdict. Then, you will deliberate. You must agree

100%—without a reasonable doubt—that the defendant, Matt Dono-hue, is 'guilty' of setting fire to the clubhouse, or he is 'not guilty' of this crime. Do you understand?"

The jurors nodded.

"All right. I'll be over by the door if you have any questions."

Justin joined Steve, Matt, and Joe as they walked to the farthest wall away from the jury. Some of the spectators opened the door and stepped out into the back yard. Jason was nowhere in sight.

Toby watched as Matt and the others approached him. When they were close enough, he said, "Listen, Matt, I'm sorry about all of this. I really thought it was you—but, now … I must have been wrong."

Matt looked at Toby and started to say something, but he changed his mind, and shrugged, instead. "Okay," he finally muttered.

One of the spectators walked up to Justin and asked, "Aren't you Justin Powell? I heard about you from some of the kids at school. I understand you plan to practice law … I was really impressed, this afternoon. In fact, all of you did a great job. When I first heard about this trial, I thought it was a big joke—but, well, if I'm ever accused of a crime, I'll come to you for help."

"Thanks … I guess," Justin said, laughing.

"I agree," a fellow student said. "I learned more about how a court of law operates, this afternoon, than I did all last semester, at school."

Just then, Marc Nicholson approached the group.

"Do you have a question, Marc?" Justin asked.

"No. I'm the foreman, and I just wanted to let you know that the jury has reached a verdict."

"Already?" Justin looked at Matt, Steve, and Joe. "Well, tell everybody to come inside—court is back in session."

'Judge' Justin returned to 'the bench' as Steve informed the rest of the group that court was reconvening.

Once everyone had taken their seats, Justin rapped the table with his gavel.

"Court is now in session," he said.

The room quieted down, and the spectators leaned forward in anticipation.

Justin looked at Marc and asked, "Has the jury reached a verdict?"

Marc smiled and replied, "We have, Your Honor."

"Will the defendant please rise?" When Matt and Joe stood up, Justin turned to Marc, again. "What is your verdict?"

"We find the defendant, Matt Donohue, not guilty of setting fire to the Eastchester's clubhouse!"

"YAHOO!" "Hooray!" "That's great!" The courtroom erupted in a variety of hoots and well-wishes.

RAP! RAP! Justin smiled at the chaos and said, "The defendant is dismissed, and court is adjourned!"

The jurors surged forward to shake hands with Matt and Joe.

Steve walked over to Matt and held out his hand in a combined gesture of reconciliation and congratulations. "I knew it was going to turn out this way ever since Joe questioned Toby. I should have dug deeper into his story. I'm sorry, Matt. I have a feeling the Eastchesters need to do some soul-searching."

Matt shrugged and shook hands to show his acceptance of Steve's apology. "Just don't let it happen, again," he added with a lopsided grin.

Marc pounded Matt on the back and smiled broadly. "What a great afternoon! We should do this more often!"

"Only, the next time, you can be the accused!" Matt replied.

Steve turned to Justin and said, "I really enjoyed studying with you, 'Judge'. In fact, the next time you plan to visit a courtroom, let me know. I'd like to go with you. Suddenly, the law has become fascinating to me."

"I'll do that," Justin agreed.

"You said that you first became interested in the law after reading about King Solomon in the Bible," Steve continued. "Tell me about it."

"Funny you should mention that," Justin said, "My Sunday school class is going to study King Solomon, tomorrow morning. Marc and I are in the same room. Maybe you'd like to come with us...you'll even get some material to take home with you."

"Sure! That sounds great. What time should I be here?"

A small voice piped up from behind them, "Can I come, too?" Toby Berger stepped into view with a hopeful look on his face.

"Absolutely!" Justin said, placing a welcoming hand on Toby's shoulder.

Matt looked up with sudden interest. "How about me, too?"

Joe grinned at Justin who said loudly, "Everyone who would like to study King Solomon at our Sunday school class, tomorrow morning— be here by 8:00 am!"

🔥 Comprehension Questions

1. Who owned the old shed that burned down in the opening scene of the story?

2. What person was accused of setting fire to the clubhouse?

3. Do you think that Justin Powell had the right character to become a successful judge? If so, please explain why?

4. Where did the boys decide to set up their courtroom?

5. Who do you think was responsible for burning down the clubhouse? Please explain your answer.

6. How did Justin Powell first become interested in studying the law?

52   *Learning To Trust*

by Ruth E. McDaniel

"Go for help, Buck! Get Mother!"

The large Golden Retriever sniffed around his fallen charge with obvious anxiety. Suddenly, he grabbed the right wheel of the wheelchair in his mouth and started to pull.

"No, Buck, don't move me! Go get Mother!"

Buck stood over the girl and stared at her as if he was thinking over his options. His intelligent eyes took in the situation. His mistress was strapped to her wheelchair which had slipped off the bike trail and slid down a steep embankment. He was strong enough to pull her up the hill, but she could be hurt. She wanted him to go for human help, instead. After a moment of indecision, Buck licked her face and ran up the embankment.

Becky watched her service dog until he disappeared. Then, she rested her head on the leaf-covered ground and waited.

The woods were filled with the sounds of rustling leaves and chattering squirrels. The wind whistled through the trees. She heard a hawk screech in the distance, and the faint sound of a dog barking. It wasn't Buck—she knew Buck's deep bark.

Becky wasn't afraid. She had placed herself in God's hands. He would see to it that Buck brought help. "I've really changed," Becky thought in amazement. She was very different from the girl she used to be, before the accident.

"Was it only a year ago?" Becky asked out loud. In the silence of the forest, Becky thought back to her fifteenth birthday.

⚜

"Happy birthday to you ..." Becky Rogers' mother, father, younger brother, Ryan, and her paternal grandparents sang slightly off-key.

Becky rolled her eyes and grinned. Fifteen years old! She wished she was sixteen, instead, so she could get a driver's license. Some of her friends already had theirs, and it opened up a whole new world for them. Becky was too embarrassed to have her parents drive her places—not that she didn't love them. But, it made her feel like a child. If her friends couldn't pick her up at her house, Becky's alternative was to walk or ride her bicycle.

Brushing auburn bangs out of her light blue eyes, Becky glanced quickly at her watch. 2:30 pm. She was meeting her best friends, Lisa and Mary Beth, at Lisa's house at 3 pm. She still had time to eat some cake and visit with her grandparents for awhile.

"So, tell me, young lady, what are your plans for the afternoon?"

Becky smiled at Grandpa Rogers and thought, once again, how much her father resembled him. "This is how Dad will look in twenty years," she reflected. "His hair would be white instead of red, and he'd be wearing bifocals, too." "My friends and I plan to go shopping at Chesterfield Mall," Becky answered.

"Can't wait to spend that money, hm?" Grandpa Rogers' eyes twinkled as he teased his only granddaughter. She was his first grandchild, and he was astonished at how much he loved her. Of course, he loved Ryan, too. But, he'd never had a daughter—until his son, Stephen, married Deborah. "What a blessing Stephen's family has been to us," Grandpa Rogers thought.

Becky laughed and shook her head. Grandpa was always teasing her—and she loved it. Her grandparents had given her a money order for her birthday.

"Now, Lawrence, you remember how money always burned a hole in your pocket when you were that age," Grandma Rogers told her husband. She turned and patted Becky's arm. "You go right ahead and buy what you want, dear. That's why we gave you money instead of buying something that wouldn't fit. You and Ryan are growing up so fast, I don't know what sizes you wear, anymore. Besides, I'd probably choose something old-fashioned, like me."

"You always look great, Grandma," Becky said, eyeing her grandmother's spectacled face, permed gray hair, trim navy suit, and orthopedic shoes. Becky thought she was the perfect example of what a grandmother should look like. But, she was glad they didn't try to buy her a present, all the same. Now, she could shop with her friends and try clothes on for a perfect fit. That was half of the fun.

Becky wished her maternal grandparents would do the same. She didn't want to seem ungrateful, but they lived out-of-state and so seldom saw Becky and Ryan that they still thought of them as small children. And, their gifts reflected that image. Becky was at least two sizes larger than the blouse Grandma Lewis sent her. "Too bad I don't have a little sister," Becky thought, "she might be able to wear it."

Glancing at her watch, again, Becky suddenly jumped up. "Oops! I'd better leave or I'll be late."

"Why don't you have the girls pick you up here?" her mother asked.

"Well, we already made these other arrangements," Becky explained. She didn't want the girls to come to the house because it would take forever to introduce them, then, her grandparents would want to talk to them for a while. By the time they left for the Mall, they'd have to turn around and come right back home or be late for dinner.

"I can drive you to Lisa's house," her father offered.

"No, that's okay, Dad. She only lives three blocks away and it won't take long to ride my bike there. This way, you can visit with Grandma and Grandpa longer."

"Wear your helmet and watch out for cars," her mother added.

Becky groaned. Her mom had been telling her that since she was a baby. "Well, thanks, again, Grandma, Grandpa," Becky said kissing and hugging her grandparents. She waved at everyone and rushed out of the room.

Within two minutes, Becky's helmet was strapped to her head and she was streaking down the driveway on her bike. She glanced right—all clear. She glanced behind Grandpa Rogers' van to her left—no traffic. With a feeling of exhilaration, Becky raced out into the street—directly in the path of an oncoming car!

Everything seemed to happen in slow motion ... Becky heard the wheels screech as the driver tried to stop. She felt the impact as the car slammed into her left side, but there was no pain—just surprise. She flew through the air and landed on her back in the middle of the street. Then, the world went black.

⁂

Becky didn't know how long she was unconscious. But, when she came to, paramedics and police surrounded her. She could see her weeping mother held tightly by her father. They were talking to a police officer. Ryan and her grandparents stood in a semi-circle with their arms around each other. Their faces were pale from shock and concern.

"I'm okay," Becky tried to tell them. Her left shoulder was sore, but, other than that, she felt no pain whatsoever. "It's a good thing I was wearing my helmet," Becky thought.

"Don't try to talk or move," a paramedic told her. He gently removed her helmet, then slid a board under her.

"That's strange," Becky thought, "I feel the board touching my shoulders, but I can't feel it under my hips. I must have dislocated something."

The paramedic strapped on a rigid collar and an oxygen mask as Becky slipped into unconsciousness, again.

∾⊕⌐

"It's okay, sweetheart. Dad and I are with you," her mother said from a great distance.

Becky's eyelids fluttered, then opened. Groggily, she tried to turn toward her parents who were standing next to the bed.

Suddenly, a surge of adrenaline rushed through her, and her eyes widened in alarm. She couldn't move! "Mom?" Becky called out in panic.

Her mother came into view with her father hovering behind. "Don't worry, Becky. We're right here."

Two nurses and a doctor entered the room.

The doctor nodded at Becky's parents, then took her hand. "Hello, Rebecca—or should I call you Becky?" The doctor paused, then continued when Becky didn't answer. "My name is Dr. Gonzales and I'm a pediatric neurosurgeon. You've had a serious accident, and you're in the intensive care ward at St. Louis Children's Hospital. Do you follow me, so far?" The doctor stopped long enough to shine a light in Becky's eyes and glance at her vital signs beeping on the various instruments.

"What's wrong with me?" Becky asked in a faint voice. She was trembling with fear. She looked from face to face and saw nothing reassuring there. Her mother was crying softly, and her father had tears in his eyes. She'd never seen her father cry. Even the nurses looked solemn and concerned.

Dr. Gonzales held up a picture of the backview of a human skeleton and began to point out various bones. "Fortunately," he said, "you were wearing a helmet, so your cranium was not injured. You landed on your left shoulder and cracked the scapula (shoulder blade), but it should heal nicely. Your cervical vertebrae (or neck) was whiplashed, so it'll be stiff and sore for a while. You'll have to wear a neck brace for a couple of weeks. That's one of the reasons why you can't move."

The doctor took a deep breath and continued. "However," he paused and looked compassionately at Becky, then pointed to the illustration, "you severely fractured your second lumbar vertebrae ... and it severed your spinal cord."

"But, I'll be all right ... won't I, doctor?"

Becky's mother turned away and her father closed his eyes as if to

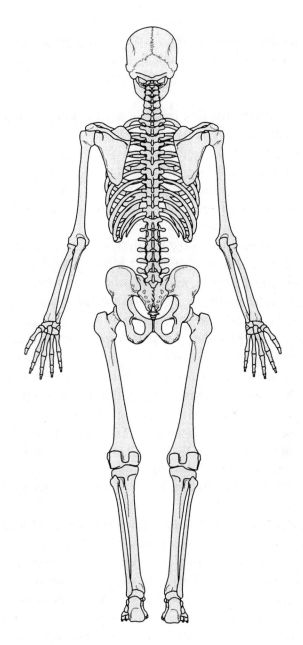

block out a painful sight.

"The other injuries will heal," Dr. Gonzales said softly, "but once the spinal cord is severed, it can't be repaired." He nodded to the nurse standing beside him, and she injected one of the intravenous tubes with medication.

"But, what …," Becky swallowed and her ears started buzzing, "what does that mean?" She tried to moved her feet and realized she couldn't feel them. Suddenly, with a terrifying certainty, Becky knew what that meant—she'd never walk, again!

Dr. Gonzales saw the growing hysteria in Becky's eyes and gripped her hand sympathetically.

Then, she felt herself falling into the dark void of unconsciousness, once more.

⚓

Becky stared straight ahead as her mother bustled about the hospital room examining and rearranging the numerous flowers and get well cards friends and relatives had sent.

"Grandma and Grandpa Rogers will visit you, this afternoon," her mother informed her. "And, here's a card from Grandma and Grandpa Lewis—they're driving up to see you, early next week."

"Tell them not to hurry," Becky said in a dull voice, "I won't be going anywhere."

"Rebecca!" Becky's mother stopped, took a deep breath, and pulled a chair close to the bed. She reached for her daughter's unresponsive hand and said, "Let's pray together, and then talk about it."

"Why bother?" Becky asked, closing her eyes. "That won't help me walk again."

Deborah Rogers stared at her stricken daughter through misty eyes. Then she replied, "Becky, we need to pray because God loves us, and He'll comfort and help us get through this."

"I couldn't have said it better, myself," a deep voice spoke up from the doorway.

Becky and her mother both looked up and saw Pastor Richards enter the room.

"Good morning, Rebecca … Deborah," the pastor nodded to both. "Deborah, I wonder if you'd mind getting me a cup of hot chocolate? You know, it's a bit nippy out there, and a cup of cocoa would take the chill from these old bones."

"Of course," Mrs. Rogers said. "I'll be back in a few minutes," she told Becky.

"Well, young lady," Pastor Richards said, sitting down in the chair Becky's mother had just vacated. "I hear you had a close call."

"Not close enough," Becky mumbled to herself.

"What's that?" The pastor leaned forward, but Becky looked away without answering. "I asked your mother to leave so we could speak privately," he continued. "I know you must have questions. Or, maybe you just want to talk about it. You can say anything to me, you know it won't leave this room."

Becky narrowed her eyes and looked at the minister. "Okay … why? Why did this have to happen to me?"

"Unfortunately, that's one question none of us can answer," Pastor Richards said, leaning forward and gripping his Bible with both hands. "Why do bad things happen to people?" He sighed and leaned back, again. "Of course, there's the law of nature—cause and effect—you rode your bicycle into the path of an oncoming car and it hit you. I wish it hadn't happened, but, there it is. However, God can help you right where you are, if you believe in His Word." He opened the Bible and read, "And we know that all things work together for good to them that love God, to them who are called according to his purpose" (Romans 8:28)."

"What good can come of this?" Becky asked, angrily.

"We may not know that for a long time," Pastor Richards replied, softly. "That's where faith comes in."

Becky closed her eyes wearily.

The minister studied Becky's bruised and pale face and patted her hand. "I know you're tired. You go ahead and rest. I'll just sit here and pray for a while." He closed his eyes and began to pray.

Lisa and Mary Beth waved good-bye, once more, then disappeared through the hospital doorway.

Becky looked up at the floating balloon they had tied to her bed rail and tears filled her eyes. She envied the way they could come and go. They took their health and mobility for granted—just as she had, before the accident. 'It isn't fair!' she cried to herself for the hundredth time. She was too young for her life to be over. How could she face the future?

"God will help you through this," Pastor Richards and her mother told her, repeatedly. "Just ask for His guidance and peace."

Becky was so tired of it all. Every night, she dreamed of running, riding her bike, skating—doing all the things she loved to do. But, every morning she awoke to the realization that she was a paraplegic. She was paralyzed from the waist down. She would have to use a wheel chair, from now on.

For the past three weeks, Becky had a steady stream of visitors:

grandparents, classmates, relatives—and they had all tried to cheer her up. 'But, they have no idea what I'm going through,' Becky thought to herself. The horror of knowing she'd never walk again filled her every waking moment. She desperately wanted peace.

Suddenly, Pastor Richards' words came into her mind. "Turn it over to God," he had said. "Remember what Jesus promised in Matthew 11:25, 'Come to me, all of you who are tired from carrying heavy loads, and I will give you rest." "Oh, God," Becky said, closing her eyes tightly, "please help me!" Tears began to flow. "I don't know what to say—I never really prayed seriously, before. But, they tell me You can help. And, Lord, I need help! Please show me what to do. I'm so angry and frightened! I feel like I'll never be happy, again." Becky thought for a minute. "I ask for Your guidance and peace, in the name of Jesus. Amen."

Becky dried her eyes and looked around the room. "Not much of a prayer," she thought. "I'd better work on it." She reached for the Bible that Pastor Richards had left on her side table. She was able to move around a little, now that they'd removed the neck brace. Her injured shoulder gave a twinge as she lifted the heavy book, but it was much better, now—sore, but flexible. She propped the Bible up on her lap, turned to Matthew in the New Testament, and began to read.

Shortly, Becky's studies were interrupted by someone knocking. She glanced at her watch and was astonished to see that 45 minutes had passed. "Come in!" she called.

Suddenly, a large, black Labrador Retriever stepped into her room. "What in the world ...?" Becky's comment was cut short by the sight of a young woman in a wheel chair. The dog was harnessed and pulled the wheel chair further into the room.

"Hi!" the young woman said, smiling broadly. "My name is Nancy, and this is Baron." The dog wagged his tail and turned to his mistress at the sound of his name. "He's my support dog," she explained. "That's why he's allowed in the hospital. May I come in?"

Becky nodded in confusion and watched Baron pull the wheel chair next to her bed. Then, he sat down, looking over his shoulder for further instructions, his big tongue hanging in a happy grin.

"Baron, say hello to Becky," Nancy commanded.

The black dog promptly placed his large paw on Becky's bed. She reached down to shake it. Then, she patted his head through the bars. "He's a beautiful dog," Becky said, smiling as Baron nudged her hand for more pats. It didn't occur to her until much later that this was the first time she'd smiled since the accident.

"He loves attention, too" Nancy agreed, laughingly. She held out her hand in a friendly gesture, and Becky shook it. "Now," Nancy said, wheeling herself even closer to the bed, "let me tell you why I'm here."

⚘

Several weeks had gone by since Becky was released from the hospital.

Dr. Gonzales arranged for her to attend the Irene Walter Johnson Rehabilitation Center for daily therapy.

"You'll need three to six months of physical therapy," the doctor had explained to Becky and her parents. "It can take up to a year for your body to heal completely. But, in the meantime, you must build your upper body strength and keep your muscles from atrophying—wasting away—due to lack of use. Your shoulder has healed sufficiently to allow you to begin therapy, right away."

Throughout the entire process, Becky prayed. She was so grateful that she had listened to Pastor Richards and her mother about praying for peace and guidance. If it hadn't been for daily Bible study and constant prayers, she wouldn't have made it … at least, not with peace in her heart. She cringed to think of what those early days of pain and anguish were like before she accepted the Lord's healing Word to comfort her. Thank God, those days were over.

"I've never had a patient as young as you handle themselves and their pain so well," Becky's therapist, often commented.

"The secret is to take your eyes off yourself and look to God," Becky would tell her. Her faith and courage became an inspiration to the staff and patients, alike.

Even so, there were days when Becky couldn't help but cry because her shoulders, arms and back hurt so much. Her mother left during therapy—she couldn't watch Becky suffer.

But, through it all, the Lord flooded Becky with a serenity that allowed her to face each ordeal following her release from the hospital. She had to overcome her pride and the embarrassment of her mother caring for her and bathing her. And, she tried to think of how blessed she was every time her father had to carry her from one location to another.

"It's no hardship for me," her father assured her. "We're just happy to have you home."

"It won't be long before I can carry you, too!" Ryan said, flexing the muscles in his thin arms.

Becky laughed at that and ruffled her younger brother's curly red hair. He had quite a bit of growing to do before he could lift her. But, it was a nice thing to say, anyway. In the meantime, he never seemed to tire of fetching things for Becky and trying to make her more comfortable. "All in all," Becky thought, "God and my family made the transition from hospital to home a joyful event."

Shortly before leaving the hospital, Jim Harrigan, a sales representative from a local medical supply store brought some catalogues for Becky and her parents to look at. They chose several pieces of medical equipment and supplies, plus, Jim measured Becky for a wheel chair. They decided on a lightweight, collapsible chair—just like the one Nancy owned.

Dr. Gonzales had contacted Nancy, a former patient of his, and asked her to visit Becky and tell her about Support Dogs.

"Because of Baron, I'm able to live alone, go shopping, and even attend school," Nancy told her. "He opens heavy doors, pulls my wheelchair, loads it into the van, carries my books and packages, retrieves objects for me ... plus, he's a loving companion."

Nancy went on to explain that Support Dogs are trained to assist people with all types of disabilities such as multiple sclerosis, cerebral palsy, muscular dystrophy, "... and spinal cord injuries, like yours and mine." Nancy was only twelve when an auto accident caused her paralysis. She related the story of her recovery and gave Becky a brochure and an application for a Support Dog, along with her home telephone number. "Whenever you feel like you need to talk to someone who understands, call me," she told Becky.

When Nancy left her hospital room that day, Becky closed her eyes in a joyful prayer of thanksgiving. After weeks of self-pity and angry rejection, God had immediately and lovingly answered her awkward prayer for guidance and peace. She had no doubt whatsoever that it was the Lord who led Nancy to her. A warmth flowed over her body as she prayed, and Becky knew—no matter what happened—God would be with her. She was learning to trust Him, moment by moment.

⚬⚬⚬

The Support Dog staff contacted Becky within a few days of receiving her application, and they interviewed her several times over the next two weeks.

"I knew it!" Becky responded when told she was accepted as a client. And, much to her family's astonishment, they discovered there was no charge for either the dog or the services ... a savings of over $10,000! God had led Becky to a nonprofit organization totally supported by contributions. The once-bitter girl glowed with love for her Lord who continued to pour out blessings upon her.

Next she prayed for a perfect match—the right support dog for her. The staff told her it sometimes took two years to match up a client with an animal, but Becky just prayed all the harder and studied God's Word even more. So, it came as no surprise to Becky when she received a phone call within a month.

"We have a Golden Retriever named Buck who entered our intensive training program, four months ago," the S.D. staff told Becky. "He's 22 months old, strong, and intelligent; we think he might be the one for you." They promised to meet with Becky, again, when her therapy ended in three months to determine her abilities. "Then," they continued, "we'll customize Buck's training for your specific needs. That's when you'll need to come to our facilities. You'll work with Buck and our staff, daily, for a month of individualized instruction."

Becky claimed Buck as her dog.

"Bucky and Becky—sounds like a team to me," Ryan said.

"Becky and Buck," his sister corrected him. "Yes," she thought, "it has a nice ring to it ... just as if God planned it that way."

Now, Becky had a new direction—while Buck was strenuously training to assist her, Becky redoubled her therapy. She wanted to be in the best possible physical condition when she met Buck for the first time.

⚜

Becky listened in stunned silence as her mother explained that she could not return to public school.

"Parkway High School doesn't have the facilities to accommodate your wheelchair," Deborah Rogers said as gently as possible. She picked up Becky's hand and held it.

Swallowing hard, Becky closed her eyes for a moment. She said a short prayer, then opened her eyes, again. It had never occurred to her that she couldn't return to Parkway High and rejoin her classmates. "But, I thought ... with Buck's help ..." She couldn't finish the sentence.

Becky's father cleared his throat. "We checked with both the principal and the Special School District. Their only alternative is to transfer you to the Special School on Clayton Road."

The stricken look on Becky's face told them how she felt.

"Isn't that where all those kids go—you know, the ones who wear helmets to protect their heads?" Ryan asked.

"Yes," Stephen told his son, "but the students aren't all mentally handicapped. There are many who are physically challenged—like Becky."

Becky looked down and her mother patted the hand she still held. "There is one other option open to us," she said quietly.

Becky looked up with an equal mixture of hope and apprehension in her eyes.

"We could start home schooling," her mother announced.

"Mother and I met with Pastor Richards, the other day," her father added, "and he referred us to Mr. and Mrs. Brown—they're the Christian homeschool support group coordinators for this area."

Becky's mother nodded and picked up the conversation. "And, we're going to a homeschool meeting, this evening at eight o'clock. We want you to come with us, if you feel up to it."

"Can I come, too?" Ryan asked.

"Of course! The whole family's invited."

Three pairs of eyes looked at Becky, expectantly.

"I ... guess so," Becky agreed with a noncommittal shrug of her shoulders.

"Homeschool?" she thought, "what's going to happen to me next?"

⚜

They drove three blocks to the Brown's home at Becky's request. She was still a little shy about being pushed down the street in her wheelchair. She decided to add prayers on "acceptance" and "overcoming pride" to her list. Her prayer list was growing daily.

"Do they know I'm in a wheelchair?" she asked anxiously.

"Yes," her mother replied. "Mrs. Brown assured me it would be no problem."

As they pulled into the driveway, a small woman with a large smile rushed out to meet them. "You must be the new family," she said, reaching out to shake hands as Deborah Rogers stepped from the car. "I'm Bonnie Brown."

Deborah introduced the rest of the family while Stephen and Ryan set up Becky's wheelchair. Becky briefly shook Mrs. Brown's hand, then, concentrated on transferring herself from the car to the chair. Her therapy was working; the transfer became easier as time passed.

"You can wheel yourself right through the front door," Mrs. Brown was saying. "My father uses a wheelchair, and he visits us quite often. So, we've had ramps and handrails installed, carpets removed, and doorways widened. You might say we're 'wheelchair-friendly'," she added, grinning.

Becky allowed her father to push her into the house and felt her neck muscles loosen somewhat. "Maybe this won't be so bad, after all," she thought. She bit her lower lip in anticipation as they entered the well-lit home. There appeared to be people everywhere.

"May I have your attention!" Mrs. Brown called. When everyone quieted down and turned toward her, she said, "Please welcome the Rogers family. Deborah, Stephen, Ryan, and Becky, meet the West County Homeschool Support Group!"

As Becky progressed slowly into a large family room, people introduced themselves to her. She glanced back and saw her family surrounded, too. Ryan grinned as several people ruffled his curly red hair.

"Do you homeschool, yet?"

Becky turned to face the man who was talking to her. "No ... not yet."

"I think you're going to be pleasantly surprised. Peter," the man indicated the person standing next to him, "has never attended a public school."

"Really?" Becky studied the young man.

"Hi!" he said, shaking her hand, "I'm Peter Brown and this is my father, Dennis."

"I'll never remember everyone's name," she said apologetically.

"Sure, you will—eventually," Peter said with a smile. "There aren't that many of us, only six families in our group—twelve adults and ten kids. If you join, that will be a total of twenty-six people. Some of the groups are much larger. We get together, on occasion—you know, for picnics and ball games." Peter glanced down at Becky's wheelchair. "What happened?" he asked.

"I was hit by a car," Becky replied.

"Boy, that's tough! Is that why you're going to homeschool?"

"I don't know ...," Becky began, but she was interrupted by Ryan.

"Wow! This punch tastes great! Do you want some, Becky?" Without waiting for an answer, Ryan shoved a cup of red punch into Becky's hand. Then, he turned to Peter and said, "Who're you?"

"Peter Brown—I live here—and I made the punch," he laughingly responded. "How old are you?" Ryan asked with youthful abruptness.

"Fourteen."

"Hm, I'm thirteen, you're fourteen, and Becky's fifteen!" Ryan thought about that for a minute, then asked, "What grade are you in?"

"Ninth!"

"Hey, that's the same grade Becky's in! You must be pretty smart!"

"Not necessarily," Peter grinned. "In homeschool, you progress at your own rate. We don't focus much on grade levels."

"Tell me about homeschool," Becky urged.

⁂

"HOMESCHOOL?" Lisa looked at Mary Beth with the same expression Becky had when she first heard about it, weeks before.

Becky laughed. "I know what you're thinking. But, it's a lot different than I first imagined."

"Is your mother going to teach you?" Mary Beth asked in a horrified voice.

"Not really," Becky said. "You see, there are several ways you can homeschool." Becky went on to explain what she'd learned at the support group about creating your own curriculum, establishing your routine, attending homeschool fairs, using correspondence courses, etc.

"You mean, there's other kids in the neighborhood going to school in their own homes?" Lisa looked astonished.

"Yes, there are ten in this area—well, twelve, now, including Ryan and me."

"Ryan! Your little brother's home schooling, too?"

Becky laughed and nodded. "When Ryan heard how you can study at your own pace—and, especially when he heard about all of the group field trips and other activities—well, he became really excited about it. He asked Mom and Dad if he could homeschool, too, and they agreed."

"But, doesn't he miss his friends from school?"

"No, he still talks to them, and they get together—just as we do."

"How do you feel about it?" Mary Beth asked, leaning forward in concerned concentration.

"At first, I was very depressed," Becky admitted. "It seemed like another important part of my life had been taken away from me."

Her friends nodded their understanding.

"There's even a homeschool term for it—it's called decompression. That's the period of adjustment between leaving public school and getting actively involved in your own education. But, I got over it pretty quickly. Now, I really look forward to each new lesson. I, even, helped choose my own curriculum!"

"You did? How?"

"Well, my family and I decided to start with a correspondence course offered by the Christian Liberty Academy in Illinois. First, Ryan and I completed the application forms. Then, the Academy sent us some basic tests to determine our skill levels and tailored our courses to meet our needs. We helped choose our own textbooks—in school we always had to take what they gave us. The counselor recommended lessons at a seventh grade level for Ryan. Mine are at a tenth grade level."

"TENTH!" both girls cried at once.

Becky laughed. "Yes, apparently I tested higher than I thought I would. So, now, I'm homeschooling after daily therapy! I'm pretty much in charge of my progress. For instance, if I have a bad day, I can postpone my lessons—or, I can complete two lessons in one afternoon! It's a great feeling to be responsible for your own education—of course, I'm guided by the people at the Academy."

"Will you receive report cards?" Lisa asked.

"And, how many grades levels does the Academy handle?" Mary Beth added.

Becky told Lisa, "Yes, they grade my work, keep records, and send quarterly report cards." She turned to Mary Beth, "And, the Academy offers courses from K3 through the twelfth grade. When I graduate, I'll receive an official transcript. After that, I think I'll attend Junior College. They have ramps and facilities for the handicapped—plus, I'll have my support dog to help me."

Both girls sat back in wide-eyed wonder and admiration.

"Ryan's not the only one excited about the field trips," Becky added with a sparkle in her eyes. "Recently, the homeschool group arranged to have us visit a photographer's studio—we visit artists, craftsmen, courthouses, etc., and write essays about them, as part of our studies. At the studio, not only were we allowed to watch the photographer take pictures, but he let us help develop a roll of film. It was fascinating! In fact, I'm thinking of adding photography to my curriculum—it would make a wonderful career—wheelchair-bound, or not!"

"But, what about all of the special equipment and resources available at the public schools? Sometimes, you'd need those, wouldn't you?"

"There are seven families in our group, and a dozen groups in our network at all age levels. We share equipment, supplies, and books. We have access to school gyms. Plus, some group-members' churches and companies allow us to use their office equipment during slow periods and on weekends. Everyone has just been wonderful; this is an entirely different world than the one I knew.

"Here! These homeschooling magazines can say it better than I can."

Lisa and Mary Beth each borrowed two magazines and promised to bring them back. They definitely wanted to learn more about their friend's new life. And, they wanted to share this information with their parents.

⚜

"I can't wait to see Buck," Ryan said, fidgeting in his seat. Deborah Rogers turned around to smile at both of her children.

"It's been a long three months," Becky agreed. It was time to meet her Support Dog. Becky found it hard to believe that her accident only happened six months earlier. It seemed so much longer.

Her physical therapy ended the previous week, and Becky couldn't say she was sorry. She'd grown fond of the therapists and knew she'd miss them, for a while. But, it was time to get on with her life. Her broken bones and torn ligaments had healed, and she'd developed the upper body strength she needed to swing herself from her bed into her wheel chair. Her father rarely had to carry her, now.

"Are you all right back there, honey?" her father called over his shoulder, as if he knew she was thinking about him.

"I couldn't be better," Becky said, smiling at his reflection in the rearview mirror. Her parents had talked about buying a new van with an electric chair-lift, but Becky reminded them that Buck was being trained to lift her wheel chair onto the special rack attached to the back of the car. Her medical expenses had been so great, she didn't want her parents to go deeper into debt on her account. With Buck's help, Becky would even be able to drive the family car, some day—with the installation of hand gears. There were so many possibilities open to her, she had even begun to think about the future, again.

"Well, here we are," her father announced as he pulled up to the entrance of the Support Dog office building and training center.

Within minutes, Donna, one of the staff, led Becky and her family into a large room that reminded Becky of the school gym. There were various obstacles scattered throughout the room, and trainers and clients, alike, were sitting in wheel chairs pulled by harnessed dogs.

"This is the training area for our service dogs," Donna said. "We, also, have Therapy Dogs, but, they're in another section of the building. Their training isn't as vigorous or lengthy because they're simply taught to assist people with therapy—or, just love them! We have a program that enables us to take our Social Dogs into hospitals and nursing homes to provide affection to the patients. You'd be surprised at how effective these animals are.

"And, now, I want you to meet Buck!" Donna signaled to a trainer who steered a large, golden retriever toward the group.

"Oh, boy!" Ryan cried, ready to run to the beautiful animal.

"No, Ryan," Donna warned, "Buck is Becky's service dog. She must meet with him, first. They have to form a close bond, and that will require everyone else to back off, for a while."

Becky's parents hugged Ryan and they stepped away so Becky could face Buck, alone.

As soon as Becky looked into Buck's eyes, she knew that, somehow, the dog recognized her as his mistress. The trainer disconnected the harness, and Buck trotted over to Becky. He sniffed her feet, then examined her wheel chair, carefully. Finally, he sat down in front of her and lifted his paw onto her knee.

"Wow!" Ryan shouted.

"It seems to be a match," Donna agreed, smiling broadly.

Becky bent over to vigorously rub the fur behind both of Buck's ears.

She held Buck's face in her hands and whispered, "God has given you to me, Buck. We're going to be one of the best teams this institution ever brought together." Buck looked directly into Becky's eyes and made a noise that sounded like, "Yep!"

※◎※

Becky glanced at her wristwatch and estimated that Buck had been gone for about seven minutes. She looked around the wooded hillside and watched the leaves swaying in the slight breeze.

Then, she moved her head slowly back and forth, and cautiously moved her arms and shoulders. She had an abrasion on her left hand, but her fingers moved easily. It appeared that she was just shaken, but not injured. Becky closed her eyes for a small prayer of thanksgiving.

Suddenly, she heard a deep-throated bark. "Buck," she thought.

"Becky! Becky, where are you?"

"Mom! Here I am!" Becky responded in a relieved voice.

Leaves and twigs scattered in all directions as Buck raced to Becky's side. He sniffed her face and groaned anxiously, as if to say, "Are you all right?" Becky hugged Buck and told him, "I think I'm fine!"

"Oh, my word … are you hurt?"

Becky lifted her head to watch her mother slip-slide down the hill to reach her side. "I don't think so. I'm able to move everything, so I don't believe there are any broken bones … just a few scrapes, here and there."

Becky's mother examined her head, neck, shoulders, arms, hands, and legs. Then, she sat back on her heels and said, "Thank God, I think you're right!"

Her worried face relaxed a little. "I'll go back to the house to call for help so we can carry you up the hill."

"Wait, Mom," Becky stopped her. "Buck can pull me. If you'll attach his harness to my chair …"

Becky watched as her mother reconnected the leather straps. "Now, try to straighten my chair … Buck, pull!" Becky motioned for Buck to grab the top of one wheel and pull on it. Her mother made sure the brakes were on, then she guided the chair to an upright position.

"Good boy! Now, pull me up the hill, Buck!"

Becky's mother flicked off the brakes, and the powerful animal began to haul the wheel chair slowly up the leaf-covered incline. "All you have to do is guide me," Becky called over her shoulder. "Buck will do the rest."

Deborah Rogers shook her head with wonder at the strength Buck exhibited. "Surely, God must have sent this animal to us," she murmured to herself. She guided the chair around limbs and rocks, and thought back through the previous year. "Your birthday is only one week from today," she spoke aloud without thinking.

Buck's ears twitched backward, but he continued to strain toward the crest of the hill.

"That's it, Buck! Keep going! Good boy!" Becky smiled as they reached the edge. One final tug, and the wheel chair was back on the hiking trail, once more.

Becky and her mother both threw their arms around the panting animal. Becky rubbed her face in his luxurious fur and said, "Thank you, Buck. Good boy!" Then, she reached for her mother's hand. "I'm really sorry I worried you, Mom. From now on, I'll wait until Ryan or one of my friends can come with me before I go hiking, again."

Becky's mother smiled with relief. "No need to lecture Becky," she

thought, "she's learning as she goes."

"Okay, Buck, let's go home. Pull!" Becky glanced over her shoulder.

Her mother guided the wheel chair as Buck pulled her along the dirt path. "Now, what were you saying about my birthday?" she said, grinning.

🔥 Comprehension Questions

1. How did Becky Rodgers become injured and paralyzed?

2. In what ways did the story reveal that Becky struggled with pride and worldliness before her accident?

3. What type of school did Becky go to after she returned from the hospital?

4. What was the name of Becky's dog?

5. It has been said that God is more interested in saving His children through problems rather than from problems. Do you think this principle held true in the life of Becky Rodgers? Please explain your answer.

53 *Only If We Have To*

by Doug Rennie

They were driving to Warrensville, out beyond the suburbs, to look at a car. They had nine thousand to spend—"but only if we have to," Mark said. He ran his free hand over his beard and looked over at Brenda who was turning the knobs on the radio. They had been married almost a year, and she was seven months pregnant. A month ago, they had put a deposit down on a two-bedroom English-style cottage in an older, but well-maintained, neighborhood. The house had a small formal garden, like the white-sided homes of Surrey and Sussex whose photographs she always scissored out of travel magazines and filed away. The kind of home she had always wanted to live in. The house was near both shopping and a large, treed park. The perfect place to raise a child.

"It sounds like a good car," Brenda said. "I mean, in the paper."

"Uh-huh. First day for the ad, I think. Sounded mechanically A-OK. Low miles, too. That's the key, Bren. Low miles. So you don't start putting money in right off."

"Ummm. Well, that's what he told you, right? Low miles?"

"Yep."

"So, how did he come across on the phone?"

"Uh, old, I'd say. Well, kinda old. His voice sounded weak, like he was talking from a long way off. Yeah. Older guy, I'd guess. Seems his wife died a few months back and he's still…what? Thinning things out, I guess. Selling off stuff he doesn't need anymore."

Brenda twisted one of her brown bangs around a finger. "She died?"

"Uh-huh. S'what he said."

She looked out the window at a station wagon they were passing. "What of?"

Mark glanced at his watch. "Five to 10. I told him we'd be there between 10, 10:30. Looks like we'll make it easy." He returned his eyes to the road. "Sorry, hon. You say something?"

"I asked you what she died of. Did he say?"

"Uh, no. Just that she'd died. That, and when. A few months back, like I said. Anyway, what difference does it make?"

A frown formed briefly on her face, then just as quickly vanished.

"And he sounded old? Like an older man?"

"Well, yeah, that's how he sounded to me. But who knows? I mean the guy could be twenty-eight for all I know. But he did sound old, you know, sort of…what? Small, I guess. Something like that."

"Poor old guy." She began to massage the back of her hand. "That's tough. Really tough. I mean they were probably married, what, forty years or something? Imagine losing someone after spending most of your life with them."

Mark laughed. "Hey, hold on, kiddo. First of all, we don't really know for sure how old this guy is. Or how long he was married. Could have been his third or fourth wife, for all we know. Don't start feeling sorry for him so soon, if you know what I mean."

The frown returned, "So soon?"

"Sweetie, sweetie." He patted her thigh. "We've got some heavy-duty negotiating to do here. Guy's asking ten K. I'm…*we're* just not going to pay that. No one pays asking price. Ever. We'll get the car for a grand, grand and a half less. At least." He tapped his front teeth. "Hey, we might even get him down to eight. Put the rest into a new kitchen. How's that sound?" He began to tighten his grip on the wheel, then loosen it, then tighten it again. "The guy doesn't need two cars anymore, probably just wants to get rid of the thing. I gotta feeling, Bren. I'm betting we can hardball this guy."

Her eyes traced his profile. The straight nose, the thin lips. She sighed, then swallowed. "C'mon, Mark. Isn't that just, I mean, a little *cold*?"

"Nah." He shook his head, slowly at first, then faster. "Like I said, he probably just wants the thing out of his hair. What's he need a second car for? He came up with the ten-K tag as a starting point, that's all. That's how it's done, Bren. Remember when we sold your old '72 Bug? We put, what, twelve hundred in the paper, right? All the time thinking if we got ten, ten-fifty, we'd be happy. Remember? And we got"— he narrowed his eyes and bobbed his head— "ten-fifty, I think. Ten-fifty, yeah. Hey, nobody expects to get asking price. I'm even thinking we're doing the old guy a favor by taking it off his hands. I mean, he probably sees her every time he looks at it."

She nodded, but said nothing. Bonnie Rait's voice came out of the radio and she moved her head to the music. She thought about what Mark had said, about the common sense of it, the undeniable logic, and she found herself thinking, almost involuntarily, that, yes, he was right. This was the way you bought a car. Even a new one. That's what her dad and older brother had said, the way it was done. Besides, you almost always had to start putting money in right away, so it was only fair. She reached over and squeezed his hand.

"Yeah," she said, "I guess you're right. I mean, he lives in Stonegate, right? So how bad can he need the money?"

"Exactly." Mark snapped his fingers. "Like I said, if we buy the car, we'll be helping him out, one less thing for the grieving widower to worry about."

They rode the rest of the way in silence, and several minutes later pulled up in front of a stucco house painted pale eggshell with a small, neat lawn and a grove of white-barked birch on one side of a bricked entry.

"Well," Mark said, looking around, "this must be, like Baja Stonegate or something. The big houses are a mile more up the road." He unbuckled his seat belt, took a deep breath, and released it slowly. "So let's get this thing started—and remember Bren, don't act excited, even if you like the car, okay? I mean don't even smile."

"Okay," she said, reaching for the door handle. "Okay, I got it."

A few seconds after they rang the bell, a man opened the door. Mid-seventies, on the small side, neatly trimmed white hair, dressed in a plaid flannel shirt and old khakis. He extended his hand to Mark. "Hello," he said. "I'm Raymond Henderson. You're here about the car?"

Mark nodded and took the hand. Brenda started to smile, but then caught herself.

Motioning them to follow, the old man walked toward the open garage. "Well, that's her." He pointed to a white Accord. "It was, as I told you on the phone, my wife's car. She drove it infrequently. Oh, I know that's what everyone selling a car says." He smiled and seemed on the verge of chuckling, but did not. "In this case, though, it's true." He paused and rubbed his fingertips over his chin. "Her eyes, mainly. They weren't so good the last few years. So most everywhere we went, we took my car."

"Uh-huh," Mark said. "Well, let's have a look."

They all walked over to the car. Mark ran a hand over the front fender, then turned suddenly toward Henderson. "So, what's high blue book on this car?"

"Blue...book?" Henderson's forehead wrinkled. "Why, I don't know. Not even a guess, I'm afraid."

"Eighty-one," Mark said. "I looked it up. Maybe eighty-three if the miles are way low."

"Eighty-three, you say? Well, I, ah, I mean—"

"So where did you come up with the ten-thousand figure, if you don't mind me asking, sir?" Mark's voice was low, the words slow and deliberate, respectful.

"Well, I...looked at the newspaper ads. There were two others of this model, this, ah, year, one a shade higher, the other one a bit lower. So I just put it in between."

Mark nodded and ran a finger over his lower lip. "Yeah. Lot of people do that. But you know, of course, that those numbers aren't at all reliable, don't tell you much about what the car's really worth. People—and I've done the same thing myself—tend to ask a lot higher than the car's real value." He laughed and turned his palms up. "And, hey, why not? I mean, everyone wants to get as much as they can, especially for a car they took good care of, right? That's what we did when we sold her old Volks, right Bren?" He nudged his head in her direction. She formed a smile and rested her arms across the arch of her stomach. "We asked twelve, took nine-fifty." Mark laughed and Henderson smiled in response. "Well, yes, I suppose that's so," the old man said. "Perhaps I should have checked this, this blue book thing, but I just wanted to sell the car as quickly as I could. No need having it around now. I can't—I won't—drive it." He looked over at the car, then off beyond it. "Still smells like her inside, you know." He put his hands in his pockets and rocked back slightly on his heels. "Besides, the funeral costs were more than I expected, so—"

"Sure, of course. You need to get a fair price out of the car. I understand that, appreciate your position. And we want to pay a fair price, too. So, let's see what gives inside." Mark opened the door and slid in behind the wheel. "Hmmm. Some play in this clutch. Feels a little worn." He turned toward Henderson and grinned widely. "Women, huh? They all like to rest their foot on the clutch. Kinda funny, you know, a stick. Most women, older ones especially, drive automatics."

"No, no. Not Eleanor. Didn't trust them, she said. Claimed they crept on her at stoplights."

Mark stepped out of the car and squatted near the front fender. "Tires look okay, not great, but okay. Good for another eight months, a year maybe." He looked up at Henderson.

"Ever replace the brakes or water pump? Timing belt?

"Well no. The miles were so low that—"

"Twenty-seven thousand, the odometer says. Those mechanicals start to go pretty fast once a car gets close to thirty. Timing belt, especially. Wham! then you're looking at a whole new engine."

Henderson licked his lips. "I really…I had no idea. It always felt so new. So solid and all."

"Well, it is, Mr. Henderson. Basically a pretty sound car. Going to need some work pretty soon, though." Mark massaged his chin. "Tell you what. I'll give you seventy-six. Have a cashier's check for you this afternoon."

"Seventy-six hundred? I…I was hoping to get more. Maybe ten thousand was a little, ah, unrealistic, but—"

"Okay, we can go seventy-eight. We just bought a house, and as you can see, Bren here's expecting." He nodded in her direction and grinned. "We're a little tight on cash right now, but I guess we can come up a few hundred. Tough time for you, too, we know that, and we don't want to drag this out. Anyone who comes out's going to tell you that you're off base to ask even nine for this car. Like I said, it's going to need more than a little work."

Henderson drew a long, deep breath and tapped his foot on the driveway. He turned and, bent forward, walked a few steps back toward the house, his head nodding slowly and rhythmically. Mark looked over at Brenda and grinned, then made a circle of his thumb and forefinger, thrust it toward her, and mouthed "Got it!" She nodded and managed to lift the corners of her mouth.

Henderson walked back toward them. "Well, you think seventy-eight is a good price, a fair price. For both of us." He jingled some coins in his pocket. "You seem like a nice young couple. I just don't know these things. I thought…I mean…." His voice faded off but he continued making gestures with his hands.

"It is Mr. Henderson. Check the blue book and you'll see."

"Oh, I don't even know what one looks like. Except, I imagine, that it has a blue cover."

Mark laughed. "So. A deal then?"

"Well, I…ah…yes. A deal."

"Good! I'll go to the credit union right away, be back here at," he looked at his watch, "1:30, maybe a little earlier, with a cashier's check made out to…to Raymond Henderson. That's with an *o*?"

"An *o*, yes." Henderson stared straight ahead, gnawing at his lower lip. "And," he said, "thank you for being so well-informed. And for being so fair."

"Sure thing. Thank you, sir." Mark looked at his watch, bobbed his head several times as if counting. "So, we'll be back shortly. If you could have all the paperwork—pink slip and all—ready to go, well, we'd be grateful."

He reached over and took her hand. "C'mon, Bren."

Minutes later they were in the car, heading back to town. "Whoa," she said, "lucky you were there. That car looked in such good shape, I mean so new-looking, I'd have paid what he asked right off. Good thing you spotted all those problems."

He threw his head back and laughed. "There weren't any, Bren. None. The car's cherry. Engine. Tires. Clutch is like new. It's in mint condition. We won't put a dime in it. Hey, I'm thinking—seriously, Bren—I'm thinking about putting it in the paper next weekend. Twelve, fifteen hundred instant profit, easy."

"But you said—I mean what about all that work, that...that belt thing?"

"All crap, Bren. Just crap! The guy didn't know beans about cars. I just pulled that out of the air!" He pounded the wheel with both hands. "You could see right off he mainly just wanted the thing out of his life. You know what? I'm thinking now we could have taken him down to the low sevens. Yee haw!"

She felt her face flush. Her heart skipped a beat. Then another. She closed her eyes, then moved her face to open the window and let the breeze hit it. "He was an old man, Mark," she said after half a minute. "Confused. Still depressed." She shook her head. "I know we're not rich, but that...that wasn't right."

"Hello. Earth to Brenda." He reached over and squeezed her cheek. "Money, babe. That's what it's all about. Life's bottom line, like it or not. Hey, too bad if he didn't check the blue book. His problem, not mine...ours." He ran his hand over her leg. "Like I told you on the way out, Bren: 'only if we have to.' "

She nodded and repeated his words twice, quietly, slowly, more to herself than to him. She remembered once before, when he had brought home a computer from work. An old one, he told her. Just taking up space. At least now someone will be using it. She had said nothing then and, as she looked out the car window toward the distant hills and slowly moved her hand over her round, hard belly, she knew she would say nothing this time either.

🌿 Comprehension Questions

1. From a Christian perspective, should it have made any substantial difference to the young couple that the man with whom they were dealing was elderly? If the man's age was a factor, in what respect was it an issue and in what respect was it irrelevant?

2. Why is it dangerous for people to place the accumulation of things on a higher scale of importance than human relationships? Read 1 Timothy 6:6–10 and Luke 12:13–21 before answering this question.

3. Did Brenda provide a biblical basis for her objections to her husband's behavior? Why is it important for moral principles to be linked or supported by eternal truths that emanate from a holy Creator?

4. How do you think Mark's attitude would have changed if he had comprehended that his wicked actions were going to be revenged by a holy God? Read Psalm 94 before you answer this question.

5. What does this story teach regarding the capacity of fallen human beings to deceive themselves? In what specific ways did both Brenda and Mark attempt to justify their phoniness and unrighteous behavior?

6. How does the "golden rule" of doing unto others as you would have them do unto you, apply in our business or financial dealings with others? Matthew 7:12

7. Was it sinful for the young couple to have attempted to bargain with Mr. Henderson in an effort to obtain his car for less than $10,000 dollars? In other words, was the sin committed by this couple tied to the fact that they tried to obtain a good deal?

54 *All Nature Sings!*

By J. Gresham Machen

As our cities spread rapidly in every direction, and as the pace of living becomes more and more hurried, people feel increasingly the need of the quietude of nature. Dr. Machen, a distinguished scholar and teacher, found not only rest but also revelation in the mountains of Europe and America. After reading his essay we may well ask ourselves. "What do I see when I go out into the world of nature? What do I hear?"

≈≈◎≈≈

The testimony of nature to nature's God comes to men in different ways. To some it speaks most clearly through the knowledge of nature possessed by the scientist. To others it comes by what the poet Browning calls "a sunset touch." To one man in one way, to another in another.

To me nature speaks most clearly in the majesty and beauty of the hills. One day in the summer of 1932 I stood on the summit of the Matterhorn in the Alps. Some people can stand there and see very little. Depreciating the Matterhorn is a recognized part of modern books on mountain climbing. The great mountain, it is said, has been sadly spoiled. Why, you can even see sardine cans on those rocks that so tempted the ambition of climbers in Whymper's[1] day.

Well, I can only say that I do not remember seeing a single can when I stood on the Matterhorn. Perhaps that was partly because of the unusual masses of fresh snow which were then on the mountain; but I think it was also due to the fact that unlike some people I had eyes for something else. I saw the vastness of the Italian plain, which was like a symbol of infinity. I saw the snows of distant mountains. I saw the sweet green valleys far, far below, at my feet. I saw the whole glorious round of glittering peaks, bathed in an unearthly light. And as I see that glorious vision again before me now, I am thankful from the bottom of my heart that from my mother's knee I have known to whom all that glory is due.

---

1. Whymper was an English Alpinist, or mountain climber, who lived from 1840 to 1911.

My mother was used by God to provide me with the capacity to love the softer beauties of nature. I wonder whether you love them with me. Some years ago, in the White Mountains,[2] I walked beside a brook. I have seen, I suppose, hundreds of brooks. But somehow I remember particularly that one. I am not going to tell you where it is, because if I did you might write to the National Park Service about it and get them to put a scenic highway along it, and then it would be forever ruined. But when I walked along it, it was untouched. I cherish the memory of it. It was gentle and sweet and lovely beyond all words. I think a man might travel through all the world and never see anything lovelier than a White Mountain brook. Very wonderful is the variety of nature in her changing moods.

Silence too, the silence of nature, can be a very revealing thing. I remember one day when I spent a peaceful half-hour in the sunlight on the summit of a mountain in the Franconia range.[3] I there experienced something very rare. Would you believe it, my friends? It was really silent on that sunny mountain top. There was not the honk of a motor horn; there was no jazz music; there was no sound of a human voice; there was not even the rustling of the leaves. There was nothing but a strange, brooding silence. It was a precious time indeed. I shall never forget it all my life.

Please do not misunderstand me. I am not asking that everyone should love the beauties of nature as I love them. I well understand that there are many people who do not love the beauties of nature. Are they shut off from finding God revealed in the world that He has made?

That is not so, my friends; indeed, it is not so. The mystery of the existence of the world presses itself upon different people in different ways. I remember, for example, a talk that I heard from a professor at an afternoon conference service many years ago. The professor said that he had had a friend who had come to a belief in God, or had come back to a belief in God, by—what do you suppose? Well, by a trip through Europe! As he went from city to city and observed the seething multitudes, the throngs upon throngs of men and women, somehow, he said, the conviction just seemed to come over him: "There is a God, there is a God."

---

2. This range of mountains is part of the Appalachian system and is located in northern New Hampshire.
3. This is a smaller range located within the western region of the White Mountains .

Was that a foolish fancy? Were those experiences in my own life of which I have been bold enough to speak merely meaningless dreams? Or were they true testimonies to something marvelous beyond? Were they moments when God was graciously revealing Himself to me through the glory of the world that He has made?

A Christian ought not to be afraid to give the latter answer. The revelation of God through nature has the stamp of approval put upon it by the Bible. The Bible clearly teaches that nature reveals the glory of God.

In a wonderful passage in the first chapter of the Epistle to the Romans the Apostle Paul says that "the invisible things of him from the creation of the world are clearly seen being understood by the things that are made, even his eternal power and Godhead." Here the Bible approves the arguments of those who in systematic fashion argue from the existence of the world to the existence of a divine Maker of the world.

But the Bible also approves those more unreasoned flashes of knowledge in which suddenly we see God's workmanship in the beauty and the majesty of His world. "The heavens declare the glory of God; and the firmament sheweth his handiwork," says the Psalmist. And what said our Lord Jesus Christ. "Even Solomon in all his glory," said He of the lilies of the field, "was not arrayed like one of these."

All that is true. The revelation of God through nature is a very precious thing. But then a serious question arises. If God has revealed Himself through the things that He has made, why do so very few men listen to the revelation? The plain fact is that fallen human beings are no more interested in finding out about a personal God through a study of nature than they are from a study of the inspired Scriptures. Even those skilled scientists who are about the business of selling their pantheistic religious views to careless Christians are often found, upon closer examination, to believe only in a God who is identical with a spiritual purpose supposed to be inherent in the world process itself and are found not to believe at all in the living and true God who created the heavens and the earth.

Why is that so? If God has revealed Himself so plainly through the world that He has made, why do men not see?

Well, when men do not see something, there are two possible explanations for the fact. One is that there is nothing there to see. The other is that the men who do not see are blind.

It is this latter explanation which the Bible gives for the failure of men to know God through the things that He has made. The Bible puts it very plainly in that same passage already quoted from the first chapter of Romans. "Their foolish heart," says Paul, "was darkened." Hence they did not see. The fault did not lie in God's creation any more than it did in His written revelation of his son Jesus Christ. Men were "without excuse," Paul says, when they did not see what nature had to show. Their minds were blinded by sin.

That is a hard saying, but like many other hard sayings it is true. We all of us, so long as we stand in our own right, and have not had our eyes mysteriously opened, are lost and blind in sin. This spiritual blindness makes it impossible for lost sinners to rightly comprehend or appreciate the physical world, the testimony of Scripture, and ultimately, God Himself.

❧ Comprehension Questions

1. Contrast two scenes that made a deep impression on the author.

2. Where did J. Gresham Machen find complete silence? How did it affect him?

3. What two widely different ways of seeing God in nature does the author mention in the first paragraph of this selection? Describe in your own words these two ways.

4. Nature tells us much about the power and wisdom of God. What vital truth about Him, and His relationship to us, can nature not reveal? Read 1 Corinthians 2:1–14 and Romans 10:13–17 before you answer this question.

5. In your own words explain the meaning of the following verse: "For the invisible things of him since the creation of the world are clearly seen being understood by the things that are made, even his everlasting power and Godhead; so they are without excuse:" (Romans 1:20).

❧ About the Author

It may safely be said that in the twentieth century no one has proclaimed and defended the truth of Scripture with greater thoroughness, clarity, and courage than did John Gresham Machen. He it was whom God led to defend the historic faith in the face of growing unbelief and theological liberalism in the Presbyterian Church, U.S.A. So intense did the conflict become that out of it was born a new seminary—Westminster Theological—and a new denomination—the Orthodox Presbyterian Church.

Born in Baltimore in 1881, the second of three sons, Gresham enjoyed a happy childhood in a home rich in cultural influences and blessed with the fear and love of God. He received his education at Johns Hopkins University, at Princeton Theological Seminary, and in graduate study in Germany. A Greek scholar of great ability and distinction, he became instructor and then assistant professor of Greek New Testament at Princeton with the status of an ordained minister in the Presbyterian Church. During the first World War Machen went to France with the Y.M.C.A. to do Christian work among the soldiers at the front; however, much of his time was spent in the canteens, taking care of men's physical needs—a service he performed with cheerfulness and patience.

His distinguished teaching career at Princeton, in which he unfolded the riches of the New Testament to scores of appreciative young men, came to an end in 1929 with his withdrawal to Westminster in Philadelphia. There he continued his inimitable teaching until his death on New Year's Day, 1937, in Bismarck, North Dakota, where he had gone to encourage a new congregation and fill a speaking engagement.

Dr. Machen was in great demand as a lecturer in his field and as a speaker in the controversy with modernism. Twice he made lecture tours in Great Britain at the urgent request of Christians there. He also lectured in France in the French language.

Besides the institutions he helped to found, Dr. Machen left several volumes of his writings embodying the essence of his study and thought. *The Origin of Paul's Religion* and *The Virgin Birth of Christ* are scholarly works, the fruits of his lifelong studies in the Greek New Testament. *Christianity and Liberalism* is directed to the general reader. Dr. Machen wrote a Greek grammar, *New Testament Greek for Beginners*, whose usefulness has gained increasing recognition through the years. All his writings remain alive and significant, a treasury for scholars and for all who would increase their understanding of God's Word and their love for Him.

55

Our Parents Are Growing Old, John

by Jean Richter and Michael J. McHugh

1. Our father's growing old, John!
   His eyes are growing dim,
   And years are on his shoulders laid—
   A heavy weight for him.
   And you and I are young and strong,
   And each a stalwart man,
   And we must make his load as light
   And easy as we can.

2. He used to take the brunt, John,
   At cradle and the plough,
   And earned our meals by the sweat
   That trickled down his brow.
   Yet never heard we him complain,
   Whate'er his toil might be,
   Nor ever lacked a welcome seat
   Upon his sturdy knee.

3. And when our days of childhood came, John,
   And solid grew each limb,
   He brought us to the yellow field,
   To share the toil with him;
   But he went foremost in the work,
   Tossing aside the grain,
   Just like the plough that heaves the soil,
   Or ships that cleave the main.

4. Now we must lead the work, John,
   Through weather foul and fair,
   And let our weary captain read and doze,
   And tilt his easy-chair;
   And we'll not mind it, John, you know,
   To look duty in the eye,
   And honor him who cared for us
   While our childish days waltzed by.

5.   I heard you speak of ma'am, John;
    'Tis Gospel what you say,
    That caring for the two of us
    Has turned her hair to grey!
    Yet, John, I do remember well
    When neighbors called her fair,
    And like a gleaming sheaf of grain
    Did shine her long blond hair.

6.   Her lips were cherry red, John,
    Her cheeks were round and fair,
    And like a ripened peach they swelled
    Against her wavy hair.
    Her step fell lightly as the leaf
    From off the summer tree,
    And all day busy at the home,
    She sang to you and me.

7.   She had a righteous arm, John,
    That wielded well the rod,
    Whene'er with willful step our feet
    The path forbidden trod;
    But to the compassion of her eye
    We never looked in vain,
    And evermore our yielding cry
    Brought down her tears like rain.

8.   But this is long ago, John,
    And we are blessed indeed,
    Tho' her fading cheek and hair,
    We, day by day, no longer heed:
    And when beneath her faithful breast
    The tides no longer stir,
    'Tis then, John, we the most shall feel
    We had no friend like her!

9.   Yes, father's growing old, John,
    His eyes are getting dim,
    And mother's treading softly
    Toward her heavenly home with him;
    But you and I are young and strong,
    And each a stalwart man,
    And we must make their path as smooth
    And level as we can.

❧ Comprehension Questions

1. How has your attitude toward your parents changed after you read this poem?

2. Write a short poem that expresses a theme of thankfulness for the sacrifices that your parents have made on your behalf.